Praise for the Groundbreaking Bestsellers of Harville Hendrix, Ph.D.

GETTING THE LOVE YOU WANT

"Harville Hendrix offers the best program I've seen for using the love/hate energy in marriage to help a couple heal one another and to become whole together."

—T. George Harris, founding editor, *American Health* and *Psychology Today*

"This book will help any couple find the love they want hidden under all the concealing confusion of a close and intimate relationship. I have seen these principles in application and they work!"

—James A. Hall, M.D.

"A solid book for married couples looking for a good balance between insight and practicality that can help make a marriage better."

—Bonnie Maslin, Ph.D., coauthor of *Loving Men for All the Right Reasons*

KEEPING THE LOVE YOU FIND

"The very best book we have seen on how people can establish a long-term, monogamous relationship. This book will be a classic in the field of human relationships."

—Bob and Mary Goulding, Western Institute for Group and Family Therapy

"*Keeping the Love You Find* could put marriage counselors and divorce lawyers out of business. . . . Dr. Hendrix teaches individuals how to create and keep healthy, happy primary relationships."

—Frederick L. Covan, Ph.D. chief psychologist, Bellevue Hospital

"A marvelous book that singles will love. If every person read and pondered this book before marriage, the divorce rate would plummet and marital happiness would soar."

—Don Browning, University of Chicago

Books by Harville Hendrix, Ph.D., and Helen Hunt, M.A.

The Couples Companion: Meditations and Exercises for Getting
   the Love You Want
The Personal Companion: Meditations and Exercises for Keeping
   the Love You Find
Giving the Love That Heals: A Guide for Parents
The Parenting Companion: Meditations and Exercises for Giving
   the Love That Heals

Books by Harville Hendrix, Ph.D.

Getting the Love You Want: A Guide for Couples
Keeping the Love You Find: A Personal Guide

The Couples Companion

Meditations and Exercises for
Getting the Love You Want

HARVILLE HENDRIX, Ph.D.,
and
HELEN HUNT, M.A.

Illustrations by Beatrice Benjamin

POCKET BOOKS

New York London Toronto Sydney Singapore

Day 15: Quotation by Lillian Hellman, excerpted from THE QUOTABLE WOMAN, © 1991 by Running Press, Philadelphia. Reprinted by permission of Running Press.

Day 65: Excerpted from THE COMPLETE LIFE, by John Erskine, Ayer Company Publishers, Inc.

Day 126: Excerpted from THE BOOK OF NIGHTMARES, © 1971 by Galway Kinnell. Reprinted by permission of Houghton Mifflin Company. All rights reserved.

Day 272: Excerpted from SEXUAL INTIMACY, © 1973 by Andrew Greeley. Reprinted by permission of Thomas More Press, Chicago, Illinois, 60606.

Day 327: Excerpted from THE BRIDGES OF MADISON COUNTY, © 1992 by Robert James Waller. Reprinted by permission of Warner Books, Inc., New York.

Day 364: Excerpted from GIFT FROM THE SEA by Anne Morrow Lindbergh, copyright Pantheon Books, New York. Reprinted by permission of Pantheon Books.

An *Original* Publication of POCKET BOOKS

POCKET BOOKS, a division of Simon & Schuster Inc.
1230 Avenue of the Americas, New York, NY 10020

Copyright © 1994 by Harville Hendrix and Helen Hunt

Hendrix, Harville.
    The couples companion : meditations and exercises for Getting the love you want / Harville Hendrix and Helen Hunt.
      p. cm.
   ISBN: 0-671-86883-7 (trade pbk.)
    1. Marriage—United States—Psychological aspects. 2. Love.
3. Interpersonal relations—United States. I. Hunt, Helen, 1949–
II. Hendrix, Harville. Getting the love you want.
HQ734.H488   1994
306.7—dc20   93-23670
                                       CIP

First Pocket Books trade paperback printing February 1994

10 9 8 7 6 5

POCKET and colophon are registered trademarks of Simon & Schuster Inc.

Cover design by Patrice Kaplan

Text design by Stanley S. Drate / Folio Graphics Co., Inc.

Printed in the U.S.A.

To our children:
Josh, Mara, Kathryn, Kimberly, Leah, and Hunter,
whom we watch grow into maturity
with a true sense of wonder.

We acknowledge
Laura Torbet
for her
special contribution
to this project.

Acknowledgments

Expressing appreciation to those who have inspired us is especially appropriate in a book of inspiration. There have been many, both close at hand, and at a distance.

I (Harville) recall with deep appreciation the emphasis on the value and necessity of prayer in my teenage years as a minister. Through my theological education I was introduced to the mystical tradition of western civilization and came to appreciate the distinction between theological thinking and personal transformation through the direct experience of God. The workshops of John Lilly and Lawrence LeShan introduced me to the science and technology of meditation, the concept of altered states of consciousness, and to the essence of meditation as "doing one thing at a time with your whole being." I also am indebted to certain couples in my practice who experimented with the process and reported the benefits.

Two theorists I (Helen) read years ago influenced the perspective I have wanted this book to embody: Edward Edinger, whose book *Ego and Archetype,* articulated an analysis of religious symbology as a depiction of an individual's psychological development; and Martin Buber, whose I-Thou Relationship hypothesized that the love between two persons contains the presence of God. Also, I want to acknowledge five women with most special appreciation—Carole Angermier, Nell Martin, Florence Pert, Joan Thorne, and Sara Waterbury. Our weekly meetings over these last five years, which always included twenty minutes of silence for prayer and meditation, demonstrated to each of us the importance of regular time spent in openness to our inner spirit, and to our fuller selves.

Among the other persons who contributed directly or indirectly to the book we want to especially thank Beatrice Benjamin for her creative illustrations; Elizabeth Neustadter for her many suggestions and her unfailing sense of humor; Joan Minieri, who assisted in research; and Lisa Joy Kelvin and Natasha Federal, who assisted in editing and organizing. Thanks also to Debra Dadd-Redalia, Mariah and Stephen Marvin, Yvonne Ginsberg, Diane Wakelin, and John McNally.

Special thanks is due to Pocket Books for their support of this project, especially to Claire Zion, our editor, who pushed us to strengthen the book's structure and suggested the idea of the Units, and to Barney Karpfinger, our agent, who supported this project from the beginning.

Note from the Authors

The enthusiastic response we received to the initial publication of *Getting the Love You Want: A Guide for Couples* demonstrated to us that couples were hungry for practical information to assist them as they navigated the difficult waters of relationship. But in the years that followed, we began to realize that while couples understood the basic ideas of the Imago system described in that book, some had difficulty implementing the exercises in their relationship on a day-by-day basis.

Several years ago, Helen began to structure daily prayer and meditation into her life in a way that wedded it to the Imago process. Within his practice, Harville had for years given couples a sentence to focus or meditate on between sessions. The beneficial results for our marriage and for the couples who followed Harville's guidance led Helen to suggest that we share what we were learning. So we conceptualized *The Couples Companion* as a tool to assist in using the Imago system on a daily basis. We hope the meditation format will encourage you to consider your relationship as a means of spiritual development.

The Spiritual Essence of Relationship

The term *spiritual*, as we use it in this context, means the innate drive in nature—and thus in all of us—toward healing and self-completion. To us, spiritual development is the goal, the *telos*, of our species. We are the apex of nature, that part that has developed self-consciousness. But we are in pain because our connection to the whole was ruptured in childhood. Our inner as well as outer worlds are fragmented. We find ourselves the walking wounded, armored with adult coping mechanisms that thinly veil the scarring of childhood. Our belief is that in healing the wounds of our relationships, we become the primary means through which nature heals itself. From our view, the mutual healing of childhood wounds that can be achieved in a relationship is a deeply spiritual process. It moves us through the intense pain and alienation that characterizes most relationships and restores our interconnectedness and interdependency with each other, as well as our original union with the greater whole.

Our Story—Relationship as a Path for Spiritual Growth

We began our journey together after the failure of our first marriages. During our five years of courtship, and into our early married years, we shared a mutual desire to build a rewarding relationship. We incessantly discussed the ideas that gave birth to *Getting the Love You Want*, valiantly did the exercises, doggedly engaged in the processes. But our zeal left many problems unsolved.

Although we both possessed a thorough intellectual understanding of the process, we discovered that insight was not the same as cure. Because our self-protective defenses, the adaptations we had made to our childhood wounding, had become frozen into our character, our problems were more deeply entrenched than we had imagined. At one point, we made a significant discovery—that what one of us needed most, the other was least capable of giving. We were at an impasse that would not yield to insight.

At the time, we were convinced that the changes required to meet one another's need represented capitulation for our own self-development. But soon, we found that encoded in our struggle was an exact blueprint for the growth we each needed to remobilize our arrested psychological development. Within our mutual frustrations were clues pointing the way to greater consciousness about ourselves and our relationship. We came to see that the growth essential for our relationship's survival would bring restoration to our own fragmented state, thus becoming a path for spiritual healing and wholeness.

So with time, we learned that responding to each other's needs was not so much a sacrifice of our selfhood as much as an invitation to personal as well as spiritual growth. We began to see our marriage as a means of recovering our original self, as a path to self-completion—essentially a spiritual process. And we discovered that opening ourselves to a meditative process fostered the inner receptivity so that the specifics of the Imago process could take deeper root in our lives.

Why an Exercise/Meditation Combination?

As we assessed our own process, we realized that there was a theoretical basis for flanking specific Imago exercises with a meditative practice. Whereas the Imago *exercises* were targeted to the conscious mind, the practice of *meditation* gave access to unconscious states. We felt that in combination, they had the potential to produce deeper and more permanent levels of relationship growth.

We all want a better relationship. But most of us become bogged down in despair and disillusionment and reach the point of giving up, claiming that we just don't know what to do anymore. The daily use of Imago exercises appeals to our conscious minds. They offer tangible, measurable ingredients in the recipe for change, fortifying the conscious mind with specific, doable, concrete tasks. They may not change your relationship overnight, but you will experience a cumulative effect over time. Ongoing, cognitive work will strengthen your ability to develop *intentionality* in your relationship, to will a desired outcome, and to carry out actions that achieve a goal. This in itself is an empowering experience.

We believe that a meditative practice is also a form of personal empowerment. You will find that working with the deeper self will produce the unconscious attitudinal shifts essential to flank the cognitive work you are doing on your relationship. Current research on meditation lends support to the claims that the practice of this ancient discipline can tap into our deeper levels of awareness to bring about changes in the unconscious part of the mind. There are varied forms of meditational practice from many religious traditions, and with a variety of purposes—spiritual development, ego transcendence, and inner healing. In past centuries, Brother Lawrence spoke of the meditative state as "practicing the presence of God," and Saint Teresa of Avila offered the definition, "Contemplation is divine union." It is the modern researcher Lawrence LeShan who described meditation as "doing one thing at a time with your whole being." Whatever your tradition, the practice of quiet on a daily basis will help you discover and integrate your innate personal as well as spiritual resources.

It Takes Time

There isn't one of us who wouldn't like a quick fix—the one secret formula, the one weekend seminar, the one therapy session that would solve all our problems. The truth is that meaningful change takes time. Be patient. And be assured that the ongoing practice of meditations combined with cognitive exercises can allow for gradual but profound change—the kind that's often the hardest to achieve.

We all must accept the reality that permanent change comes about slowly, requiring large doses of understanding and a ready sense of humor. We encourage you to sprinkle lightheartedness into the process whenever possible, which is why we've accented the book with occasional opportunities for a smile. After all, we're only human. And a gentle forgiving moment of humor can be a healing balm for the tensions that beset most relationships.

Within these pages, you will learn some of the essential lessons in the art of love. The small, incremental steps suggested in the daily entries that follow should increase your chance of succeeding at the changes you desire. Our hope is that in accessing the inner power necessary to move through the fires of relationship, the process itself will become the path to recovering your innate spiritual and human potential.

Introduction

Every relationship travels a predictable path from the bliss of romantic love to the nightmare of disillusionment and conflict. Yet every relationship, with the addition of conscious intentionality, has the potential to be a transformative journey toward spiritual growth and wholeness.

Imago Relationship Therapy, the means for achieving a conscious relationship, facilitates the conscious mutual healing of childhood wounds between two partners. At its theoretical core is the idea that we pick our partners based on an unconscious image—called the Imago—of "the person who can make me whole." This image is a composite of our caretakers, especially the negative traits that were most wounding to us, and of the original aspects of ourselves that got lost in the process of conforming to social expectations. We seek in our partnerships to re-create the context in which we were wounded, so that we can finish the business of our childhood. Thus we seek from someone like our caretakers what we didn't get in childhood in order to heal old wounds, thereby restoring the joyful aliveness with which we came into the world.

But because this agenda is unconscious, and because we are carrying around the character defenses we've built up all our lives to protect ourselves against further pain, our old wounds are reopened by our Imago partners because they are similar to our parents, and we react in the same old childish ways. In a conscious relationship, we recognize this unconscious agenda and make its completion our conscious intention.

The Imago process involves committing to understanding our own wounds and those of our partner, to learning new skills and changing our hurtful behavior, in the course of which we meet our partner's needs and restore the lost and denied parts of ourselves, thus achieving spiritual wholeness.

Organization of *The Couples Companion*

Each entry of *The Couples Companion* takes a quote or illustration as the subject for a brief discussion of some aspect of a conscious relationship, followed by an exercise and a meditation.

This combination of exercises and meditations will guide you through a year of Imago therapy, in which the basic skills of the Imago process are taught at intervals throughout the book in step-by-step learning "units" of from two to seven days. Unit entries are indicated by a series of hearts at the top of the page; the shaded heart indicates the day within the unit. What follows is a brief overview of the Imago process. (A list of the units in order of their appearance can be found on page xvii).

There is *one precondition* for going through the Imago process: *commitment* to the unconditional safety and healing of your partner. An essential ingredient of commitment is the Exits agreement, which reclaims time and energy that belong in the relationship but are currently being dissipated elsewhere.

There is *one foundational skill* that must be mastered: The Couples Dialogue, the components of which are Mirroring, Validation, and Empathy. The couples dialogue is simply a tool for direct, intentional communication, and is the basis for all other skills.

There are five key areas in which the couples dialogue must be applied:

- *Revisioning your relationship* involves reframing your relationship as a spiritual journey to wholeness, which includes understanding the nature of the Imago (and specifically your own and your partner's Imagos). This activity is covered in the learning units labeled Relationship Vision; Unmasking the Imago: Childhood Agenda; Unmasking the Imago: Childhood Frustrations; The Power Struggle: Partner Profile; The Power Struggle: Partner Frustrations; and The Power Struggle: Summing Up.
- *Reimaging your partner.* Seeing your partner as a person who is wounded, like yourself, whose hurtful behavior is the result of childhood pain, opens the door to mutual healing. This activity is addressed in Reimaging Your Partner as Wounded, Positive Flooding, and Visualization of Love.
- *Reromanticizing your relationship.* Actively re-creating the fun, passion, and aliveness of your courtship can diffuse negative feelings and restore the open, caring atmosphere necessary for resolving conflict. The pertinent learning units are Reromanticiz-

ing; Caring Behaviors; Target Behaviors; The Fun List; Reromanticizing: Surprises; and Sexuality.

- *Resolving rage.* Learning to contain spontaneous, destructive anger and criticism, so that we can both express and receive it consciously, creates safety and sets the stage for the resolution of our frustrations and self-hatred. You will be working with this activity in the Containment Process and Container Days units.
- *Restructuring Frustrations.* Moving from criticism and anger to understanding the need behind our frustration, asking directly for what is needed, and changing our behavior to meet our partner's needs allow us to reclaim our shadow selves and become whole. Behavior-Change Request, The Lost Self, The Denied Self, The Disowned Self, The Hidden Self, The Presentational Self, and Core Scene are the learning units here.

Tips for Using *The Couples Companion*

- Entries are arranged to offer topical variety from day to day. Lighter "fun" days are interspersed with the more complex learning units.
- We suggest that you keep a notebook for the tasks that require writing. Because there are several places where you will be asked to refer back to information collected in earlier units, you will find it helpful to note the number of the day at the top of each notebook page.
- We recognize that the demands of this book are at times strenuous and that sometimes we haven't the physical, psychological, or emotional stamina to "work on the relationship." We can easily become discouraged with our progress, or our inability to change, or our perceived failure to measure up to our dreams. We need time off. The entries are numbered sequentially, rather than dated, to enable you to take a break as needed, and be able to come back to the process where you left off.
- Each day's entry will take about twenty minutes of your time. Time is not always easy to find in a busy life, but we urge you to make this time a priority. It is a way to honor your commitment to your relationship and your partner, and to care for yourself. Martin Luther King, Jr., made an important point when he said, "There's so much to do in a day, if I didn't pray two hours a day, I don't know how I would get it all done."

- While many of the daily entries are directed to the individual partner, we want to stress the importance of working through *The Couples Companion* together—mutuality is, after all, at the core of a conscious relationship. Even many of the individual tasks will be enhanced when done together, and the sharing of one's experiences and insights as you go is itself a way of connecting, of keeping the dialogue and the love—and the fun—flowing. It is of course possible for just one partner to use the book, if they are prepared for the resulting imbalance in care and intention; for the solo partner the self-care inherent in the meditations may be of particular benefit.
- We also want to make clear that this book is designed for couples who are committed to creating mutually healing relationships but who may find themselves at an impasse. We all have varying degrees of relationship problems. Couples with serious problems should seek out professional help to support the work being done with this book at home.

On the Path to Real Love

The process of attaining real love has a beginning and a middle, but no end. The need for relationship maintenance and reinforcement endures. Using the approach of *The Couples Companion*, a meditative or contemplative practice is encouraged, so that from a position of calm and safety, attention is given on a deeper level to the relationship, and more time is devoted to pleasurable pursuits that promote joyfulness and intimacy.

With the passing of time and diligent attention, the two of us have seen our own yearnings fulfilled. Just in the last few years, we have truly moved into a place of grace and safety, becoming "passionate friends." We have a relationship we can be proud of. It feels as if we have come to a place where we know and accept each other deeply, where we are organically bonded, with a sense of loving trust that enables us to move with confidence and assurance and love, individually and together, out into the larger world, with something to contribute. Our hope is that some of what we have learned will help you as you work with your partner to transform the struggle into a rich source of mutual healing. We wish you well on your journey to real love.

But the beginning of things . . . is necessarily vague,
tangled, chaotic and exceedingly disturbing.

—KATE CHOPIN

We all enter our partnerships with our minds full of pictures—
dreams, movie fantasies, beliefs—a detailed Technicolor extravaganza
of "how it's going to be." But reality has a way of undermining our
fantasies, and soon enough we find out "how it is." The shattering of
your fantasy may be the reason you picked up this book. You may feel
you're in uncharted waters. What now?

Here is where our journey of relationship truly begins. All the
pretty pictures that we managed to sustain through courtship have
become contorted into images we hardly recognize. We may find
ourselves married to someone we don't like, or worse yet, a virtual
stranger, with a seemingly unbreachable gulf between them and us.
Reconnection seems a near impossibility. We don't know which way
to turn.

When we lose the way, when we acknowledge that we don't *know*,
then we have taken the first step on our journey to real love.

The purpose of *The Couples Companion* is to provide a daily
compass for direction. For right now, just trust the process.

🏵 *Ask your partner to talk with you about working through this*
book together. Get a notebook for keeping records, and make a
plan that includes time to do the reading and tasks, ways of
sharing what you learn, and commit to encourage each other to
stay in the process.

Taking twenty minutes to simply sit in stillness today, I acknowledge
that I'm often groping in the dark when it comes to my relationship.
Letting go of my preconceptions of how it ought to be is the beginning
of the journey to what can be. I hold this thought as I take my first
step: "This is the beginning of tomorrow."

Take a rest; a field that has rested gives a beautiful crop.

—OVID

When our lives are too busy, when conflict and ill will seem insurmountable, it is hard to work on your relationship. Exhausted and spiritually depleted, we run out of solutions and hope and ideas and caring. We have no interest in examining our relationships, no energy for having fun—or sex—with our partners. What we need is calm and rest. As a field periodically needs to lie fallow, we need to retreat, to rejuvenate, to reenergize.

There is a place within you that is a source of renewal. Finding twenty minutes a day to relax and access that place is a vital aspect of relationship maintenance. Depending on your temperament or inclination, you may want to spend that time in prayer, doing a form of meditation that you know, or just sitting with your eyes closed, possibly as part of your routine ride to or from work, or as you run an errand. Even quiet exercise can be a form of meditation. Whatever your preference, it is important to do it. Most days you will be asked to use part of this time to think about something specific in connection with a daily task, but this is primarily your time to restore your spirit, to revitalize, to find the strength to go on.

&❧ *Identify a place in your home or at work where you will spend your daily twenty minutes of quiet time. This could be a comfortable chair in your bedroom, a spot beneath a tree in the park across from your office, a cushion on the floor, your seat on the bus.*

Taking time in my chosen place, I breathe slowly and deeply, entering the still place within. From there, I acknowledge: "It is in letting go that new life, the God-essence within, has space to be born."

Out of the ashes of the past, new life is born.

—WHITE EAGLE

As years of ill will and criticism, unresolved conflict, and disappointments mount up, we look around and feel as if we're standing in a pile of rubble that can never be cleared away. We thought we would fight to the death. But nobody won. We're exhausted and ready to surrender. The damage is irreversible, and there isn't enough faith or goodwill to turn the situation around. The illusion of love has given way to despair. The fires of passion have turned to ashes. The only way out seems to be to walk away from the whole smoldering mess.

Paradoxically, sometimes that fight to the death is the conflagration that is needed to bring about the dissolution of the old and clear the way for rebirth. By persevering through our most frightening and ferocious conflicts, we exorcise our lifelong demons and come out, alive and whole, on the other side. As our past goes up in flame, the ashes of the conflagration fertilize and nurture the ground of the new life emerging. To trust in this process is to honor the cycles of life.

In conversation with your partner, share your hope for a new relationship. Together, identify three qualities you hope will be born in your relationship as you work through this book. Write them down in your notebook.

I open my spirit in a time of renewal today. Here I access greater courage and strength so as to move through conflict, with its hope of rebirth. I focus my thought on this wisdom: "It is only when the fire has been reduced to ashes that the phoenix rises."

It is good to have an end to journey towards, but it is the journey that matters.

—URSULA LE GUIN

If you had been born two hundred years ago, you would have been in an arranged marriage; your parents would have picked your partner. But marriage has changed radically in the last century. What used to be a static institution that made economic and social sense has now become a powerful psychological and spiritual journey with the potential for self-understanding and growth.

This journey of a conscious relationship offers the kind of intimacy we dream of, the restoration of our wholeness and sense of connectedness to the world. If we stay on course in the hard times, work through the conflicts, hone our skills, and overcome resistance and boredom, the process itself becomes the therapy we need to heal. The day-in-and-day-out attention, the continual learning about our partner, every act of caring, every conflict resolved, every bit of self-knowledge, every act of stretching, opening, healing, peels off a layer of the defenses and makes us safe with each other, bringing us closer to the essence of real love.

❧ *Think of your relationship as a journey rather than a static state. Imagine how you can make that journey safe for you and your partner. Consider doing something especially caring for your partner today. Set aside ten minutes to talk together quietly, share a little laughter, declare a moratorium on criticism.*

Today, as I enter a time for stillness, I see my relationship as a journey to real love. I hold this thought in prayer: "The longest journey begins with a single step."

Joy is the most infallible sign of the presence of God.
— PIERRE TEILHARD DE CHARDIN

The yearning to feel relaxed and safe in the world is universal. Every culture has some version of the myth of an idyllic place of peace and abundance, where all beings live in harmony—the Garden of Eden, nirvana, El Dorado. And every culture talks about the loss of this idyll—a disturbance, the fall from grace, cataclysm. Then begins the quest to return to paradise. These are clearly metaphors for our yearning to recapture the innate joy and wholeness that we dimly remember from birth.

Traditionally, religion has been the path to that restoration, as people sought to revitalize their spirits through prayer, devotion, and good works. In this past century, with the recognition of the power of the unconscious, some people have also turned to psychotherapy to resolve their pain and alienation. And now we recognize that our intimate, committed relationships could have a larger purpose and can become a third structure for healing and wholeness. The struggle toward a conscious relationship can be seen as a deeply vital spiritual path, for it has the potential to restore our original joy—our wholeness, our feeling of connection to others and to all else.

❧ *In your notebook, remember two or three times when you felt true joy—even for a moment—with your partner. Tonight, share your memories of these moments together.*

Allowing petty agitation to flow away, I move into twenty minutes of deep quiet and begin the cultivation of my own inner Garden of Eden. I celebrate this spiritual reality: "Love is the recovery of paradise."

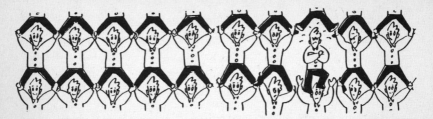

At birth, although we couldn't report it, we experienced a wondrous reality: we were whole. We had a sense of relaxed joy and a feeling of interconnection to the entire fabric of the universe. So, what happened? Why don't we feel that way now?

Well, we had parents who, like all parents, were less than perfect, wounded by their own life experience. Even with the best intentions, they passed their wounds on to us. Now, fearful and defended, our primal energy no longer flows freely; we are no longer whole. We are afraid to laugh, too inhibited to dance and sing; we don't know how to express our anger directly and appropriately; we've lost touch with the parts of ourselves we gave up.

What has this to do with relationships? When we were wounded, we became self-absorbed and lost awareness of our connection to the tapestry to which we belong. But when, in the course of our relationship journey, we restore the sense of aliveness that is our birthright, we can repair the frayed connection and thereby heal not only ourselves but the wound in nature as well.

❧ You and your partner may want to do this exercise together. Stand with your feet apart, arms relaxed at your sides. Feel your heart beating, touch each other's pulse, put your hands on each other's chest and feel the rhythmic pulsations. Now look at the sunlight and think about the fact that you and the sun are made from the same pulsating energy. Share your sensations and thoughts with your partner.

In my time of solitude today, I see my own unique life as one small area of a complex tapestry of beings. As I expand my focus, I see my life interconnected with and enriching the broader tapestry. I joyfully focus on these words: "I am one with the universe."

Have you ever wondered why you picked your partner? It's a complicated story, and it goes like this: Each of us was wounded in very specific ways, depending on our temperament and our caretakers, and the societal rules by which we were raised. Thus for each of us there exists a particular recipe for healing, specific needs that must be met for us to feel whole and loved. And guess what? The necessary ingredients for that healing are possessed by our partners.

Yes, this partner who frustrates you or ignores you is the key to your healing. Not only that, but the very traits that hurt and infuriate you are the most vital ingredients in that recipe.

Your partner was the choice of your unconscious, which scanned the candidates you encountered for a mate that matched the image formed in childhood of "the person who can make me whole." This image, or Imago, is composed of both the positive and negative traits of your caretakers, though the negative traits, which had the most profound effect on your wounding, tend to dominate. You see, the unconscious has an agenda—to finish childhood; that is, to get from a partner who resembles our caretakers what our caretakers didn't give us, so that we can correct that early experience and heal those old wounds.

❧ *Make a list of three negative traits that your parents had. Now list three negative traits of your partner. Compare them. Can you see the similarities?*

Drawing hope from a time of solitude, I see my partner and myself as a perfect fit. I acknowledge this thought with a reverence: "In spite of all our differences, we belong together."

*Conflict is the alchemical soup that transforms raw
emotion and instinct into pure gold.*

— HARVILLE HENDRIX

Just because we understand the agenda of our unconscious doesn't
mean that our defenses disappear. No, understanding is just the
beginning. We are still devastated by conflict with our partner, still
caught in pain and ill will, and we still have to learn to talk with each
other. This can be discouraging, and we despair of ever attaining the
love we seek.

But conflict is supposed to happen. Everything in nature is in tension,
which is an essential condition for change. The hard truth is that
incompatibility is the ground for marriage. Conflict needs to be
understood as the norm, a sign that the psyche is trying to get its
need met and become whole. It is in the crucible of conflict with your
Imago partner, in the restructuring of your frustrations, and in the
resolution of your rage that you will heal the wounds of childhood.

*❧ In your notebook, list the current conflicts in your relation-
ship—the fights about chores, your unhappiness about your sex
life, your partner's sabotaging comments about your income. Now
disengage from your emotions for just a short period and imagine
how working to resolve your conflicts can lead to growth.*

**Today, as I go within to my deepest resources, I enter the place of
courage. I see our conflicts as growth trying to happen.**

Love is blind; marriage opens its eyes.

> —ANONYMOUS

Relationships are born in the illusion of romantic love. We chose our partners not so much because we fell in love with them as we fell in need—a nonnegotiable *need* to recapture the joyful aliveness that is our birthright. The bells and whistles and fireworks that went off when you met your Imago partner was a signal from your unconscious that the person standing before you had the unique qualifications to help.

Romantic love *is* blind. When the veil of illusion falls, the realities are all too apparent. Real love does not give birth to relationships; real need does. Real love, if it appears at all, is born in the midst of conflict. It rises from the ashes of conflict worked through together, born in the perception of the other as a person in need of healing. This mutual commitment to meet each other's needs is the beginning and end of love. Partners in a conscious relationship welcome this awareness with open eyes.

&. *Look at your relationship today with your eyes open. Is the illusion gone? Are you working through your conflicts, or are you stuck? Talk with your partner today about the idea of a mutual commitment to meeting one another's needs and creating real love.*

In a place of contemplation, I shift into that deep place from which I see the needs I bring to my relationship rather than the love. While keeping my needs in mind, I allow my spirit to draw strength from my core, and I feel myself transcend the obsession with my own concerns. I see instead my partner's needs, and lovingly offer the gifts of comfort and healing.

*Everybody thinks of changing humanity, but nobody
thinks of changing himself.*

—LEO TOLSTOY

One of the hardest things about a conscious relationship is that we
have to give up our fantasy that the right partner will come along and
magically make everything okay. Once we accept the reality of our
Imago partner, we have to give up the next fantasy—that if our
partner would just change what is wrong with *them*, everything would
be fine. We have to accept the hardest truth of all: that in order to
have the relationship we want, *we* have to change.

There is, happy to say, a hidden benefit behind this grim reality. In
making the changes that should happen to meet our partner's needs,
in doing what is called for to have the relationship we want, we
restore our wholeness. That's the irony: in the process of stretching
beyond what is comfortable for us, we are transformed.

🔊 *Write down three changes you could make in yourself that
would improve your relationship—for example, cutting out criticism, being more punctual, expressing appreciation.*

**Taking time for quiet meditation, I move to a place of inner courage
and accept the reality that I must change. I hold this truth in faith:
"Healing my partner makes me whole."**

Luck is a matter of preparation meeting opportunity.

—OPRAH WINFREY

When we look at happy couples, we are tempted to feel that somehow they got lucky—they chose the right partner, or they haven't had to face hard times, or there is some kind of charmed fate involved.

Hardly. There are really only two kinds of relationships: those that are unconscious and those that are conscious. They both have the same agenda—to finish childhood by getting needs met with the partner that were unmet by our caretakers. But in the unconscious relationship the couple is unaware of this agenda; they don't understand either the nature of their needs or how to get them met, so they become locked in a power struggle, trying to get what they need through various forms of coercion—anger, withdrawal, complaints, withholding.

In a conscious relationship, the couple understands what is going on, and the partners make that unconscious agenda their conscious intention. They *decide* to do what is necessary to heal each other's wounds.

&. *Are you ready for a better relationship? Are you willing to step beyond your anger and denial and purposefully commit yourself to doing the work necessary to heal yourself and your partner? If so, it is time to make a vow. (Treat this as a ritual; it works better that way.) Write this in your notebook: "I vow to keep my eyes and mind open, to be aware of myself and my patterns, because I want to achieve a conscious relationship."*

I visualize myself willing to learn how to create a dream relationship. Acknowledging that the skills I must acquire are a part of my own spiritual path, I commit to this thought: "I am willing to learn what I need to know."

Marriage is our last, best chance to grow up.

—JOSEPH BARTH

We come to our partnerships with an unspoken agenda: to finish childhood. We have chosen partners with qualities of our caretakers that caused us pain, hoping to get what our parents were unable to give. Most people haven't a clue about this unspoken purpose in their partnerships, however. All they know is that their partners aren't making them happy. In word and deed, they set out to prove how unhappy they are. Pretty soon they're both much more unhappy. Perhaps they change partners, or change locations, hoping that the outcome will be different. It never works. The central characters remain pretty much the same. The same scenarios get reenacted, with the same dialogue.

Real love can happen only between adults. Committing ourselves to the Imago process results in the maturing of character as partners agree to do what is necessary to heal each other's wounds. It is a tall order, but it is also the best shot we have to finally grow up and to reclaim the spiritual and psychological parts of ourselves that we gave up as children. In a conscious relationship, we rise to the challenge of growing up at last.

❧ *Identify one aspect of your relationship with your partner that you think is immature. How can you change it and grow up a little today?*

As I move into an inner sanctuary, I see an image of myself as immature, sometimes acting like a child in my relationship. I commit to growing up in this area and relating to my partner as an adult. This wisdom becomes mine: "My relationship provides me with the opportunity to finish growing up."

I will show you a love potion without drug or herb or
any witch's spell: if you wish to be loved, love.

—HECATO

When we fall in love, our hope is that we will be loved as we've never
been loved before, and that the pain we carry within us will be healed.
Then we are disappointed when our partner is unable to give us what
we need and is frustrated with our shortcomings to boot. It turns out
that both of us have needs that arouse expectations, and both of us
are wearing protective armor that keeps us from giving, or receiving,
love.

Children need to be loved, but as adults, in order to *be* loved, we
must learn *to* love. Love is not instinctual. Our life energy is neutral
unless we are threatened; then it becomes self-protective. Real love
must be learned, for it transcends our survival instincts, requiring us
to let down our defenses, even in the midst of conflict. In a conscious
relationship, we stretch to transcend our fear of "otherness" of our
partner; we treat them as equal in value to ourselves, and guarantee
their safety in our presence. And we do this unconditionally, without
expectation of anything in return.

In order to be loved, in other words, you must become a lover.
Real love is not an emotion; it is a decision to act unconditionally in
the interest of your partner.

❧ *Think of one act of unconditional love that you have received*
from your partner. Tell your partner about it. Now think of one
act of unconditional love you have expressed toward your partner.
Don't talk about it.

Drawing hope as I sit in stillness, I send unconditional loving
thoughts to my partner. I gently hold in mind these words: "Love
begets love."

Here is an important strategy and etiquette tip about using the Imago process: all expressions of criticism or anger are done *by appointment only.*

Now this may sound like an unnecessary (and near-impossible) formality. But think about it. You know how distracting or downright irritating it can be when your partner interrupts you in the middle of something—even if that something is just relaxing after a hard day— because they're so upset that they're about to explode. You feel intruded upon, ambushed, and unprepared to think straight or respond calmly. Even if you weren't upset before, you've thrown up your defenses before you know it, and you're in a pitched battle.

Making an appointment shows respect and consideration for our partner, and it prevents spontaneous combustion. Making an appointment gives the person who's angry or frustrated a cool-down period to organize their thoughts. The person on the receiving end has a chance to prepare for the onslaught and doesn't feel invaded. Moreover, making appointments guarantees that we will find time in our busy lives for the important business of relationship maintenance, and more time for love.

&. In dialogue today, make appointments with each other for the work you will do together on this book, for at least a week in advance if you can't set aside a regular time. In addition, make an agreement that all expressions of criticism or anger will be done by appointment only.

In my retreat time today, I recognize that expressing my frustration or criticism to my partner by appointment is a sign of my respect for myself as well.

People change and forget to tell each other.

—LILLIAN HELLMAN

We lead such busy lives—each of us pursuing our own interests and career, attending to our responsibilities—that we don't always find time to keep our partners current. Some separateness is fine, of course; it stimulates and enlivens our relationship. Without continuous, ongoing communication, however, we lose touch—sometimes dramatically, detrimentally—while we're preoccupied with other things.

There is one core skill in the Imago process: the couples dialogue. It is simply an intentional, structured way of communicating, but it is the trunk of the tree from which all other skills branch off, the basic technique for keeping in touch and working through problems. It is a three-part process consisting of mirroring, validation, and empathizing. In the four days ahead you will learn the foundational skill of mirroring. This quiet, unassuming skill is a powerful one, with the potential to transform your relationship. It is a way, to paraphrase Lillian Hellman, of remembering to tell each other how you're changing.

❧ *Make a list of the current issues in your life that you've neglected to run by your partner: plans, secrets, minutiae, those items you think your partner won't understand. Once you start, you may be surprised how long the list is!*

Keeping this list in mind, I move into quiet meditation. I see myself opening all of myself to my partner and feeling safe. I honor this wisdom: "Safety is possible only through honesty and openness with my partner."

The first duty of love is to listen.

—PAUL TILLICH

The way many couples go about it, you'd think the first duty of love was to talk. Even when our partners are talking, we're often so distracted preparing what *we* want to say next that we don't really hear them. This isn't dialogue; it's *parallel monologue.*

If you and your partner hope to be more open with each other, you will need to master the primary skill that will enable you to make contact: listening. The ability to listen is the heart of mirroring. As you practice listening today, you may find out that you're not as tuned in as you thought you were.

❧ *Today is a day to practice active listening. Be still within yourself and alert to the world outside. Tune in to the gentle hum of the air conditioner, the low-decibel roar of cars a block away, the whooshing sounds as you slowly brush your teeth, the ubiquitous chirping of a sparrow, the conversation at the next table in the luncheonette, the idle chatter of your partner. Note how many of these sounds you normally miss.*

Today, I go inside to the still center of my being and pledge to understand and be available to my partner. In contemplation, my mind focuses on this truth: "Listening to my partner is the first requirement of love."

See what happens when we're not paying attention? We think we hear perfectly well what our partner is saying, but we're slightly distracted and, sure enough, we misunderstand. *If our feelings weren't sometimes being bruised in the process, it would be comical.*

This is where mirroring comes in. Language is a powerful tool of communication *if* we follow certain simple rules to ensure that we hear what our partner says—both the words and the meaning. Mirroring is simply a matter of carefully repeating back what was said for verification, and repeating the process until we get it right.

Here's how a simple mirroring of the above transaction looks:

"Don't forget to bathe the dog, sweetie."

"Did you say 'don't forget to shave the knob?' "

"No, 'don't forget to bathe the dog.' "

"Oh, of course, bathe the dog. I won't forget."

Admittedly, that's a bit tedious. In the beginning you may find that mirroring sets your teeth on edge, but it guarantees understanding and a feeling of being heard, and *that* is wonderful. With practice, mirroring will become second nature. You'll hardly notice that you're doing it.

  ે *Today, mirror at least three of your partner's communications between dinner and bedtime. Simply reflect back to your partner, as accurately as possible, their words and feelings. You might preface your replies with "Let me see if I heard you right. . . ." or "I hear you saying that . . ." Ask "Did I get it right?" to confirm that you listened correctly and understood.*

In peace and meditation I become attentive to my partner, aware of their total otherness. I focus on this thought: "In listening, I make room for my partner's reality."

*To talk easily with people, you must firmly believe
that either you or they are listening. And even then,
it's not easy.*

—MIGNON MCLAUGHLIN

We spend a great deal of our lives talking, and yet many of us are
not very good at it. We don't say what we mean, we habitually
interrupt, or we have little to say. Yet good conversation is so
delightful, and the intimacy—the feeling of being connected—that
good communication creates is more delightful still. Isn't it worth the
time and effort to learn this new skill?

Simply reflecting back one another's statements is a powerful
technique whereby two people can make contact with each other's
interior world. And until this happens, marriage doesn't really happen.
It's conceivable that your partner has never had anyone truly listen to
them before. So be aware that you're beginning to engage in a
process that could, over time, be transformational.

❧ *Continue to practice mirroring your partner today. Keep it
light, warm, caring. Remember, the point is to make your partner
feel safe and honored.*

**For twenty minutes today, in deep relaxation, I imagine myself and
my partner together, perhaps holding hands, talking freely and
without fear of whatever is in our minds and hearts, openly sharing
secrets and dreams, fascinated by all there is to know about each
other.**

Good conversation is as stimulating as black coffee,
and just as hard to sleep after.

—ANNE MORROW LINDBERGH

You've now had a few days to experiment with mirroring, the first step of the couples dialogue. You're on your way to mastering the foundational skill for creating the relationship you desire. Congratulations are in order! You survived the tedium, you didn't pull all your hair out, you didn't disappear in the process of putting yourself aside in order to listen. Perhaps you even feel a little closer to your partner.

In the coming weeks you will move on to validation and empathy, which complete the process. But you'll find that mirroring alone goes a long way toward shifting the energy of your relationship to one of healing and wholeness.

As mirroring becomes a more natural and automatic response, you'll find that your conversations take on qualities of warmth, excitement, and unpredictability. It may get a bit intoxicating. So later tonight, think of serving up some black-coffee conversation, laced perhaps with a bit of sugar.

❧ *Have that black-coffee conversation. Make an effort to have something interesting to say—a story about something in the news, a tale about the kids, an idea for a vacation. Don't forget to mirror, today and every day.*

In quiet prayer, I let my worries slip away and become aware of the patience and attention that lie deep within. Relaxing in the safety that is building within my relationship, I absorb the truth of this thought: "Full openness leads to true intimacy."

*In matters of love, the beginning of the end often turns
out to be but the end of the beginning.*

—ANONYMOUS

Every relationship reaches the point where it looks as if it's going to come completely unraveled. We move from wanting to be together constantly to looking for other, more exciting things to do. When your first passion cools, every conversation seems to end up in a fight, and our dream mate looks more and more nightmarish by the minute. It feels like the beginning of the end—of romance, of our dreams, perhaps even the relationship. It can be a time of terrible disappointment, of questioning and reevaluating our lives and our choices.

But couples who understand the Imago process know that things are happening as they should. What looks like the beginning of the end is really the predictable terminal stage of the first phase of relationship—romantic love. It's grand while it lasts, but it's only meant to be a phase. The difficulties that provoke your despair are good indicators that you *are* with your perfect Imago mate, that together you have what it takes to make a new beginning. You've only just begun the journey to real love. There's so much more to come!

❧ *Make a point to mirror back any frustration that your partner expresses today, especially if it is about you.*

In my time of quiet today, I contemplate the fact that our relationship, like everything else in nature, goes through a process of evolution. Right now, my partner and I are in the staging area that leads onto the path to real love.

Hidden deep in the heart of things, Thou carest for growth and life: the seed becomes shoot, the bud a blossom, the flower becomes fruit. Tired I slept on my idle bed in the illusion that the work had an end. In the morning I awoke to find that my garden was full of flowers.

—TAGORE

In this culture of instant breakfasts, express mail, and one-hour cleaning, very few of us have had the need or opportunity to cultivate patience. So when we find that a happy partnership doesn't happen overnight, that there are no one-stop therapies or quick-fix answers to our problems, we can get pretty discouraged.

We need to remember that our relationship is often like a small seedling, struggling to take root. It needs time, the proper fertilizing, before it opens in full flower. Each day, one bit of the Imago process provides the needed structure and nourishment. If you skip a day, don't beat yourself up about it; just pick up again the following day. Applaud yourself each time you mirror your partner, or go out of your way to do something caring for your partner. At first the results may seem meager, and you may fall into bed exhausted and discouraged. Keep on. One day, you will awaken to find your garden abundant with bright blossoms.

❧ *Take a minute to think about the past few days and the tasks you've performed each day. Have any of them been beneficial? Have they led to even small or subtle improvements in your relationship? Make a list of all these new beginnings in your notebook. Does that list help you see that the end of the journey will come if you are patient and just keep working one step at a time?*

Taking twenty minutes of time for renewal today, I celebrate the seeds I have sown to become a source of love for my partner. I honor this wisdom: "One seed at a time. Soon the flowering of love."

> *I finally figured out the only reason to be alive is to enjoy it.*
>
> — RITA MAE BROWN

Let's hear it for pleasure! How about a good word for plain old fun? We spend so much time trying to figure out the meaning of life, trying to survive, trying not to be hurt, to make ends meet, making sure nothing goes wrong. With this kind of attitude, we could die of dullness. We forget that, whatever our circumstances, we are here, and we are alive.

Our natural state of full aliveness was lost in childhood, and we have an innate drive to reclaim it. All around us, tangled up with everything else, there is love and laughter and children and chocolate and kissing and bubble baths and a thousand other reasons why life can be a pleasure dome. Having fun should be high on your list of priorities.

🕊 *Today, enjoy being alive. Whatever your troubles and distractions, make a special effort to ferret out the moments of pleasure, to savor those morsels of enjoyment. Share with your partner a few simple pleasures—a minute to step outside and see the moon or a new-bloomed flower, an extra kiss or caress, something to laugh about.*

Today I enter the place of the spirit within and, feeling my energy pulsating and joy coursing throughout my body, I celebrate these words: "The world is alive and I am a part of the world."

Beauty is in the heart of the beholder.

—LILLIAN HELLMAN

What is our partner's beauty secret? It is with neither the eye nor the mind that we fully apprehend our partner's beauty. Beauty is revealed in the accumulation of heartfelt experiences that punctuate our long journey together. It is the partner who understands our yearning, who goes the extra step, who comforts and supports, who supplies us with laughter and compassion, that we find beautiful. There is no artifice involved.

❧ *Make a list of at least five ways your partner touches your heart. Tonight, tell your partner how beautiful they are.*

Closing my eyes in silence, I recall in detail the many ways in which my partner has warmed and healed my heart during our journey. From this vantage point, my partner's beauty is revealed to me anew.

When conflicts arise in our relationship, we tend to draw back. We wait and see, trying to be sure that we're not going to get hurt. Our involvement is not total; there's still a part of us looking around for a fallback position.

But in this half-hearted stance, nothing gets resolved. We don't make the effort to show our care; we let conflicts slide; arguments fester. We spend more time with our friends, more time reading bedtime stories to the kids; we bury ourselves in work or books or hobbies. Then we notice that our partner has one foot out the door too, and we feel vulnerable and unsafe. These avoidance behaviors are called exits.

In a conscious relationship, both feet are planted firmly in the relationship. We commit to taking the journey together and to learning the skills of the Imago process we need to heal our partner. By closing our exits we create an atmosphere of safety in which we can talk freely and be ourselves, without fear of reprisal or abandonment. We put all our eggs in one basket and nurture them until they are fully hatched.

❧ Recommit today, not only to your partner and your relationship but to the Imago process that you are learning in this book. Acknowledge your commitment to your partner, but do not ask your partner for a commitment. Leave that decision for your partner to make without pressure.

As I relax in quiet contemplation today, I summon the resources to honor my commitment. I hold this thought: "The journey to love requires commitment to the process."

All, everything that I understand, I understand only because I love.

—LEO TOLSTOY

With all the big questions we have about life and relationships, all the serious issues we confront, the tiny steps we take each day in the name of relationship maintenance sometimes seem frivolous, a drop in the bucket. Day after day, we faithfully do a little something to move things forward, when what we want is a bolt of lightning to illuminate the path, a jolt of instant transformation. What we're doing each day doesn't even seem to generate sparks.

Instant transformation is for sci-fi movies and fairy tales. In a conscious relationship, we pay attention to the faint light of illumination that comes with each day that we take a small step. We take responsibility for creating excitement, in small but regular installments. Those small changes and mini-doses of loving build up. One day you'll discover that all you have done has reached some kind of critical mass. You've crested the hill, passing the halfway point. All the love that you've accumulated serves to illuminate the road ahead, and the journey makes eminent sense.

࿔ *Think about one way in which you feel bogged down in your relationship. Identify one specific small act that you can do to turn that area of boredom into an opportunity for excitement.*

In my quiet space today, I identify and value the small steps that I am taking to create a conscious relationship. I celebrate the work that I have accomplished. This becomes my truth: "It is by taking one tiny step after another that we eventually learn how to walk—and then run!"

Darkness reigns at the foot of the lighthouse.

—JAPANESE PROVERB

Some days feel so bleak and hopeless. Our relationship seems a shambles, and though the sun is shining, we've lost touch with its warmth. Unable to see a way out of our unhappiness, afraid that our partnership will never change for the better, we become lost in a fog of hopelessness and depression. Caught in spiritual or emotional crisis, we forget that even in such periods of darkness there is movement, and eventually we will emerge into the light. We forget that darkness holds gifts for us, that there is richness and wisdom in coming face to face with our shadows. For the darkness holds the key to the mysteries of our lost and disowned selves.

Recall a past crisis in your relationship, a time of darkness. Think about how long it lasted, and how it ended. Was it darkest just before you found a solution to your problem? Share your memory of this past crisis with your partner today, and let that experience of emerging from crisis reassure you as you talk about any current darkness in your partnership.

Accessing courage in my quiet time today, I allow myself to experience the contours of darkness inside of me. I let go of my impulse to carry this weight alone by pretending that nothing is wrong. I focus on this phrase: "With trust, the process of moving into my darkness will one day deliver me into the light."

*Darkness within darkness. The gateway to all
understanding.*

—LAO-TZU

After years of failing to work out our problems, years of unhappiness
and discouragement, the dearth of kisses and compassion seems
crushing; we want to give up. In the dark hours when we feel most
hopeless, the unconfronted shadow issues of our partnership rumble
ominously just beneath the surface, and we feel the situation is
hopeless. This is the predictable endgame stage of the power struggle, when partners either sink into the passionless accommodations
of a parallel marriage, or break up, or choose, in desperation, to
finally confront their demons.

Despair can be a turning point for couples, a gateway not only to
understanding but to a new direction and recommitment. It can lead
to the acceptance of the truth that you are connected to an incompatible person who is in your life to be healed and to be a source of
healing for you. When you are about to give up, when your defenses
are weakening, a breakthrough can come—an insight and a resolve to
let go of the impasse, to surrender your fear and take the risk of
change. Sometimes our relationship is darkest just before the dawn.

❧ *In your notebook, describe the darkest night in your relationship. If you are at an impasse now, describe it. Then use the
couples dialogue to discuss it with your partner until you see the
good hidden in the conflict.*

In these dark times, I realize all the more the importance of my
twenty minutes of quiet. It's critical that I move into a centered place
within, and find an inner peace of mind, and let that centered place
restore my beleaguered state. I see that my difficulties with my
partner are obstacles I must surmount on my journey toward spiritual
wholeness.

Does this scenario look familiar? Most couples have a here-we-go-again argument in which the same scene is played out each time, with the same ending—an impasse that reopens old wounds and leaves them exhausted and angry.

In the Imago system, this eternally replayed conflict is called the core scene. Core scenes occur when the childhood adaptations of one partner are pitted against the childhood adaptations of the other, making the encounter particularly emotionally charged and doubly wounding. As the couple repeats their core scene fight over and over, they come to know their roles so well, and their next lines and the outcome become so predictable, that it is as if they are following a script.

In this unit, you will learn how to identify the underlying cause of your core scene and rewrite the script so that in the future, when your core scene opens, you can change the script in a way that reduces the destructive impact of your rage and has a happier ending.

⏀ *Have a conversation with your partner in which you identify the nature of your core scene and its basic dynamics—what provokes it, what takes place, how it usually ends. Be sure to mirror each other.*

Today I relax into my deep place of courage, the place that allows me to look at myself, and I see those parts of me that react mechanically to certain provocations from my partner. Knowing this reaction comes from fear, I relax more deeply into this prayer: "Becoming more conscious frees me from blind repetitiveness."

*Nothing can keep an argument going like two people
who aren't sure what they're arguing about.*

—OPRAH WINFREY

A core scene argument seems never to end—it just goes on and on until both partners are exhausted or one gives up or leaves the scene. Because its root cause is not consciously understood, there is never a resolution. Over time a rigidly repeated stimulus-response pattern develops: one line leads to the next, and pretty soon they're fighting the same old battle. Here's the basic story line of one couple's core scene:

Act I: Husband comes home from work and is confronted by wife, who wants him to do something, anything—some yardwork, read the mail, help plan their vacation. Husband says he'll be happy to do it . . . later (first he has to go jogging or read the paper).

Act II: (Later that evening.) Wife asks again for husband to do something. Husband says he'll be happy to do it . . . later (first he has to take a shower or watch his favorite show on television).

Act III: (Later that evening.) Wife asks again for husband to do something. Husband says he'll be happy to do it . . . later (first he has to have a drink).

Act IV: Husband has several drinks. Wife is angry that husband is not doing what she asked and he agreed to do. Husband ignores wife. Wife gets angrier, screams at husband. Husband leaves and goes to local pub.

Act V: Husband comes home hours later. Wife continues fight. Husband goes to sleep alone on the sofa.

❧ *Today you and your partner should write the script of your core scene. If you and your partner disagree on the basic lines, use mirroring to understand each other's point of view.*

In my time of quiet today, I see a movie screen on which our core scene is playing. I simply watch objectively and dispassionately, allowing myself to feel serene and loving toward my partner. I hold this thought: "We are trying to heal ourselves."

We are too little to be always able to rise above difficulties. Well then, let us pass beneath them quite simply.

—SAINT THERESA OF LISIEUX

After reenacting your core scene many, many times, and ending over and over again in the same old stalemate, it may seem that your impasse is so big and unchangeable that it is impossible to rise above it. Well, that's true enough; the only way out is to go *through* it, by looking inside to identify the childhood wounds that are stirred up whenever your core scene is played out. As an example of how childhood wounds are replayed in our core scene, let's look beneath the surface of the fight our couple had yesterday.

In this drama, the husband is secretly angry at the wife because he thinks she is intruding. If he looks deeper, he sees that as a child he had to care for his alcoholic mother, who wasn't capable of doing things around the house for herself. Instead of recognizing what is going on and expressing this frustration directly, he takes full advantage of all the exits he has built into the marriage—jogging, watching TV, drinking. This is similar to what he did at age ten when he spent his after-school hours reading alone in the library instead of going home and being her servant.

The wife's anger is really disguised panic—she is terrified of being left alone because as a young child her mother worked at home giving piano lessons to other children instead of giving her the attention she needed. So she does what she used to do to get her mother's attention: first she pesters, and then she has a temper tantrum.

If you look deeply enough, you too will find that your core scene is only a childhood scene being reenacted, a wound crying out for your attention and healing. Understanding the deeper hurt will allow you to end your impasse and restore love.

🔊 *Using mirroring, share the childhood wound behind your core scene with each other. Later today, give each other some comfort.*

As I sit in contemplation today, I relax completely and reenter our core scene. I prayerfully acknowledge: "I am wounded, and my partner is wounded, too."

*In this world there is nothing softer or thinner than
water. But to compel the hard and unyielding, it has
no equal. That the weak overcomes the strong, that the
hard gives way to the gentle—this everyone knows, yet
no one acts accordingly.*

—LAO-TZU

It is nature's way to follow every difficulty with a resolution—
sometimes winter seems to last forever, but spring always comes.
As sure as the rainbow follows the storm, so too can you and your
partner find a way out of your core scene impasse.

The unfinished business of our childhood is to fill those needs that
our caretakers failed to meet. Once our partner addresses those
needs *by behaving toward us differently from our caretakers*, we begin
to heal.

Identifying that we need to resolve the impasse of our core scene
involves identifying the frustration and the deep, unmet need that lies
behind it. As you work through this book, you will have many
opportunities to give each other what is needed and resolve your core
scene conflict.

❧ *Spend a few minutes thinking about what you would like from
your partner to have a happier ending to your core scene. What
specifically do you want your partner to say or do that would
avoid the usual core scene episode? Write it down as a very
specific, doable behavior: "When I ask you to do something, be
honest with me if you don't want to do it, and if you really are
intending to do it, tell me specifically when you are willing to do
it—don't just say 'later.' "*

**Today I take time to enter my deepest place of spiritual strength.
There I become aware of my hurt and pain and the difficulty I have
asking for what I need. I honor my humanness: "It is okay to have
needs and ask for what I want."**

*The block of granite which was an obstacle in the
pathway of the weak, became a stepping-stone in the
pathway of the strong.*

— THOMAS CARLYLE

When we understand the deep, unmet need that is at the root of our core scene, we can use it as a stepping-stone for healing, instead of letting it be an obstacle to love.

To break the impasse of the core scene, it takes only one or two new lines, especially during the first act, to take the situation in an entirely new direction. Even if only one partner is able to introduce a new line, it is impossible for the old script to proceed, because you don't have the old familiar cues to respond to.

Here are two ways our conflicted husband and wife could handle their core scene differently:

The wife could honor the husband's request to back off. After asking him once or twice to do something, she could stop making demands. Then the husband's automatic response to withdraw would no longer be necessary. He would have to respond differently—perhaps he will stay home or have fewer drinks. Eventually he might even decide to do those things the wife asks because he doesn't feel pressured.

Or, the husband could be honest with the wife and say, "No, I don't want to go shopping with you tonight, but we can go together on Saturday morning. I just want to rest and watch TV tonight. Would you come cuddle and watch TV with me?" The wife would be so relieved that her husband is filling her need for reassurance and togetherness that she would be happy to wait to go shopping.

❧ *Together with your partner, go over your old script and discuss different ways you can rewrite your script, taking into consideration each other's needs. If it seems too difficult at first to meet all of each other's needs, agree on something you think you can do. Any change at all is beneficial.*

In my period of quiet today, I close my eyes and relax and bring my partner into my safe place with me. In this sacred place, I feel strength and love toward my partner and see a golden light encircling us.

The final step to resolving your core scene is to write a new script so that when the curtain comes down, the lovers are embracing. Here's one happy resolution:

> Act I: Husband comes home from work; they greet each other with a hug and kiss. Wife says, "I'd like to plan our vacation tonight. Is that okay with you?" Husband says, "Fine, but I'd like to go jogging before dinner, if that's all right." Wife says "That's fine," and husband goes off to jog.

> Act II: After dinner, wife says, "Ready to talk about our vacation?" Husband: "Yes, but let's see if we can wrap it up in time for me to get a little reading in."

> Act III: Husband and wife poring over brochures and timetables. Husband says, "That was great. I'm looking forward to this vacation. I think I'll go read now. Why don't you come in and sit with me after you make your phone call and we can snuggle up a little?" Curtain closes.

&❧ *With your partner, write out your new script. Read the new script together out loud over and over again so that the new lines will be available for you to use when the core scene comes up, replacing your habitual old ones.*

Today in quiet, I treasure these words: "It is possible to live in the relationship of my dreams."

Now, there's just one more little thing to do with regard to your new core scene script. You've got to remember your lines! This is easier said than done; the compulsion to repeat our old patterns, to respond in the same tired way, is mighty strong.

There are two specific things you can do to avoid a repetition of the past. First, be alert to the warning signs of an oncoming scene. People who get migraines talk about the aura that precedes them. Animals run from storms long before humans sense their approach. Core scenes, too, have their warning signs, if we can but tune in to them. Second, memorize those opening lines, so that the old scene hasn't a chance to get under way. When a core scene threatens, force yourself to say your lines, even if they don't sound quite natural. "Yes-dear-that-is-fine-with-me.   I-can-un-der-stand-your-feel-ings." Sounding like a robot is better than blowing your lines.

❧ *Read over your new core scene script until it feels familiar to you, and memorize at least your first few lines. Rehearse them out loud in front of a mirror.*

Today, in the inner theater of my mind, I see myself onstage learning the lines of a new play. As I repeat them until they become natural, I create a new scene with my partner that brings applause from the audience. I look to this potential: "I can make all things new."

Grow old along with me!
The best is yet to be,
The last of life, for which the first was made.

— ROBERT BROWNING

It can seem as if the future is unknown and unpredictable, but in fact, it's simply a response to what we do today. Right *now* we are making the first part of our life, which will determine the last of it. We are acquiring particular habits and preferences, cementing friendships, reinforcing each day certain patterns of behavior. We are stockpiling experiences, to be turned into memories years from now. Will they be recollections of trust and laughter or of fear and resentment?

You and your partner are co-entrepreneurs in the creation of the physical, spiritual, and psychic structure in which you will spend your future. All that happens along the way, from your first glance to your most recent touch, and everything in between, creates your future together. All that you are experiencing with your partner today is preparing the way for the best, which is yet to come. If you stick with the Imago process, you will have the precious experience of sharing each day, throughout your life, with someone you truly know and care about. Life expectancies are getting longer and longer; you might as well start today to make those years ahead golden.

☙ *Tell your partner today one thing they did yesterday that you appreciate. If you are apart, call your partner now.*

Relaxing and breathing deeply, I inhale the exquisite feeling of power I have to determine tomorrow through my actions today. This thought is my focus: "Today creates my tomorrows."

Love is the great Asker.

—D. H. LAWRENCE

An intimate relationship in which partners are afraid to ask for what they want seems to be a contradiction, but it's all too common. We don't ask because we're afraid we'll be turned down or thought weak and needy; because we don't want to "owe" our partner anything or suffer their anger or disdain. It's not unheard of for partners to create a crisis—illness, depression, collapse—in order to feel entitled to get the attention they're afraid to ask for under normal circumstances.

The reluctance to ask our partners for what we need is the predictable outcome of a childhood in which we were ridiculed or punished for asking for attention, or in which our requests were ignored or refused. Asking for what we need directly feels risky, so we learn either not to ask at all or to ask in indirect and subtle ways that are irritating or easily misunderstood. We are still under the spell of the inner child who needs attention but is afraid to ask.

How relieved our partner would be if we could learn to ask for what we want from them—without demands or innuendo. They would love to know just what it is we want without having to guess. Simply asking is one of the most intimate and loving gifts we can give to another human being. And it makes giving much easier.

❧ *Allow yourself to ask for one specific sign of affection from your partner today. Think of something that would really make your inner child feel loved—perhaps a back rub or a giant hug.*

In a quiet space today, I recognize how often I fail to ask for what I need because at times it feels so scary. I also realize that how I ask is as important as what I'm asking for. I acknowledge this wisdom: "A request made with love will be answered with love."

You've undoubtedly had the experience of giving your partner a gift or doing something special for your mate and receiving merely a lukewarm response or show of appreciation. If you look carefully, you will discover that your gift had strings attached. You were making a deal, expecting something in return—appreciation, credit, a gift in kind. Some unspoken expectation triggered your partner's unconscious "bullshit detector" and activated their defenses. Their joy was tempered by your expectations, and your anticipated pleasure and appreciation were short-circuited. The unconscious receives only unconditional gifts.

🌢 *Make a gift to your partner with no strings attached: write a love poem, rake the leaves, bring home a bouquet of balloons, do the dishes, serve breakfast in bed. Note how your partner feels and how your unfettered gift makes you feel.*

As I surround myself with a nurturing environment, I imagine myself with a pair of scissors cutting all the strings of expectation attached to the things I give my partner. Breathing slowly, I hold this prayer in my heart: "Love asks nothing in return, nor draws attention to itself."

Grumbling is the death of love.

—MARLENE DIETRICH

Over time, love is eroded by chronic criticism, unhappiness, or disapproval, buried under a blanket of insult and grievance. Eventually our partner is worn down by our complaints, the constant focus on what's wrong with them. They give up trying to make things right, and their feelings for us dwindle and die.

Criticism not only fails to get us what we want; it's a form of self-abuse. Because the traits we criticize in our partners are often projections of unpleasant truths about ourselves, our nagging has a boomerang effect. Our old brain absorbs the criticism as though we were directing it at ourselves. Then nobody feels loved.

Be aware today of the repetitive criticisms or negative thoughts you have about your partner. Restrain yourself from grumbling out loud just for today; instead, write down your criticisms. At the end of the day, experiment with converting each complaint into a desire—delivered in a simple, lighthearted way. Lace your desire with tenderness, maybe a dash of humor. Convert "You never come home on time" into "It means so much to me when you call me when you're late." See if you don't feel better about yourself.

In my time of stillness today, I gently hold this thought: "Every criticism of my partner is an act of self-abuse. To praise my partner is an act of self-love."

Earth's crammed with heaven.

—ELIZABETH BARRETT BROWNING

When we're weary, beset by worries, when the news is filled with stories of man's inhumanity to man—and animals and rain forests— we long for a kinder, more beautiful world. The idyllic heaven that we've been told about seems an altogether better place.

The world can be almost unbearably harsh, and circumstances sometimes conspire to blind us to all but its meanness. But we live in a mysterious universe: everything—good and bad, beautiful and ugly, love and hate—is everywhere, all the time. We create reality, fix it in time and space, by observing it.

How easy it is to overlook the many miracles of our lives, to gloss over the simple blessings of being alive, being loved, the smell of babies, the taste of apricots, the beauty of the moon, our partner's touch. As we learn to love day by day, as intimacy deepens, we begin to exist in a partnership enveloped by the spiritual. Heaven is here, within us, all around us, in this moment. To love is to be able to see it.

❧ *Take a walk with your partner in nature today. Go to the park, sit on the back porch, take a drive in the country, walk on the beach. Look for heaven together in everything, your partner and yourself included.*

In a joyful meditation, I tune in to my own body and feel the miracle of my heartbeat and, tuning in to the outside world, savor the sounds and smells around me. In wonder, I celebrate: "Heaven is mine for the taking."

*I'm suggesting we call sex something else, and it
should include everything from kissing to sitting close
together.*

—SHERE HITE

When you and your partner make love, what do you *do*? Does your sex life include a passing pat on the cheek, the fond look across a crowded hardware store, intimate soul-baring conversation? If not, you're sex starved.

Couples run into trouble when they separate sex from everything else in their lives. When the sex act is disconnected from the ways in which they are otherwise intimate, it degenerates into a ritualized performance—the proverbial "getting your rocks off." Divorced from kisses, from the tender touch, the loving glance, the shared joke, and fraught with expectations and role-playing, it becomes compartmentalized.

Taking sex out of the bedroom and into every room of the house and into all of our activities takes the pressure off performance and puts a lot more fun and closeness into doing the dishes. With this broader, more sensualized definition of what it means to make love, you may find you're having sex every day.

❧ *Bring sex into your daily life today—try a cuddle in the kitchen, fondling in the laundry room, a double entendre over the phone, a come-hither look across the dinner table.*

As I move into a quiet time today, I focus on the word *intercourse* and, freeing my mind from inhibitions, I experience a rich and varied flow of sexual and nonsexual images. I savor this thought: "Making love is limited only by my imagination."

"**W**here were you at lunch today? I came by your office and you weren't there. Whom did you have lunch with? Did you go to that new French bistro? What did you have? Was it expensive? Who paid for it? How long were you gone? What did you talk about all that time? Why didn't you tell me you were going out to lunch?"

This line of questioning reveals a great deal about the childhood wounds of the interrogator. It is a sign of insecurity and mistrust and a need to control or approve of our partner's every move.

There's a big difference between cross-examination and genuine concern. We may think we're showing interest, but our interest smacks of authoritarianism or prying, and our questions come across as if we're giving our partner the third degree.

Pretending we're Perry Mason or Columbo may add to our knowledge of our partner in some sense, but it subtracts from our intimacy. When we treat our partners with suspicion, we are subtly encouraging them to act out our distrust. Partners in a conscious relationship show interest in their mate's daily activities, but they show support for their partner's freedom by not pressing for every little detail.

🍃 *As you talk with your partner today, practice asking your partner about their day without prying. Mirror back your report and share your day, asking your partner to mirror you.*

Today I ground myself in my own life and well-being, releasing my partner from the burden of my fears. I hold this thought in faith: "I trust my partner to tell me all I need to know."

Play consists of whatever a body is not obliged to do.

— MARK TWAIN

As children we had an unlimited capacity for play. For hours on end, we'd make angels in the snow, stockpile pine cones, chase frogs in a creek bed, wriggle ourselves silly with our Hula-Hoops, write our initials on frosted window panes, until we returned home dirty and exhausted.

But something happens to our natural playfulness. We lose the joy of childhood and become serious. When we do play, it's with goal-oriented intensity; our toys and diversions are complex and costly. The wild, free-for-all playing of children now makes us self-conscious; we try to calm them down, and regulate their exuberance.

Better we should learn from our children the joy of pure play—the ability to enjoy ourselves with unfettered abandon, to play without goals or rules, winners or losers. When we relearn how to play spontaneously and aimlessly, we recapture the joyful aliveness that is our birthright and participate in divine revelry.

🍂 *Find some time today for pure, childlike play with your partner. Rent a favorite childhood movie. Stock up on the makings of a double banana split. Play with your old stuffed animals. Have a water-pistol duel. Dance the hootchie-kootchie.*

In time alone, I let the weight of my responsibilities fall away and feel my spirit growing lighter. I envision myself in joyous revelry with my partner and celebrate this thought: "Revelry and joy express the God within."

But the bravest are surely those who have the clearest vision of what is before them, glory and danger alike, and yet notwithstanding go out to meet it.

—THUCYDIDES

Have you ever felt that you and your partner weren't in the same relationship? It happens all the time. We enter our partnership with our own pictures of what we expect it to be like based on our conditioning, experiences, and desires. Unless your partner has the same vision, you're bound to run into difficulties.

For the next few days, you and your partner will be invited to create a shared vision of your relationship. A vision focuses your energy and efforts on a goal. It is a road map of your commitment, a view of the whole of which you both are a part; it gives direction to each decision and shapes each action. You can't get there without it!

Today begin the envisioning process by writing down your vision for your relationship. At the top of a new page in your notebook, write "My Relationship Vision"; then draw vertical lines to create four columns. Make column one about an inch wide, column two about five inches wide, and columns three and four an inch wide each.

At the top of column two, write "In My Ideal Relationship." Below that write a series of short, positive sentences that describe your personal vision of a deeply satisfying love relationship. Put each sentence on a separate line. Include qualities you already have that you want to keep and qualities you wish you had. Write each sentence in the present tense, as if it were already happening: "We have fun together." "We have great sex." "We are financially secure."

In quiet time today, I imagine myself in our dream marriage. Holding this image, I breathe its fragrance, hear its sounds, see its colors and forms, touch its textures. I offer this prayer in faith: "I can live in the marriage of my dreams."

*Dreams pass into the reality of action. From the
action stems the dream again; and this
interdependence produces the highest form of living.*

                                  —ANAÏS NIN

You and your partner have been trying to bring your individual
visions into reality, which can be a very frustrating experience if
neither of you knows the other's dream! To have a successful
relationship, you must cocreate a shared vision as a conscious
intention. A shared vision synthesizes separate dreams, desires,
values and needs. This joint creation becomes your conscious dream
and your new reality; it influences your actions and decisions. As you
articulate your dream, remember that your partnership is unique; it
need not be bound by convention or imitate the models provided by
your parents or society. This is the relationship that *you* want; it
should fit the two of you like a glove.

🖎 *Take out your relationship vision list and share it with your
partner; exchange lists or read them to each other. Then, at the
top of column one of your list, write "Similarities" and place a
check mark next to the items that you have in common. It doesn't
matter if you have used different words, as long as the general
idea is the same. If your partner has written sentences that you
agree with but did not think of yourself, add them to your list and
give them a check mark in column one, too.*

In meditation today, I return to the deep place within. I summon the
vision of my dream marriage and acknowledge this wisdom: "Without
a vision, a relationship perishes."

The best and most beautiful things in the world cannot be seen or even touched. They must be felt with the heart.

—HELEN KELLER

As we change and grow, different things become important to us. A young woman describing her perfect partner might say, "He's a hunk who graduated from an Ivy League college and drives a red sports car." As we mature, we value other things. Now we are more likely to place a premium on qualities such as kindness, sensuality, tenderness, honest communication, a sense of humor, or dependability.

As you and your partner try to articulate your relationship vision, try to be very clear about what is truly important to you. Is it more important that "we have a big house overlooking the ocean" or that "we listen to each other and respect each other's point of view"? That "we alternate vacations with our kids with vacations for just the two of us" or that "our kids go to the most prestigious school"? Our society focuses on goods and status, but keep in mind the value of things that can be touched only with the heart. As you clarify your vision, be sure to ask the important questions! What gives you most joy? What lights up your life?

Working alone with your relationship vision list, at the top of column three write "Importance." In column three, rank each item (including the ones that are not shared) with a number 1 to 5 according to its importance to you, with 1 indicating "very important" and 5 indicating "not important." Circle the two items that are most important to you.

At the top of column four, write "Difficulty." In column four, put a check mark beside those items that you think would be most difficult for the two of you to achieve.

In my time of quiet today, I summon the courage to move from the marriage I am in to the marriage of my dreams. I hold these words in faith: "Dreams are the seeds of reality."

A happy marriage is not a gift; it's an achievement.

—ANN LANDERS

Good relationships are not delivered gift wrapped to your door; they require ongoing, conscious creation. But when you are creating something that involves another person, it is essential to have a common vision. Without it, your relationship can become aimless and chaotic, and you will make random, often fruitless attempts to cope with your problems and conflicts. Defining your vision will divert your attention from past and present disappointments and point you in the direction of your dreams.

&❧ *On a new sheet of paper make the same four columns as before. Title this page "Our Mutual Relationship Vision." At the top of column one write one partner's name and "Importance"; label column two "In Our Ideal Relationship"; at the top of column three write the other partner's name and "Importance"; label column four "Mutual Difficulty."*

Take out your individual relationship vision lists and work together to create a mutual relationship vision. Start with the items that you both agree are most important and fill in your importance rating numbers in columns one and three. Put check marks in column four next to those items that you both agree would be difficult to achieve. At the bottom of the list, write items that are relatively unimportant. If you have items that are a source of conflict between you, draw a line partway down the page and list them below the line, or leave the item off your combined list.

As you create your shared vision, remember to write each item as a short, positive, descriptive sentence in the present tense.

When you have finished cocreating your mutual relationship vision, read it out loud to each other.

In the stillness at my core, I feel joy rising as I envision our mutual dream of love. I hold this joy until it floods my whole being.

Congratulations! You now share a vision of your ideal relationship and are cooperating to achieve a common goal. Read your mutual relationship vision with your partner periodically as a reminder of your intention. Refer to it when you are feeling angry or discouraged and need some reinforcement. Add to it or refine your statements as your goals change.

For now, a celebration is in order, for this is a new beginning. Plan something special today to acknowledge your passage to a new phase of your relationship—a toast, three cheers, a little slow dancin', candlelight at dinner?

❧ *Together, post your mutual relationship vision in a place where you can see it daily. This is an important document, for it is a guide to your future. Take some time to make it attractive, neat, legible, and inspiring. Make it truly yours, both in words and presentation.*

Today I acknowledge the effort my partner has made in creating a shared vision. With a celebrative spirit, I give thanks for having my partner in my life.

Friendship between two persons depends upon the patience of one.

—NATIVE AMERICAN PROVERB

Because we come to our relationships with habitual patterns that insidiously dovetail with those of our partners, we often end up in a holding pattern of argument, frustration, boredom, and discouragement, which seems unbreakable. No matter how we try, we seem to return to the same conflicts, with the same results, chasing each other around in circles until we're exhausted.

Even when we become aware of the destructive pattern, we don't always have the energy or ability to do something different. But we can change the course of events simply by *not* doing what we have always done—which is to react unthinkingly in the usual way to the usual provocation. With increased awareness, we can withdraw from the drama. Fortifying ourselves with spirituality keeps us from impulsively reacting to the stimulus that usually sends us spiraling into conflict. Rather than reacting, we can simply bear witness to our partner's distress. When we are able to hold their projections—their accusations or name-calling—rather than respond in kind, we remove the screen on which the usual movie plays.

This is more easily said than done, but it is essential to the process. The withdrawal of one partner from the tension can be a turning point. When your partner sees that you are hearing them, bearing witness to their communication without retaliating or retreating, their own energy will shift in response. It always takes two to tango, but it only takes one person to change the tune.

&. *Without telling your partner, be the receiver, all day today, of your partner's complaints or frustrations, just listening, not reacting.*

In wordless prayer, I draw on my resources of strength. Just for today, I hold my partner in complete acceptance.

There is always something left to love. And if you
ain't learned that, you ain't learned nothing.

—LORRAINE HANSBERRY

As we plow through the difficulties of the power struggle, we may come to a place where we can see only the negative in our partners. We become experts on their flaws; we could go on for hours about the nasty things they say, their lack of fairness, their bad breath, their compulsive gum chewing, the nights they didn't come home until the wee hours. We can't remember what we ever loved about them. What happened to their kindness, their generosity, their constant attention and interest in us, their affection, their passion? At the moment, we can't think of a thing in their favor.

This is a dangerous place to be. It diminishes us as well as our partner. Are we so worthless as to be with someone with no redeeming qualities? Are we really unable to find something salvageable to build on? When we are up to our necks in negativity, we may think we have lost what we once loved in our partner, but this loss is largely a matter of perception. Your partner is still the person they were when we met them but mired now, like ourselves, in their own anger or unhappiness.

What we need to do is to love—love any little thing, in any way that we can. We can love the way they clean their plate, or the cute way they yawn, their habit of pushing their glasses back on their nose ten times an hour. If we can find something that is still lovable, we learn that loving itself, not what we love, is what will rescue us from our impasse.

❧ *No matter how troubled your relationship is, find something to love in your partner today. Visualize it in your mind, go out of your way to notice it. Tonight, say to your partner, "I love you because . . ." and tell them just what it is that's lovable.*

Entering my inner sanctuary, I recognize the sacred behind all aspects of my relationship. I celebrate this insight: "Whenever I love the unlovable in my partner, I love the same in myself."

*Don't you think I was made for you? I feel like you
had me ordered—and I was delivered to you—to be
worn—I want you to wear me, like a watch-charm or
a button hole bouquet—to the world.*

—ZELDA FITZGERALD

How true that we are made for each other. We both love Italian food
and living in the country and "Star Trek." One of us hates to cook,
but the other loves to; one of us is very shy, but the other pulls us
out of our shell. On top of it all, you're just the right height, your hair
is the perfect color, you wear the right clothes, have the right job.
We belong together. Our similarities are uncanny, our differences
complementary.

But our unconscious has had a hand all along in this tongue-and-
groove construction, doing its own puzzle solving, bringing us together with a partner who fits as well the negative traits of our
Imago. Someone who knows just the right things to say to push our
buttons, who has just the right behaviors to awaken our fear of
abandonment. Someone who is adamant that we find a better way
than whining to get what we want, someone who demands our
tenderness during lovemaking. Someone who will make us learn
tolerance, patience, compassion, trust. Someone who will see, and
eventually, accept, our flaws *and* make us change to heal them. Oh
yes, we were made for each other, but not only in the ways we first
saw.

🙠 *What is the most personally challenging way in which you and
your partner were made for each other—your most difficult
conflict, the hardest change your partner asks of you? Tonight tell
your partner "You are the perfect partner for me because . . ."
(fill in the blank!)*

**Although I have always wanted a conflict-free, perfect-fit relationship,
I enter a place of inner wisdom today, acknowledging that the most
valuable resource in our partnership is our differences. I honor this
insight: "Healing is the goal of the attraction of opposites."**

The only way to speak the truth is to speak lovingly.

— HENRY DAVID THOREAU

We ask for the truth from our partner, but are we willing to hear it? Can we tell the truth to our partner in a way that is loving and not hurtful? And can we accept our partner's truth in good faith?

Truth-telling is a skill that must be filtered through love, for without love the truth can be needlessly painful. There is no honor in "telling it like it is" at the expense of our partner's feelings. All too often, truth is a double-edged sword, a lethal weapon ostensibly wielded in the name of clarity or forthrightness but having the effect of demeaning or undermining its victim.

Kindness and tact can make all the difference between hurting your partner's feelings and giving them some constructive feedback. "Your red dress is so much more flattering" is a far better response to your partner's question than "That dress makes you look fat." There's a fine, but crucial, line between helpful and hurtful critique. For loving and supportive partners, truth and kindness are intertwined.

❧ *Is there something you haven't been telling your partner because you don't want to hurt their feelings—they need to go on a diet, it's time to pluck their nose hairs, their best friend is boring? Tell your partner the truth today, with love and kindness.*

I relax into gentle prayer today. Surrounding my partner with a white light of love, I see myself sharing a difficult truth without causing pain. I ponder this thought: "Truth without love is abuse."

It is always shattering when romance begins to fade and problems begin to mar our fantasy of perfect bliss. But the days of romantic love are always numbered; this is nature's design. Romantic love delivers an important message: if you can figure out what it is that your partner secretly needs, the two of you can feel like this forever. In a way, romantic love is a kind of preamble to the real thing, a foretaste of what you will experience when you have negotiated the mine field of the power struggle and come out into the clearing of real love.

The passion of romantic love is based on fantasy and fueled by expectation, whereas the passion in a conscious relationship is rooted in our memories of our healing experience with our partners. Romantic love is a time bomb; sooner or later, the explosion comes. But this is a part of the overall process. The end of romantic love heralds the beginning of deeper spiritual evolution.

❧ *How about a surprise for your partner today—perhaps one of the things that came so easily during those early days of romance. Bagels and the newspaper in bed? Some serious necking? The new book or movie or garden rake your mate's been hinting about?*

Moving into a still clearing, away from the wars of the power struggle, I relax into the reality of what is and let go of disappointments. I hold this prayer in my heart: "Loving the reality of my partner is the door to my own spiritual awakening."

*Here's to matrimony, the high sea for which no
compass has yet been invented.*

—HEINRICH HEINE

In the early days of exploration, cartographers' maps would show
territories that were as yet uncharted. These unexplored areas would
often bear the cautionary warning: "Here Be Dragons."

Intimate relationships also have their uncharted areas, the unknown
places within each partner that will need to be explored bravely in
order to make the whole territory known and safe.

The territory of love and marriage has been pretty well mapped by
the psychologists and social scientists, and we have a pretty good
understanding of our partners when we make a commitment to them.
Even so, it's hard to generalize about relationships, harder to make
rules. Each relationship is like no other, for each combination of two
people creates a particular chemistry.

The Imago system provides a compass of sorts, guidelines that
explain basic concepts, tools, and strategies that we can apply to our
own situation, a rudder by which we can steer through the high
waves. How that system applies to your particular relationship can
only be approximate, however. No one has ever seen your and your
partner's dragons. But the basics of the Imago system are likely to
be useful. Everything we learn before we enter the uncharted waters
will help us to slay the monsters we meet.

🞋 *With your partner, reaffirm your commitment to learning the
skills of the Imago process. Have a couples dialogue about the
processes you have used so far and recall your successes.*

**In quiet contemplation today, I visualize the map outlining the
journey to a conscious relationship. Knowing I cannot reach my
destination on my own, I record these words as key to successful
navigation: "My partner's needs point the way to my destination of
wholeness."**

When we begin to emerge from the fog of romantic love, and after we get over the shock of our partner's imperfections, we still hold out the hope that our partner will ultimately change somehow to conform with that pretty picture we once imagined. We hope they'll stop smoking, curb their temper, wear Italian shoes, or be more aggressive in bed. What often happens is that, as we intensify our commitment to our partners, these hopes harden into expectations. Our fervent wishes turn into solid "shoulds" and finally into feelings of entitlement.

Shoulds are dangerous to partnerships. They define an imaginary partner, blinding us to our real mate. They dwell in a hypothetical future rather than a potentially satisfying present. They create unhappiness for us, and surefire frustration and feelings of rejection for our partner. With our love and acceptance, our partner may turn out as we hoped, but only when we least expect them to.

❧ Make a list of at least three shoulds you've been laying on your partner. Then pick out the one most important to you and reframe it as a behavior-change request for your partner tonight. In your mind, turn the rest of those "shoulds" back into "hopes."

In the serenity of time alone, I access my deep courage to acknowledge the part of myself that expects my partner to be somebody else. I visualize peeling away the shoulds like the layers of an onion to reveal my partner's reality. I rejoice in their truth.

Everything else you grow out of, but you never recover from childhood.

—BERYL BAINBRIDGE

Like it or not, childhood influences who we become as adults. The image of the person we will choose as a life partner begins to be etched on our brain in the first few minutes of life. This image, or Imago, is created by our unconscious mind in response to the way our caretakers treated us and the demands made on us by society. This core premise of Imago therapy contrasts with the popular view that we consciously choose our partners on the basis of looks, social class, profession, or sex appeal.

There are several components that, taken together, comprise the Imago—your caretakers' characters, the ways in which their parenting frustrated or encouraged you, and the ways in which you gave up parts of yourself to be accepted both in your home and out in the world. Over the next few days, we'll look at the central piece of the Imago puzzle, those experiences with your caretakers in childhood that have been influential in your choice of partner, and how they contributed to an unconscious agenda you bring to your relationship.

❧ *In your notebook, title two facing pages "Parental Traits" and divide each page into two vertical columns (so that you have four columns across two pages). Label column one "Positive Traits," and list in that column all your mother's positive traits as you recall them from childhood (not as she is today). Describe her with simple adjectives or phrases such as "kind," "musical," "patient," etc. Label column two "Negative Traits," and list all your mother's negative traits in the same manner ("grumpy," "fearful," "petty"). Label column three "Unfulfilled Desires" and in it write what you most wanted from your mother but never got. Label column four "Positive Feelings" and write about what you most enjoyed about being with your mother.*

In these moments of silence I access the courage to enter into childhood memories to discover the roots of my needs and unravel the mystery of my choices. I hold this truth in compassion: "I am the product of my childhood."

It may surprise and distress you to know that all the important people in your childhood still live in your head. They comprise your Imago, a composite picture of all the people who were responsible for caring for you. Whoever they were, a part of your brain recorded everything about them—the sound of their voices when they were angry, the way they smiled when they were happy, what they ate and wore. Along with these impressions, your unconscious mind recorded all your significant interactions with them.

The primitive old brain is intensely interested in survival. So the most vivid impressions it stores are the ones of our caretakers early in life, when we were most vulnerable. The most deeply engraved of those impressions are the negative encounters that seemed to threaten our existence. Your brain didn't simply enter the information into your data bank like a computer, however; it assigned a meaning to each experience, laying the foundation for how it would view the "world."

🍂 *Today you are invited to revisit your father (or father figure) as you knew him in childhood.*

On the two facing pages you began yesterday, add your father's positive traits as you recall them from childhood below the list of your mother's traits in column one. (There's no need to separate the two lists.) Again, use only simple adjectives or descriptive phrases. In the same manner, list your father's negative traits in column two. In column three, write what you most wanted from your father but never got. Write in column four what you most enjoyed about being with your father.

Entering the stillness within today, I open my mind to more knowledge of my childhood, relaxing into the joy of unraveling more of the mystery of who I am and the world I designed as a child.

We are not at home where our dwelling is, but where
we are understood.

—CHRISTIAN MORGENSTERN

Everyone's childhood is unique because patterns of childhood differ
from family to family, especially these days, when the traditional
nuclear family seems nearing extinction. When both parents work
full-time, the children's primary needs are often met by relatives,
nannies, baby-sitters, or day care workers. Sometimes an older
brother or sister, the boyfriend of a single mother, an aunt or
grandparents, even a group of people sharing a communal home fill
caretaker roles. In broken or troubled homes, the strongest influence
may be someone the child befriends on their own—a kind elderly
person who lives down the street, the local librarian, a teacher, a "big
sister."

Our unconscious records everything we experienced with those on
whom we were dependent for our needs, but it does not record
where it came from. All the incoming data goes to the same central
processing point and is integrated, without reference to gender, age,
creed or color, into the ever-evolving Imago.

ช *Today you are invited to bring any other people who were*
influential in your early childhood into the picture, one at a time,
noticing their traits and your feelings about them.

Then add to your lists their positive and negative traits, what
you wanted most from them and never got, and what you enjoyed
most about them, in the same manner as before.

In the stillness of prayer, I reenter my memories of childhood,
amazed at the panorama of experience I find there, and I acknowledge
the elegance of the way my unconscious has combined all my experi-
ences into one coherent reality.

Once we had it all! In the womb, all of our needs were instantly and automatically taken care of. We were in a constant state of blissful fulfillment. Then, abruptly it ended. From the moment of birth, gratification of our needs is no longer automatic or instant. Even if you were fortunate enough to grow up in a safe, nurturing environment, you still bear invisible scars from childhood, because from the very moment you were born you were a complex, dependent creature with a never-ending cycle of needs—"feed me," "hold me," "change my diapers," "play with me," our cries implored. And no parents, no matter how devoted, are able to respond perfectly to all of these changing needs, *all* of the time. So we are all wounded. But the nature and degree of our wounding depends on how well our caretakers understood and responded to our needs.

↜ *Referring back to the pages on which you have been recording the traits of your caretakers, circle the three positive and three negative traits that seemed to affect you the most; it doesn't matter which caretaker you associate them with. In column three, circle the most influential things that you did not get from both caretakers, and combine them into a single sentence ("What I wanted most and did not get was enough affection" or "attention," or "praise"). In column four, circle what you most enjoyed from your caretakers, and synthesize them into one sentence.*

As the mystery of choice unfolds, I relax into my inner sanctuary, allowing the images of my unconscious to inform my conscious mind. This ancient truth is mine: "With knowledge comes power."

Don't think that fate is more than the density of childhood.

—RAINER MARIA RILKE

We are products of our past, no matter how free we think we are. When we begin to see the connections between what happened to us as children and what is happening in our relationships, we see that there are no coincidences. The conflicts in our relationship are no accident; it is no quirk of fate that our partner is "just like" our mother or father, or some other significant person in our childhood. We are reliving our childhood in the hope of getting it right this time.

This happens because our unconscious mind seems to have no sense of linear time. Our adult Imago partner literally *is*, in our timeless unconscious, our early caretakers. In unconsciously choosing a partner who has the same wounding behaviors that our caretakers had, we are unconsciously trying to correct that early experience and get them to meet the needs we did not get met in childhood. But we can only do this if we understand what's going on. In becoming aware of your Imago, you take the first step in learning what needs to be healed.

✺ Title a new page in your notebook "My Childhood Agenda" and write out this sentence, filling in the blanks: "I am trying to get a person who is" . . . [fill in the three negative traits you circled in column two yesterday]; "to always be" . . . [three positive traits from column one]; "so I can get" . . . [unfulfilled desires from column three]; "and feel" . . . [positive childhood feelings from column four].

In dialogue tonight, share this information with your partner.

Breathing deeply, I access my inner courage and allow myself to experience my yearning to recover my wholeness. I acknowledge my innate spiritually with thanksgiving.

*You can't expect insights, even the big ones, to make
you suddenly understand everything. But I figure: Hey
it's a step in the right direction if they leave you
confused in a deeper way.*

— LILY TOMLIN

Since you've purchased this book, you've been working so diligently on various tasks and journal entries that your eyes may be glazed over a bit. Consciousness this. Intentional that. It can get pretty overwhelming!

If you're like most of us, you need some down time when you don't have to make sense of things or feel responsible for making it all work. So relax. Chill out. And let your psyche and spirit have a day off. You don't have to be doing this process perfectly, and it's okay if you give out now and then. In the down time, you may feel you're unproductive. Not so! You're simply giving your body and soul a chance to self-restore.

🐦 *Announce to your partner that there will be absolutely no task today. No unit work. No record keeping. No journal entry. Don't even let them mirror you back.*

Taking time in utter stillness, I feel the weariness of my body and soul. Breathing deeply, I allow the repetitions to calm my frazzled spirit. Focusing on each slow inhalation and exhalation, I confess: "The renewal of my own interiority is essential to the process."

When male and female combine, all things achieve harmony.

—TAO TE CHING

Gender issues are a hot topic of the day. We've now come to understand that all men and women possess masculine and feminine qualities. Each of us, for example, has the capacity to be aggressive, a trait commonly thought of as masculine, and each of us also has within us the capacity to be nurturing, a trait considered typically feminine. But our culture conspires against this harmonious balance of *yin*, or male energy, and *yang* female energy, in favor of more rigidly defined gender stereotypes. Girls have traditionally been given dolls, and boys chemistry sets. Girls are praised for their sensitivity, boys criticized for it. Over time those traits that don't fit our gender designation—our "contrasexual" traits—are repressed in the service of our acceptability in society. These missing qualities are part of our lost self, which will be explored on Day 224.

To be whole we need to acknowledge both our masculine and feminine traits. When we bring these complementary energies into balance, we increase harmony, both within ourselves and in our relationships.

❧ *Make a quick list of at least twenty of your personal traits or qualities. Go back down the list and write M next to the qualities that are usually labeled "masculine" and F next to those usually labeled "feminine." Add up the Ms and the Fs. If there is an overabundance of either group of gender-specific traits, you could use a bit of attention to bringing them into balance. See what you can learn from watching your partner.*

Moving into a time of solitude, I see the ways in which my partner and I have developed our male and female energies at the expense of our contrasexual traits. I visualize us merging and then separating, with each of us possessing the qualities of the other. I ponder this wisdom: "Becoming more like my partner restores my missing self."

Reliability sounds so lukewarm in comparison to hot passion or vacations in Spain, but it's a fundamental ingredient of lasting love. Reliability has to do with being responsible for your behavior, answerable for your words and deeds. It means that if you're supposed to do the grocery shopping for the week, and the cupboard shelves are bare, you're accountable. Likewise, if you agree to close an exit, or to change a behavior, or to come home at a certain hour for dinner, you can be counted on to come through.

Reliability is the foundation of security in a partnership. It means we act responsibly toward our mates, own up to our actions, admit our mistakes, keep in touch, stick to our promises, and generally do what we say we're going to do. We become someone our partner can rely on completely, which is an incredibly lovable quality.

➢ *Spend a few minutes thinking about the things that your partner relies on you for, with regard both to the commitments you have made to the relationship and to the instrumental chores and responsibilities that make your life together run smoothly. On a scale of 1 (unreliable) to 10 (totally reliable), where are you? Are there areas where you need to take more responsibility? Do one specific thing today to change your present evaluation — do the laundry, pay the overdue bills, be home for dinner on time.*

In stillness today, I resolve to be faithful to my commitments and become trustworthy for my partner. I focus my spirit on this truth: "Being reliable for my partner deepens my reliability for myself."

Marriage is not just spiritual communion and passionate embraces; marriage is also three meals a day, sharing the workload and remembering to carry out the trash.

— DR. JOYCE BROTHERS

Alas, we cannot live on kisses and words of love alone, though they provide their own special nutrition. It is the nature of life that 90 percent of our time is spent not with candlelight dinners or mind-blowing sex but in taking care of business. Our daily acts of caring for each other's needs are the real demonstration of our good intentions. Willingly doing our share of errands and chores and housework is the proof that we value our partners as equals.

Loving words, flowers, passionate embraces are just empty rhetorical devices unless they are backed up with truckloads of mundane toil and effort. Kisses may be a welcome accompaniment to doing the laundry, but they are no substitute. When we fully share the responsibilities of daily existence—income, chores, child care, bill paying, home maintenance—the spiritual communion and passionate embraces become entangled with everything else in our daily lives. They take on an authenticity and power that we have infused with meaning through our actions.

Is there a balance in your relationship between acts of communion and taking care of everyday chores and responsibilities? In dialogue today, discuss this with your partner. Correct any imbalance that is uncomfortable for either of you.

Moving into my inner sanctuary, I open myself to awareness of any split I have made between abstract "loving" and concrete sharing of the daily tasks. I absorb this thought: "The spiritual is present in the concrete acts of the moment."

When times are tough and our partner is driving us crazy with demands, our fantasy is that there is someone else "out there" who will understand us perfectly, treat us better, love us as we are. Romantic notions dance through our heads, and we dream of starting over with someone new. Somewhere in the world, we think, there must be someone with whom we can live "happily ever after."

Reality is a bit grimmer. Though we may leave our partner, we don't get to leave our problems behind. We cart them along with us, and they inevitably show up and create havoc in our perfect new relationship. However, our fantasy partner can tell us something about what's missing in our relationship, for our fantasies are indications of unmet needs. In taking an objective look at our fantasy of the perfect partnership, we gain insight into what needs to happen in our real-life relationship.

❧ *Daydream for a few minutes today about your dream mate; spin fantasies of your life together. Identify three qualities of your fantasy partner that you can develop in yourself and can express in your current relationship.*

In my time of quiet today, I contemplate this thought: "My wish for a trouble-free relationship without the hard work is a pipe dream." Today I choose to celebrate my reality and accept the challenge of a conscious relationship.

*The body travels more easily than the mind, and until
we have limbered up our imagination we continue to
think as though we had stayed home. We have not
really budged a step until we take up residence in
someone else's point of view.*

— JOHN ERSKINE

"**I**'ll never understand how you can watch those ridiculous horror films." "How can you say such a thing?" "Why do you waste your time with her?" If you go around making statements like this, you're suffering from tunnel vision. You need a lesson in looking from the other end of the tunnel.

It's called validation, the second part of the couples dialogue. Validation is simply the act of recognizing that the inner experience of your partner makes sense from *their* perspective. In validating your partner's communication, you put yourself in their place, look at the situation from their point of view, and convey your understanding that what they say is true for them.

This is not as simple as it seems, because we are threatened by our partner's divergent opinions. We tend to absolutize our own views, afraid that if we acknowledge the worth of another's perspective, it will mean that our own outlook is invalid. But such fear hardly makes sense. After all, even if you understand your partner's love of horror movies, for example, you're still free to dislike them. If you watched one so that you could try to comprehend your partner's enjoyment, would that mean you were losing the battle for your soul? Of course not, but we are trapped in an old childhood survival mode that says that if we give up our point of view, we surrender ourselves and die.

🍃 *Spend a few minutes today imagining that you are your partner. Imagine yourself literally under their skin, behind their eyeballs. Picture them going through their typical day. Explore how they might experience life because of the road they've traveled—their sex, height and weight, age, attitudes, interests, and childhood experience.*

Today I shift away from frustration at my partner's differences to the awareness that accepting my partner's worldview will expand my own. I contemplate this with gratitude.

*In love the paradox occurs that two beings become one
and yet remain two.*

— ERICH FROMM

No matter how intricately bonded we become with our partner, we
remain distinct individuals with our own ways of doing things. Like
love, validation exemplifies the paradox of two beings becoming one
and yet remaining two. The process of validating our partner's point
of view acknowledges their personal experience and at the same time
expands the territory we can mutually share.

After mirroring your partner's communication, as you've been
practicing, validation additionally involves a verbal acknowledgment
that you accept your partner's experience as true for them. Validating
phrases typically contain phrases like: "It makes sense that . . . ," "I
can see that . . . ," "I can understand how you would think (or feel)
that . . . ," all of which communicate: you make sense.

❖ *Practice validation today. You can do this during dinner, if
there are no distractions, or set aside a time and place to practice
for at least ten minutes. Start with something mundane. Save the
heavy stuff for later.*

*Decide who will be the sender and who the receiver. The
sender starts by saying a simple sentence that begins with the
word "I" and describes a thought or feeling, such as, "I thought
the plot of that movie we saw last night was totally unrealistic."
The receiver mirrors the statement and asks, "Is there more?"
and continues to mirror until the sender has completed their
thoughts. The receiver then validates: "You thought the movie we
saw last night had an unrealistic plot. I can see how you thought
that." The sender then acknowledges the validation by saying,
"Thank you." If you feel resistance, remind yourself that validating your partner's view in no way compromises yours.*

**I draw strength to validate my partner's views without strain or
resentment. Stretching into a broader consciousness, I celebrate my
partner's uniqueness.**

We want people to feel with us more than to act for us.

—GEORGE ELIOT

If you ask ten people (with their eyes wide open!) to describe an event or object, each will recount it differently according to their own interpretive filter. Yet each description is the truth for that person. In any communication between two people, there are *always* two points of view. Successful dialogue comes from hearing and validating each other's views, so that you can reach agreement from a place of mutual understanding—even if the agreement is to disagree while honoring each other's differences.

To validate your partner's perspectives, thoughts, and feelings is to recognize that your partner is a separate person, equal in importance and value to yourself. It tells them they are worth listening to, and loved. Validation is far more than a conversational ploy. It has the power to transform two self-centered people who are trying to promote their own views into an I-Thou partnership of equals who share the center. As you continue to practice validation, it will feel increasingly natural, and you may be surprised at the growing openness between you.

❧ *In all conversation with your partner today, focus on validation. When your partner expresses a feeling or opinion, say, "I can see how you would think that (or feel that)" or "You make sense." Notice how you don't need to change your own view and how good it feels to allow your partner theirs.*

Today I transcend myself and see that my partner's point of view has a logic of its own. Seeing that enlarges my world and frees me from the prison of having only one perspective.

Our lives are but an accumulation of moments. The way we live tomorrow, next week, and next year will be the product of what we are doing right now. If we are critical and angry toward our partner today, too busy to chat over dinner, we are spending the currency of our lives unwisely.

Our relationships have the power to transform our lives. Transformation occurs not with the wave of a magic wand but through the daily stockpiling of small acts building to a critical mass that we end up labeling a "life" or a "relationship."

In a conscious relationship we spend time wisely, taking responsibility for the future by intentionally designing actions that move us closer to our goals. Each day counts; the whole can never be greater than the sum of its parts. The appreciation clearly expressed today, or the time spent in idle chatter, is giving weight and definition to your life.

Today, change a behavior that is dissonant with the way you wish to spend your life. This might be a habit of indirect criticism, a tendency to slack off chores, a reluctance to compliment your partner.

In my time of quiet today, I take stock of the ways my partner and I interact with each other, and notice where there is dissonance with the way in which I want to spend my life. I hold this thought in prayer: "If I change my life today, I change my future."

Are you furious with your partner because they have, yet again, made an insensitive comment? Are you outraged because you've been diligently working with this book daily, and your partner has been lax and seemingly uninterested? Has this been a week of back-to-back crises? Do you feel as if you're about to explode because your partner seems oblivious to how difficult this time is for you?

Our partners are not always as supportive as we'd like them to be. The more insensitive and uncaring they act, the more upset we become. The more upset we become, the more we escalate the blame and acrimony. When things reach this point, it's time to disengage and find time when we can simply focus on nurturing ourselves and getting the rest we need. It is vital to protect regular time for self-restoration and renewal. We are entitled to be comforted and cared for, but if we neglect to care for ourselves, we cannot expect others to care for us. After you recharge, you can return to the process.

&. *Make time to rest today. Take several small time-outs from your usual schedule for rest and recuperation, for self-nurturing. Stare out the window, have a tall glass of iced tea, walk around the block, read the funnies.*

Today I clear away all obstacles, taking time to focus on the deep God-essence within myself that keeps me connected to the universe. In this space I can remember: "I was born to enjoy life and to give and receive love."

*I have lived long enough to know that the evening glow
of love has its own riches and splendour.*

—BENJAMIN DISRAELI

If all we know of love is hot passion and peak experiences, we assume
the relationship has burned itself out when the excitement and novelty
dim. Even when we've made a commitment to our partner, we may
look back longingly on the romantic phase of our courtship, wishing
for that rush of blood coursing through our veins. Some of us engage
in fantasy or affairs to keep this feeling pumped up.

But what we are seeking—surrender to the emotional ocean of
feeling and pleasure in an atmosphere of total safety and validation—
is only temporarily and superficially available in an affair. In a conscious relationship, couples make this their goal. Only those who
have stayed the course of commitment in an atmosphere of safety
and full disclosure know the glory of a seasoned relationship. Such a
relationship has an incomparable beauty all its own. Until you begin
to get glimmers of the kind of deep-brewed passion and intense
pleasure that is the prize of the hard work of a conscious relationship,
you cannot fully appreciate what lies in store for you: the end of
longing.

🐾 *Are you longing for excitement? Envious of your single
friends? Tempted by an affair? Today bring to mind the moments
you and your partner have shared that have hinted at the riches
and splendor that love bestows over time. Tell your partner how
much you love them, and see what kind of excitement you can
stir up at home!*

In the serenity of this time alone, I identify the ways I am not true
and faithful to my partner. I confess these areas and pledge to marry
my partner on a deeper level. I contemplate the riches and splendor
our relationship could amass in the years ahead.

Love is an act of endless forgiveness, a tender look
which becomes a habit.

—PETER USTINOV

A forgotten promise, a casual slight, a withering glance, an over-looked kiss, an unintended insult, an accidental spill on a favorite oriental rug—we all make mistakes. We do things that are foolish or mean or hurtful, with and without the intention to cause pain. We do them again and again, and our partner does them to us, too. Nobody's perfect.

What's needed is not an escalation of the pain and blame but a little forgiveness. It takes a large and tolerant heart to forgive our partner, but it is a necessary ingredient to their safety. Like us, they need to know that they can do or say something wrong and we will not hold a grudge or make them pay for it somehow.

Forgiveness is a powerful heart opener, for both giver and recipient. Once you make it a habit, you will be surprised to find a major reduction in the seemingly innocent slights and apparently innocuous insults that were once laced through your conversation. One day you may notice that there's nothing more to forgive.

❧ *On a new page in your notebook, make a list of five old hurts and grudges still taking up space in your heart, keeping you from loving your partner. Can you forgive your partner for these lapses? If so, rip the page out of your notebook, say out loud, "I forgive you, my love, for these mistakes." Tear up the paper into little pieces and throw it in the garbage. If there is something on your list you can't forgive, look more deeply and find out why.*

Today in my time of quiet I visualize a large garbage can labeled MISTAKES, ACCIDENTS, OMISSIONS, OVERSIGHTS . . . that is filled with everything I need to forgive my partner for. I see myself digging a big hole in the earth and emptying the contents of the garbage can into it. Then I plant a tree of forgiveness that fills the hole with love.

Many waters cannot quench love, neither can floods drown it.

—SONG OF SOLOMON 8:7

Every relationship has its share of stresses and changes—illness, job layoffs, the arrival of children, the departure of children, separation, a death in the family, infidelity. Romantic love goes out the window at times like these; the illusion of perfection, of effortless passion, cannot be sustained in the face of real life. It is during such times of crisis that real love is born and becomes the tenacious glue that holds the relationship together. When the troubles are resolved, the relationship is even stronger than before. Love based on illusion can often be pasted back together after a crisis, and it may even look pretty much the same as before, until you hold it up to the light and see the sunlight streaking through the cracks. When the glue of real love seals the cracks after the crisis, a tighter bond is formed and the cracks become invisible.

❧ *Select a period of stress or a crisis that you and your partner have weathered. Using dialogue, have a talk with your partner about this topic tonight and list every way in which difficulties have created more love and closeness between you.*

Taking time for soul restoration, I renew my commitment to endure all troubles in our relationship, knowing that each problem presents an opportunity for growth. I focus my prayer on this thought: "Love endures all things."

*Before falling in love, I was defined. Now I am
undefined, weeds are growing between my ribs.*

— JOYCE CAROL OATES

When we are single and unattached, we have a clear picture of who
we are. We are pretty much able to control the image we present to
the world; it changes little from day to day.

But under the microscope to which intimacy subjects us, there's
no place to hide. New aspects of ourselves are revealed, and we see
ourselves reflected many times a day in the mirror of our partner.
Our carefully delineated self-image keeps shifting. Change comes fast
and furious; there's little we can do to control it and little we can do
to keep our partner from seeing it all. Our edges become fuzzy,
weeds grow wild, we can no longer say who we are with such
certainty. We feel lost.

In fact, we've been found. Our self-definition is a trap that keeps
us from understanding who we really are; it acts as a restraint on our
self-exploration. When we are unhampered by preconceived definitions, when we can surrender ourselves to being the person who our
partner calls forth, we open the way to experiencing our whole, true
selves.

&❧ *Spend a few minutes today thinking about the ways that being
in relationship has "undefined" you, forcing you to reconsider
your self-image. Are you comfortable with being more fluid in
your self-definition? You may want to dialogue with your partner
about this and hear their experience also.*

**Today I offer thanksgiving for the continual change that is the natural
state of partnership. I revel in the ever-changing mirror that my
partner holds up to me.**

Do you have a psychological, emotional, or literal foot out the door of your relationship? Does the possibility of your leaving hang in the air? Sometimes, despite our protests to the contrary, our commitment to our relationship is provisional or tenuous. Though we think we've convinced our partner, and even ourselves that we're committed, there is still some part of us that is waiting to see how it will work out, some part of our heart that never unpacked its suitcases and settled into the relationship. Leaving is still an option.

There's a catch-22 here: the safety we seek in our partnership can never happen as long as we hold out the option of escaping to safety. Until we have convinced ourselves, and our partner, that we are in it for the long haul, there will always be some resistance, some drawing back, some provisional status to what we do and say. We feel stuck because we feel it is still possible for the relationship to come unglued. When we close our exits, take a deep breath, and plunge in wholeheartedly, we become unstuck. The possibilities reveal themselves.

🙠 *Look at your feet today and see if both are firmly planted in your relationship. Examine your ambivalence and, using the couples dialogue, put your fears of commitment into words to your partner. You may find that a sympathetic ear will help you rule out the option of leaving.*

Relaxing deeply, I recognize that my doubts and hesitancy are like tears in the fabric of our relationship. With needle and thread, I sew up the rips and torn places as a reaffirmation of my commitment.

> *One can never speak enough of the virtues, the danger,*
> *the power of shared laughter.*
>
> —FRANÇOISE SAGAN

Of all the things we do with our partner, there is something unique and special about the things we laugh about together—our own foibles, our private jokes, our secret sillinesses. Laughter *is* the best medicine for us and our relationship.

When couples have exuberant fun together they identify each other as a source of pleasure and safety, which intensifies their emotional bond. Almost like magic, fun reminds partners that they are allies.

So what is fun? In the Imago process, fun is defined as any high-energy interaction that requires no skills, has no rules, can't be done wrong, and produces deep pleasure in the form of laughter or an orgasm or both, in a short period of time. Just a few minutes of an exuberant fun activity have an energizing effect. For example, telling jokes, chasing each other around the yard, dancing to lively music, squirting each other with hoses, giving each other a massage, or making love create more high-spirited feelings than quietly watching TV or reading together. We can pepper our lives with fun activities to jump-start our feelings of aliveness and get those endorphins pumping. And pleasure is a bonding agent.

❧ *Make a list of high-energy activities you would like to do for fun with your partner. Write down as many ideas as you can think of—things that create deep laughter; activities that involve physical movement and deep breathing, activities you enjoyed with your partner in the early stages of your relationship. Use your imagination!*

I settle into a peaceful time today, aware that to feel fun at my core I must relax the tension that holds me in its clutches. With each exhalation I release, one by one, these issues that preoccupy me, and relax into the joyful state beneath my worries. As my breathing deepens, I feel space for my joy to surface.

As children, we naturally played and laughed, expressing our innate drive toward full aliveness. As adults we have mostly forgotten these pleasures in favor of more passive adult activities.

The often paradoxical result of our childhood experience of fun is fear of pleasure. On a conscious level, we go to great lengths to seek happiness. But unconsciously, many of us blow it when we get there because we are afraid to experience our own aliveness. Why is that? Somewhere along the journey from childhood to adulthood, we lost our natural joy. We were told to limit or give up fun in favor of work, pressured to conform to social norms. If this was done in punishing ways, we not only redirect our energy as adults but we associate intense pleasure with emotional pain, having learned that to be fully alive is dangerous. Don't get too old and forget that inside each of us there is still a child that wants to come out and play with their best friend.

Read yesterday's individual lists of fun activities out loud together and make a new list of things you can do together that combines the ideas of both of you. Pick one activity on your combined list to do tomorrow. If it is an activity that you need to schedule time for, do so now. If it requires any special equipment, get everything ready in advance.

Today I relax my neck and shoulder muscles as I enter into my center, my place of full aliveness. Here I find the God within. I let go of all manipulative or critical thoughts about my partner and focus solely on fun. I hold this thought: "We are alive and one with the all."

Today you're invited to do the first of regular fun activities. While this may sound simple, don't be surprised if you feel some resistance or create some excuse to avoid enjoying yourself. If there are conflicts in your relationship, it may feel artificial and contrived to have fun together—after acting like enemies for years, it can feel strange to dance.

If you're feeling resistance, tell your partner, and openly listen to their feelings of resistance too. If it is easier for one of you to get into the spirit of things, that person can take the lead. Whatever your hesitation, try to put your feelings aside and just go do it! Push through your discomfort. Once you start doing a fun activity, your feelings will begin to shift as the endorphins start pumping, and you'll find you're enjoying yourself after all. *Doing* fun activities generates fun *feelings*. Don't be surprised if you wake up one day to discover you actually are enjoying your relationship.

☙ *Have fun with your partner! Do the fun activity you chose yesterday. If you feel any resistance, just make note of it and try to do it anyway. Remember, the point here is to feel good! Put your fun list in a handy spot and plan to take a few minutes to share some energetic fun at least once a week.*

I ask myself in time of quiet: Is it better to hold on to my righteous stance in my relationship or to simply enjoy my partner? I relax into knowing that a lighthearted evening may signal a forgiving attitude that could make a world of difference to my partner. With new insight, I honor this truth: "The joy I bring into my partner's life will spill over into mine!"

In the beginning, we make our habits. In the end, they make us.

—ANONYMOUS

Think about the things you usually do that really don't work very well in your relationship. Do you routinely say, "I can't talk to you now" when your partner calls you at work? Does everybody know by now that you just don't pick up after yourself? Is your habit to badger your partner until they do what you want, or withhold sex to get your own way? These habits have evolved over time. They are adult versions of the childhood behaviors that seemed to work for you. Up until now, they have defined who you are.

Habits begin in infancy. Responding to our experiences in ways that seemed necessary for our survival, we used the only tactics within our power to protect us from harm and ridicule. Those defense mechanisms, immature as they were, kept us alive. But these coping mechanisms become entrenched. They become who we are, and our lives are molded by others' response to them. Our rote adherence to our habitual patterns makes it hard to be flexible in our relationships, to respond to each unique situation in the moment and not to our history. We're too frozen in habit to try something new that might be more effective. Are you happy with your habits? Why not change a few?

&. *Break a habit today: hold your temper, say what's on your mind instead of sulking, do something for your mate without expecting something in return.*

In a time of prayer today, I see myself with all my habits, and I thank them for their help and protection in the past, but then I let them go in the wind one by one. I focus my thought on new, healthy behaviors, done in love, that express my needs directly and enable me to get the love I want from my partner.

The more I wonder . . . the more I love.

—ALICE WALKER

Ours is a pragmatic world where science reigns. We're impressed with facts and figures. We want to know and quantify everything. This holds true in our relationships: we want to know all about our partners. We press them for details, analyze their dreams, keep track of their whereabouts. But no matter how many facts we collect and how closely we scrutinize them, mysteries remain.

Life, our partners, and our relationships, are full of impenetrable wonders that we cannot fully understand. The deepest workings of our hearts are no more knowable than the origins of the stars. Really, isn't this wonderful, that there is always something new to discover, that we can never exhaust the possibilities, never unearth some final, conclusive fact? Can we not appreciate the magic of life, the unknown forces that draw us to our partners, that keep us in orbit? Can we not love the sheer mad mystery of it all?

❧ *Forget the facts today. In dialogue with your partner, dwell on life's wonders, the unsolved mysteries—the imponderable movements of the stars, the cycle of birth and death and love, the dazzle of deep-sea creatures, the unknowable depths of your relationship.*

Today I open my spirit to the wonder of life and existence. I offer thanksgiving as I embrace this truth: "Life's mystery is my connection to the ultimate."

*Do not hurt your neighbor, for it is not him you
wrong, but yourself.*

—SHAWNEE PROVERB

The idea that we can get our partner to love us by criticizing or
intimidating them, by pointing out their Achilles' heel or punishing
them for their neglect or insensitivity, is obviously absurd. If this
strikes a chord, it's because you, like probably most of us, have
stooped to using these tactics at one time or another.

What you want is for your anger or criticism to have a direct effect
on your partner—to get them to change. You are convinced that it
has no effect on you. You couldn't be more wrong! Ironically, it has a
more direct effect on you than on your partner. They can use their
conscious mind to defend themselves, write you off as irrational, or
change to meet your needs. You, however, have no such protection.
Not only do you sabotage the goodwill in your relationship, diminishing the chance of being loved and decreasing your partner's respect
for you, you inflict on yourself the pain you attempted to visit on your
partner. Your unconscious mind directly receives what you express
through your conscious mind. When you whine at your partner, your
unconscious receives it as if it were a special delivery letter addressed
to itself.

 *Take a few minutes today to identify your most typical coercive
behavior—avoidance, rage, the silent treatment? Even if you can
think of no new behavior to replace it at the moment, refrain from
the old behavior today.*

**Today I open my mind to a deep truth: that what I do to others is
done to me as well. In this time of contemplation I allow this truth to
fill every cell in my body, and prayerfully hold these words: "When I
hurt my partner, I wound myself."**

At some point in our relationship, we realize that things are going to work out. The partnership may be far from perfect, but we realize that the bottom line is that we are going to stay together, for better or worse. So we stop worrying and relax. But before we know it, we've slipped into predictable, lackadaisical routines. There's little excitement, less surprise. Ho hum.

A committed relationship is ours to actively cultivate. We shouldn't be taking chances with ruining a good thing. Keeping the sense of wonder and spontaneity alive is a part of our commitment that is too easily forgotten. We need to liven up the mix from time to time, turn things upside down. When we throw our partner the occasional curveball, we're telling them that we're not fool enough to take them for granted.

Do something today to make your partner's jaw drop: start a tickling match while they're still in the shower, scatter Hershey's kisses in their underwear drawer, drive them blindfolded to a new restaurant for dinner. As your partner gets swept up in this new behavior of yours, you'll probably be having more fun than they are!

I take time for renewal today. Tapping into the joy of meditation, I focus on delighting my partner, stirring the aliveness of our love.

Let there be spaces in your togetherness . . .

—KAHLIL GIBRAN

Togetherness is a main topic of relationships, but part of togetherness is apartness. Not surprisingly, many couples find themselves in conflict around finding the right balance of time together and time alone, since they have chosen each other for their opposite approaches to intimacy. One feels shut out by the other and clings. The other feels intruded upon and withdraws. Each partner has developed the opposite coping mechanism for handling the feelings of rejection or abandonment they felt as children, and each must stretch to meet the other someplace in the middle.

As much as partners need to be committed to their relationship, they also need privacy—time alone or with friends, time to pursue their individual interests. Each partner is entitled to personal space and possessions, privacy of thought and feeling. Couples need to define boundaries that are fluid, neither too rigid or too loose, that neither shut each other out nor permit smothering intrusion. They need to understand that in composing a relationship, the spaces are as important as the togetherness.

❧ *Have a dialogue with your partner today about privacy in your relationship. Do you have enough time alone? Do you intrude on each other's personal space or property—your desks or private correspondence or phone calls? Do you allow each other your private thoughts and feelings, encourage each other's interests? Allow each other free expression of your fears or irritation around this subject, and make an agreement to do one specific thing to honor each other's desire for separate space or time.*

I access the inner courage necessary to be both in the relationship and true to myself. I honor the need for my partner and me to have private time and space. I smile as I hold this thought in prayer: "In creating the proper balance between our togetherness and the spaces between us, we become more bonded as partners."

Imagination is the highest kite one can fly.

—LAUREN BACALL

If you look around at the couples you know, you will find that even though they share somewhat similar backgrounds or income, some of those couples lead pretty dull, predictable lives, while others seem to be having a much better time. They go more places, they laugh more, they've got ideas for a dozen vacations.

What they have is imagination. They're not limited by rules or circumstances. If things get dull, they change them. They realize that their ability to have what they want depends on their ability to conceive of it and the intention to make it happen.

What is your dream of love? Are you able to articulate your highest hopes for yourself, for your partner, for the world we live in? Are there limits to what you can do, the places you can go, how much love you can have in your life? Of course not. Can you have more sex, more money, more time with the kids? Of course. You only have to clearly image what you want, so that you have a blueprint to follow. Mix imagination with love, courage, and perseverance, and all things become possible.

ᨠ *Write down ten sentences today that begin "If I could have our relationship be any way I want, with no limitations . . ." You might complete them by writing "We would have the time to fix all our own meals from food we grow in our garden," or "We would travel two months out of every year," or "We'd start a center for homeless children." Make a list of your wildest imaginings, no matter how improbable they seem. Tonight, share your dreams with your partner in a couples dialogue.*

In prayerful contemplation today, I cradle this hope: "My dream relationship can become reality, if I only dare to dream it."

Are you or your partner a missing person in your relationship? It's natural for each partner to spend time alone, with their own friends, or pursuing individual interests. But when solo activities become an escape from the day-to-day intimacy of the partnership, they sabotage the journey to real love. What we end up with instead is a parallel marriage, in which each partner goes their own way, and the relationship becomes more of an arrangement. We might as well be living alone, except that it's a convenience for our children, our career, or our social life.

For the next several days, we'll be talking about exits, by which we mean any activity, thought, or feeling that decreases or avoids emotional or physical involvement with your partner. In a conscious relationship, we must—slowly but surely—close the exits by which we squander energy that belongs with our partners.

🍋 *Have a conversation today, using the couples dialogue, to reflect on the gap between your current level of togetherness and the kind of intimacy you would like to have. Share with your partner your desire to create more intimacy by closing your exits.*

In a time of stillness, I relax deeply and visualize our relationship as a balloon with holes through which air is escaping. One by one I touch each hole with the warmth of my committed love, sealing each rupture. I keep this thought uppermost in my mind today: "The more we do together, the closer we feel to each other."

*He who goes out of his house in search of happiness
runs after a shadow.*

— CHINESE PROVERB

When things become dull or go awry in our relationship, we often run for the exits. Instead of facing our problems headon and working through conflicts, it seems easier to look elsewhere for diversion, distraction, substitutes.

Our goal is to be rid of our psychic pain. And since our partner is the perceived source of that pain, we assume the solution is to avoid our partner. So we start working longer hours or join a health club. If our pain is unbearable, and we feel hopeless about healing it, we may even turn to desperate measures for relief. We mumble about divorce and start an affair; seek solace in alcohol or drugs; we are consumed with murderous fantasies. Such catastrophic or lethal exits must be closed immediately, with professional help. Discussion of their source and solution is beyond the scope of this book.

Today you're being asked to make a list of your functional exits. Functional exits are the things we *need* to do: go to work, take care of the kids, clean the house, shop for groceries. Their intent may not be to diminish intimacy, but that is their effect.

⁂ *Label a new page in your notebook "Exits," and divide the page into two vertical columns. On the left, make a complete list of all the functional activities you engage in that diminish the time you spend with your partner. On the right, list all those activities you perceive as your partner's functional exits from your relationship.*

Today I see a wall separating me from my partner. As I move into the quiet of my time alone, I discover that the wall is composed of hectic activity that limits intimacy with my partner. Absorbing strength from my deep spiritual source, I decide to tear the wall down and both share with as well as listen to my partner.

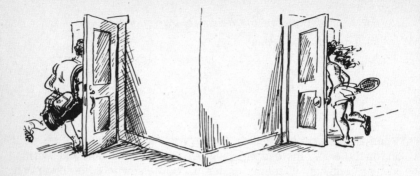

There's another kind of exit that takes up space in our everyday life. These are our "motivated" exits—the ways we *choose* to spend our time. As with functional exits, they are not harmful in themselves, but they serve, consciously or unconsciously, to allow us to avoid involvement with our partner in order to avoid emotional pain. Examples of motivated exits are watching TV, reading, window shopping, hanging out with friends, sports, emotional withdrawal, hobbies, and religious activities. In all cases, the activity itself is innocent. It's the motivation that may be suspect.

Couples who want to stay together, who dream of lifelong intimacy, need to *be* together. Quality time counts in a relationship, but it's the *quantity* time—just being together in the same room, chatting idly, hanging out, day after day, and talking . . . reading . . . touching . . . doing the chores side by side—that creates intimacy. If all our energy is spent in activities separated from our partner, the relationship soon runs out of fuel.

🔊 *Using the "Exits" list that you started yesterday, continue by adding all the activities you would call motivated exits from your relationship, those you use to avoid being with your partner emotionally and physically. Then write down in the right-hand column what you perceive to be your partner's motivated exits.*

In my time of quiet today, I confess the superficial protection my exits afford me. I move into a deeper place where I find a well of inner protection from which I can draw. Here, drawing waters of resilience, I envision safe ways we can unite.

This is what happens when couples go their own way too often. It may look as if they're on the same track, but those tracks are actually running parallel to each other, and the distance between them keeps increasing.

Many of our exits seem so innocent. We have a dozen good reasons for working out at the gym, for just wanting to relax in front of the TV with a beer after a hard day's work, for agreeing to chair the recycling drive. We don't stop to consider the dozen good reasons why we shouldn't, or rather, why we should be more judicious about how we choose to spend our time.

Today you are invited to talk with your partner about the exits you both use to avoid intimacy. Be sure to use the couples dialogue, for talking about exits converts feelings that you have been acting out into language. Paradoxically, just the increased involvement of talking about these feelings that you have been expressing as behavior can turn things around. Soon you'll be riding in the same direction again.

❧ Exchange "Exits" lists with your partner, using the couples dialogue. Add to your list any additional exits that your partner suggests. With your completed list, put a check mark next to the exits that you are willing to eliminate, or to begin to reduce, at the present time. Mark with an X any exit that would be difficult for you to close now.

Today I acknowledge the tensions involved in living intimately with my partner. I move to my own spiritual depth and draw upon it for the strength to be vulnerable. I allow this thought to permeate my being: "My partner can't grow to love all of me unless I offer my full self."

I am his mistress. His work is his wife.

—MARION JAVITS

Workaholism is only one of our society's addictions. Many of us worship work; others are obsessed with exercise, their children, public service, or a spiritual path. Busy, busy, busy. The motivation may be economic survival, cultural values, or childhood wounds. But the results are the same: our obsessions or addictions drive us, effectively forcing our relationships to take a backseat.

In a conscious relationship, the partnership comes first. Partners see their relationship as a resource for the energy they need for work, service, and parenting. They make their life-style choices accordingly.

Today you are invited to have a conversation with your partner about your life-style choices and their impact on the closeness in your relationship, and to close your first exits. Remember, you're not making all-or-nothing choices. You are *selectively cutting down* on the amount of time you spend at work, watch television, attend evening meetings, work out at the gym, or read bedtime stories to the kids. You are paring down on these activities only to the extent that they are used to avoid spending time together, so that you can slowly find your way to the pleasures of each other's company.

🍃 *Today have a conversation with your partner about the exits that need to be closed in order for your life-style to support the kind of intimate relationship you desire. Select an exit you are willing to close today and share the fear that motivated you to use it. For example: "Because of my fear that you would criticize me for not doing more around the house, I make business calls after dinner. I will close that exit."*

Today, in my twenty minutes of solitude, I think back to the rich closeness that we had during our courtship. From a place of inner potency and love, I commit to the changes in our life-style that will be needed to re-create that atmosphere of intimacy.

Congratulations! Over the last week, you have been doing some hard work on your relationship. This is a day to celebrate.

You have learned about exits, those activities through which we avoid involvement and intimacy, which can threaten the very existence of our partnership. You have identified your functional and motivated exits and begun to close them. Through dialogue with your partner and commitment to changing your life-style to reflect the intimacy you desire, you have already begun to heal the feelings of alienation and hurt that your exits were acting out.

Today, toss your heart to your partner, and receive your partner's heart gently. Remember that the couples dialogue is your safety net. Today, take a break from lists and agreements. Do something together just for fun.

❧ *Join your partner in some activity or ritual that celebrates the exits you have closed in your relationship and your continuing commitment to close those that remain. Shop for a friendship ring. Share a single glass of fine wine. Have your picture taken together. Make love. Light a candle.*

I relax in my interlude of quiet today with the image of the couple tossing a heart back and forth. I feel their pleasure in being together, the safety they must feel in their commitment. In my mind's eye, I slowly replace this couple with the image of my partner and myself.

*It seems necessary to completely shed the old skin
before the new, brighter, stronger, more beautiful one
can emerge. . . . I never thought I'd be getting a life
lesson from a snake!*

—JULIE RIDGE

When we begin to make the changes that put us on the path to real
love, we slowly edge out our old, unproductive habits. We give up the
heavy sighing to show our displeasure, stop blaming others for our
bad moods, give up the bullying tactics that get us out of chores. For
a while, before we learn a new behavior to replace the old, before it
takes hold, we may feel naked and vulnerable. We're in what might
be called an identity crisis. We're not sure who we are without our
comfortable old habits.

New behaviors do not emerge full-blown. Rather, they take hold
slowly, through repetition, from the inside out. We learn them first in
our minds and then put them into practice in our relationship. This
in-between stage, where the old behavior has fallen away and the new
is not yet firmly integrated, is unavoidable. It doesn't work to paste
healthy new behaviors over old ones. They don't stick. The old must
be cleared away so that the new behaviors, learned in love, can take
hold.

&● *Before a snake sheds its skin, little pieces start to flake off as
the new skin grows beneath. Which old behavior of yours is
coming loose and ready to be shed? What new behavior is ready
to emerge? Watch for or create an opportunity today to shed an
old behavior and replace it with a new one.*

**Today in a quiet awakening, I envisage myself covered with old skin;
I see it as my ossified character defenses, cracking and peeling,
revealing underneath a beauty unknown to me before, which I recognize as my true self. I hold this truth in faith: "In changing to love
my partner, I am restoring my original self."**

Life is what happens to you when you're making other plans.

— BETTY TALMADGE

How human it is to fantasize about the future, to dream about what will happen when, or what life would be like if . . . "Next year will be better when we'll be able to afford a vacation," "If only Alice were more affectionate," "When the kids are out of school . . ." "When I lose that weight . . ."

Plans and daydreams have their place, but they can steal from our enjoyment of the present. When we get the feeling that life is passing us by, it's often because we're not paying attention to what's happening in each moment. We drive to the store and don't notice the scenery. We've finished our lunch and haven't savored a single bite. How can we appreciate what we have when we're not paying attention to it?

Life has a way of altering even the best-laid plans. When we are consumed by "what if . . ." we cannot enjoy what is. This, *today*, is your life. Live it fully.

❧ *Spend today in the here and now. Don't think about the past; no daydreaming about the future. Resolve to pay attention, moment by moment, with all your senses alert, to everything that is happening today. Smell the flowers, feel the softness of your partner's skin, notice that your coworker smiles. You may be surprised to find how wonderful your life already is, when you pay attention.*

Taking twenty minutes of quiet today, I notice what is—the sounds and smells around me, the sensations in my body, the thoughts that come and go through my mind like the waves of the ocean. Entering more deeply into prayer and relaxation, I experience eternity in the now.

We're so wounded—by love lost or withheld, by neglect or abandonment—that we have a hard time trusting that our partner really loves us. After all, we reason, if our caretakers and our teachers and our chums found fault with us, we must not be lovable. So our partner must be faking it. Terrified of more loss, we seek to reassure ourselves that our partners are telling the truth about their feelings for us, that they're really not going to leave us. So we put them through their paces, demanding that they pass a series of tests. Walk the tightrope, jump off a cliff, go to the store for ice cream at midnight, make impossible promises. Nothing is too much to ask, and nothing is ever enough. Our lack of trust says more about our own woundedness than about our partner's love and loyalty.

⊱ *On a new page in your notebook, write down at least ten ways that your partner shows their love for you. "Comes up behind me and nuzzles my neck," "Takes the papers and cans to the recycling center," "Learned to play softball," "Holds me in the middle of the night when I'm worried and can't sleep." Tell your partner about the ways you feel loved. Ask them to mirror.*

It's so easy to see the glass as half empty, but today I clearly see it as half full. In my time of quiet today, I relax my demands for reassurance, take down the tightrope I have asked my partner to walk, and trust the love my partner gives. I celebrate deep within my spirit: "I am loved, and I have no further need of proof."

When we love someone our love becomes demonstrable
or real only through our exertion—through the fact
that for that someone . . . we take an extra step or
walk an extra mile. Love is not effortless. To the
contrary, love is effortful.

—M. SCOTT PECK

Some people just *love* to be in love. They want all of those loving feelings—the shortness of breath, the pounding heart. But what they've got—three meals a day, a peck on the cheek in the morning, the same old position when we make love—well, they'd rather go to the movies and see the R-rated version on the big screen.

But that pounding heart, the breathless words are not real love; they are indicators of our need, barometers of our fantasy level. Real love is not puppy-dog feelings but acting unconditionally to heal both our partner and ourselves.

The depth of our love can be measured by our efforts. We demonstrate our love when we take that extra step, when we act in our partner's best interest even when we don't feel like it—listening to their worries at four o'clock in the morning when they can't sleep, making love when *they* want to, confronting their worst monsters. Then, one day, we look up at our partner and see stars in their eyes, and hear the strains of a violin in the background. At last we've found real love, the reward for our efforts.

꙲ *Take an extra step, walk an extra mile for your partner today.*
When your mate makes a request—to take out the garbage, pick
up the mail, rush downtown to pay a bill—do it with a smile,
regardless of how you feel.

I close my eyes in quiet today and acknowledge the fear that restrains
me from meeting my partner's needs. Opening myself to the courage
at my core, I commit to this truth: "The love I give makes me whole."

She did observe, with some dismay, that far from conquering all, love lazily sidestepped practical problems.

— JEAN STAFFORD

When we fall in love, we're on our best behavior. We're so kind and helpful, we hang on every word, we do more than our share to make life grand. But there are lots of things we *don't* do. We don't have to deal with who does the laundry twice a week, who cooks three meals a day, and who does the shopping. Either we're still living separately, or we're so in love that we do *everything* together. We blithely gloss over the fact that one partner isn't making much money and doesn't seem to be too anxious about it. We're able to set aside our concern about the fact that we live in different cities and one of us will have to move; that one of us is a nightowl and the other an early riser. It will all, we are sure, work out.

Get real. Romantic love doesn't conquer all; it only conquers *some*, and only for a while. It's a dismal fact of life that falling in love only avoids our problems with an almost willful blindness. Sooner or later, we have to open our eyes and solve our practical problems with our hearts and minds and valiant efforts. This is how we build real love, which *does* conquer all.

&❧ *Is there a practical problem in your relationship that you've been sidestepping? Are the two of you in agreement about how the grocery shopping gets done, how the sheets on the bed get changed? Are you both satisfied about how much money you spend on food or entertainment, at whose house you'll spend Christmas? Using the couples dialogue, solve a practical problem today.*

I enter a quiet place of courage that allows me to look at our everyday problems as an opportunity to express love. I honor this truth: "Confronting the mundane provides opportunity to awaken."

One's life has value so long as one attributes value to the life of others, by means of love, friendship, indignation and compassion.
— SIMONE DE BEAUVOIR

"I was so angry when I heard what happened to you." Isn't it wonderful to feel that our friends and partners understand what we are experiencing, that we are not alone in our pain or joy or confusion?

Empathy is the third (and final) part of the couples dialogue. After mirroring your partner's communication and validating their point of view, empathizing is the process of imagining, and sometimes experiencing within yourself, the *feelings* your partner is expressing. In the act of empathy, both partners transcend for a moment their separateness and experience a genuine oneness. This deep level of communication has remarkable healing power.

The difference between empathy and validation is subtle but very important. Validation simply acknowledges the other's experience as being true for them and having value equal to yours. "I can understand that you were upset when I didn't call." Empathy is the expression of your ability to tune in to the emotional experience of the other and, even for a moment, experience their happiness or pain or irritation: "I can feel how upset and angry you were when I didn't call."

❧ *Empathizing with your partner's feelings may be difficult and awkward in the beginning, so today will be a practice session. Find a quiet place where you can practice for at least ten minutes without interruption.*

Decide who will be the sender and who the receiver. The receiver should breathe deeply and relax so that they can tune in to their partner's feelings. The sender starts by saying a simple sentence that begins with the word "I" and describes a feeling (not one about your partner), such as, "I was so upset today reading the newspaper." The receiver mirrors the statement, adds a validation, and then expresses empathy: "Just reading the news upsets you. I certainly understand that. I can feel your sadness." The sender then acknowledges the receiver by saying, "Thank you." Repeat the process until you both feel comfortable; then switch roles.

Taking time in a sacred stillness, I recognize that empathy is difficult work. I draw on inner strength, knowing that emotionally entering into my partner's feelings is an act of self-transcendence.

Love one another, but make not a bond of love . . .
Sing and dance together and be joyous, but let each
one of you be alone,
Even as the strings of a lute are alone though they
quiver with the same music.

—KAHLIL GIBRAN

Empathy is in many ways like the music that quivers between the separate strings of the lute. It brings us together in a shared experience, though we remain our separate selves.

Psychologists and child development experts feel that as infants we are instinctively empathic, able to tune in to our caretaker's moods and feelings. But as life's blows fall upon us, and we are wounded, we become self-protective and absorbed in our own survival. Our focus becomes self-centered, and our relationship to others becomes symbiotic, based on what we need to give in order to get what we need. Our natural empathy diminishes in proportion to the degree of our wounding. No wonder we have a hard time feeling compassion for our partners; we are too wrapped up in our own drama, too defended against further wounding.

But the ability to feel each other's feelings, to make that heartfelt connection on a deep emotional level, even when the feelings have to do with our hurt or unhappiness with each other, is deeply healing. In practicing empathy, you will find that the very act of allowing yourself to connect to your partner's feelings liberates you from your wounded defensiveness and isolation, and opens a door to a more powerful union between you.

🍃 *In all conversation with your partner today, focus on empathy. When your partner expresses a feeling, stop for a moment and try to tune in to their emotion until you can truthfully say, "I can imagine how you feel." Notice how sharing your partner's feeling allows you to feel closer.*

As I retreat today, I contemplate this thought: "Embracing rather than resisting my partner's experience is the key to deep connection with my love."

Make no judgments where you have no compassion.

—ANNE MCCAFFREY

It is one thing to empathize with your partner's feelings about the state of the world, or their job, or the kids. But when negative feelings are directed at us, it is quite another matter. It is difficult for us to hear that we are not perfect in our partner's eyes. When they say, "I feel as if I'm not very important to you, given the slight you made about me at the party," our first reaction is to defend ourselves, give explanations, and justify how we are in the right. But in order to empathize with our partner we need to quell those inner voices and find that place inside us where we can truly say, "I can imagine that you felt unimportant, given what you experienced."

In practice, responding in an empathic way to our partner's feelings about our behaviors is the same as listening to our partner's feelings about their boss. They are only feelings, not judgments. They do not cancel out your own feelings or make you wrong. How can we expect our partner to have compassion for our own feelings if we judge theirs? When we can detach ourselves from our self-righteousness and fear of annihilation for a moment and be open to our partner's pain, we can have compassion for their feelings and perhaps even see how our insight and support of our partner is healing to us both.

&. *Set aside some uninterrupted time again today for an empathy practice session. But this time, instead of empathizing about neutral subjects, the sender should express feelings related to the receiver's behavior. Be sensitive to each other as you attempt this more difficult step.*

As before, the receiver mirrors the statement, adds a validation, and then expresses empathy: "When I spend the evening with my friends doing something you don't enjoy, you feel left out and lonely, and you miss me. I can understand why you feel that. I can feel how lonely you are when that happens." When the transaction is complete, switch roles.

In my twenty minutes of stillness today, I recognize that my partner's negative emotions toward me reflect their childhood wounds and are a window to healing and change. This thought becomes my prayer: "To enter deeply into my partner's feelings is a healing experience for both of us."

Well, this is a milestone on your journey to real love! You have now
learned and practiced all three steps of the couples dialogue. You are
in possession of a valuable asset; as long as you maintain these skills,
they will keep your partnership running smoothly.

In future units, you'll see that the couples dialogue is the foundation
for other skills—for expressing your anger and requesting behavior
changes from your partner. As you continue to use the couples
dialogue in everyday conversations, what now feels awkward will
become second nature.

ঌ *Celebrate your new skills by using them to have some fun
together. Go out somewhere you enjoy or want to explore that
has an atmosphere conducive to lively conversation, such as a
favorite restaurant, a park bench, the lobby bar of a fancy hotel,
a beach. Use the couples dialogue to share your thoughts about
your experience there.*

**I celebrate the relationship that can be mine if only I can stick with
this process. In quiet, I commit to the patience that will be required,
focusing on this thought: "Empathy is the meeting of two hearts
through the power of language."**

Nothing is so good as it seems beforehand.

—GEORGE ELIOT

"**J**im will move into my apartment with me, and we'll put his red couch in the bedroom. Next year we'll get married and have a big reception at the club. We'll both continue at our jobs until we have enough money to buy a little house near the park, and share all the chores. Jim likes to cook, so I'll do the shopping, and we can take our vacations at my family's house at the beach, and when we decide to start a family we'll both work part-time so we can both be with the babies."

Our fantasies of living happily ever after rarely match the realities of daily life with our partner. It is the nature of the unconscious that in the throes of romance, when we feel that we have found a partner to rescue us from our hidden unhappiness, our dreams run rampant. We spin elaborate scenarios of a rosy and carefully orchestrated future. But the minute we commit to our partners—when we get married or move in together—we regress, and our childish wish to be comforted and cared for takes precedence over our desire to do the same for our partner.

The unfortunate truth is that marriage—or any new level of commitment—screws up our relationship, as our hope that our partner will heal us becomes an expectation. To live happily ever after, we have to do something day after day to make our partner's dreams, as well as our own, come true.

🐾 *Take a few minutes to remember the expectations you originally had for your relationship. Have things turned out as you imagined? If it's better, go give your partner a big hug and a kiss and tell them how much you appreciate them. If not, identify one unfulfilled hope you had for your partnership, and do one thing today to make that wish come true.*

In my period of quiet today, I think back on all the prayers, dreams, and hopes I had for my relationship. I commit to focusing my energies and spirit on transforming my dreams into reality.

Lying is done with words, but also with silence.

—ADRIENNE RICH

What we do *not* say, what we do *not* share in relationships makes us less than truthful, even when the things we withhold are less than earthshaking. Even with the best of intentions—"I don't want to bother my partner," "I don't want to make waves," "We don't have time to talk about our day," "They don't really want to hear about . . ."—we drive a wedge of silence between us.

In whatever guise, silence between partners is a loud and clear signal that we are living a lie, betraying our commitment to build up our stores of intimacy and trust, to share our inner life. Partnership demands that we tell the simple truth, that we overcome whatever qualms or resistance we feel about filling our partner in on our thoughts and feelings, every day, on all that concerns us.

&. *Throughout the day, notice the things that you don't bother to tell your partner—the money you lost playing poker, your worry about the pain in your side, your pride in the garden. In a couples dialogue this evening, tell your partner a few of these things.*

As I relax into a time of prayer today, I enter the realm of my fears and inhibitions where I hold my secret and unspoken thoughts. Taking the time to scan them one by one, I summon the courage to break the silence and share all of me with my partner.

The best proof of love is trust.

— DR. JOYCE BROTHERS

Is it so surprising that we have a hard time with trust? It's unlikely that our parents were completely trustworthy—that we could unfailingly rely on them to be there when we needed them. They implied that they didn't trust us either—"Are you sure you brushed your teeth?" In school, managed and monitored, we were indirectly given the message that we were untrustworthy. What we ended up with is a society in which mistrust is a given, a world in which we don't even blink at the idea of punching time clocks and handing in expense vouchers, of company watchdogs and oversight committees.

So we come to our relationship with a fundamental mistrust in the dependability either of others or ourselves. Suspicion is our habit, and it needs to be unlearned. This we do by being reliably available for our partners, day after day, regardless of the circumstances.

There are many ways in which we can demonstrate our love for our partner, but few can compare with the ways in which we show our partner that they are loved for themselves, we believe what they say, that we will not laugh at them or betray their confidence. Trustworthiness cuts both ways: in learning to trust our partner, we become a person worthy of trust. It is proof of our love.

ᘒ *Are you completely trustworthy for your partner? Today make a list of at least three things you can do to reassure your partner that they are safe with you. This might mean calling when you are working late, empathizing with one of your partner's concerns, being less secretive yourself.*

Relaxing, breathing calmly in this quiet place, I see myself as a rock, unmoved by wind or rain, a place where my partner can rest in safety and peace. I focus my thoughts on this truth: "Trust is the heart of love."

Have you been reading your partner's mind lately? It's so tempting: after all, our partner is *so* predictable—we're sure we know their every thought, what they like and dislike, *exactly* who they are. Aren't we clever?

Mind reading is based on the self-centered assumption that our partner is just like us. Believe it or not, our partner has a personal life separate from us, their own private thoughts and dreams. They don't think and act the same as we do, they don't make the same choices. Taken to the logical next step, mind reading can be obliterating. We begin with an assumption and then draw vast conclusions, effectively eliminating our partner from the picture.

Unless you and your partner have psychic powers, it is impossible to understand each other perfectly without direct communication. All mind-reading assumptions need to be checked out—not with a crystal ball but with the couples dialogue.

🍃 *Make a list of ten things you think you know about your partner. Then, using the couples dialogue, ask your partner for verification.*

Taking twenty minutes of quiet, I disengage from the fusion I feel with my partner and honor our separateness. Relaxing my rigid assumptions, I focus on this phrase: "I am not my partner."

*I hate to be a failure. I hate and regret the failure of
my marriages. I would gladly give up my millions for
just one lasting marital success.*

—J. PAUL GETTY

Many couples' arguments center around money—how much is coming in, who pays the bills, what kind of car to buy, and whether
there's enough for the kids' summer camp. Financial pressures can
put a real enough strain on our relationship, but often our arguments
about money are only a smokescreen for other unhappiness we have
trouble talking about. Many times money—what it buys and what it
represents—is merely a metaphor for our own feelings of being loved
and valued.

As the Beatles said, money can't buy you love. Getty's comment
is a poignant testimonial to the true value of love from a man of
legendary wealth. In the end, a successful marriage is worth its
weight in gold. Nothing can compare.

& *Write a love note to your partner. Inside a card or at the top of
a sheet of notepaper write, "You are worth a million dollars to me
because . . ." and then list at least ten reasons, such as, "you really
listen to me," "you comfort me when I'm upset," "you laugh at
my terrible puns," "you make sure we're saving money, even
when I chide you about being stingy," "you glued together my
favorite teacup," "you smell good." Put the note on your partner's
pillow so they will see it when they come to bed.*

**Today, I visualize a balance scale carried by Athena, the goddess of
wisdom. My partner and I stand on one side of the scale in an
embrace. On the other side I visualize being piled, one by one, cars
and jewels and beautiful homes and stacks of money. I enjoy seeing
them and can imagine the pleasure in having them. But no matter
how much is put on the other side of the scale, nothing can counter-
balance our love.**

Time is a dressmaker specializing in alterations.

— FAITH BALDWIN

We often resist change. Afraid of the unknown, we'd rather stay with a bad situation that is familiar than risk the unforeseeable consequences of the new. But even when we remain in one place, things change around us; we can't avoid it. Our resentment of our partner's spending habits does not go away because we pretend they're not there. Our inability to converse intimately with our partner does not improve because we don't talk about it. The sexual tension between partners does not go away because we ignore it. Regardless of how tenaciously we hang on to the status quo, many things, large and small, will be different same time next year. Unless we risk changing the situation for the better, chances are it will get worse.

Given the inevitability of change in our lives, we might as well be its instrument rather than its victim. Not that we should have grandiose ideas about being masters of the universe. All creatures and situations have certain parameters determined by their innate nature. But within those broadly defined guidelines, we do have considerable power to orchestrate our lives to our liking. We can— through thought, word, and deed—exert a powerful influence over our own universe. In a conscious relationship, couples recognize that change is their ally. Open to the spirit of awakening, they actively make alterations that move them forward in the direction of their goals.

 Ask your partner to share an unspoken wish for a behavior or a new experience. Mirror it back until you are sure you have it right. Give your partner that behavior. Be the instrument of change.

Today I let myself become aware that I sometimes feel myself a victim rather than an architect of change. In the depth of my quiet place, I find myself at a drawing board, designing a behavior that makes our home a place of safety for my partner. I confess in joy: "I have the power to make things different."

*Marriage is the nearest adult equivalent to the
original parent-child relationship.*

—H. V. DICKS

It doesn't sound very romantic, but healing our childhood wound is
the primary aim of our unconscious in a committed partnership. Our
Imago partner is the person our unconscious perceives as the perfect
re-creation of our early caretakers, and thus the person with whom
we can try again to get what we didn't get as children. In a conscious
marriage, partners make this unconscious agenda their conscious
intention. The first step in this process is to clarify for ourselves, and
share with our partner, a clear understanding of our wounds.

In this unit you will be invited to identify another vital piece of your
childhood wound: your frustrations with your caretakers and your
responses to those frustrations. These are the behaviors that you
are unwittingly reenacting with your partners.

❧ *For the next three days, you'll be invited to do an exercise that
will help you identify the childhood frustrations that you brought
to your relationship. Today you will revisit your mother (or mother
figure).*

*In your notebook, title two facing pages "Childhood Frustra-
tions" and divide each page into two vertical columns (so you
have four columns across two pages). Label column one "Frustrations," and in that column list all the frustrations you had with
your mother as you recall them from childhood (not the frustrations you might have with her today). For example: "She never
had any time for me." Label column two "Negative Feelings" and
next to each frustration write the negative feeling you had about
that frustration. Example: "I felt sad and unlovable." Label
column three "Responses" and in it briefly describe the way you
reacted to each frustration (you may have reacted in more than
one way—list all of your common reactions). Example: "I would
sulk by myself, and pretend I didn't care if she paid attention to
me." Label column four "My Deepest Fear" and write your
deepest fear about your mother. "I was afraid she would just
abandon me because she didn't care about me."*

**During this time of deep reflection, I welcome the gift of unraveling
the mystery of my relationship with my partner.**

Being guarded, armored, distrustful and enclosed is second nature in our culture.

—ALEXANDER LOWEN

All of us, no matter how stable and nurturing our home lives may have been, are wounded. As well-intentioned as our parents may have been, there were myriad opportunities for things to go wrong, and these things that went wrong had a greater impact on our development, unfortunately, than the things that went right. We remember the angry tirades more vividly than we remember the days of relative peace.

Terrified for our lives, we develop defenses against the inadequacies of our childhood over which we have no control. Through repetition, these coping mechanisms harden into character defenses that continue throughout our lives to ensure our survival. They are the only ways we know to protect ourselves in what we perceive as threatening situations. We cling to our partner or recoil from affection or crawl into a shell at the first sign of criticism. All these behaviors can be traced back to our feeble defenses against wounds suffered in the first years of our lives. As long as we remain unaware of our defense mechanisms and their causes, we will continue to be frustrated with our partner.

🍃 *Today you are invited to revisit your father (or father figure).*

On the same notebook pages you began yesterday, list in column one all the frustrations you had with your father, in column two the negative feelings you had about each frustration, in column three your responses to each frustration, and in column four your deepest fear about your father. Example: "He would lose his temper at the slightest thing; I was scared of him; I would get very quiet and try to get away as soon as possible without causing any more anger; I was afraid that he thought there was something wrong with me and didn't love me."

No longer afraid to visit my past, I relax in my place of quiet and rejoice that I am at last becoming conscious of the motives that have influenced the way I behave in my relationship.

Those who do not remember the past are condemned to repeat it.

— GEORGE SANTAYANA

As we reenact those old childhood scenarios—situations we had so hoped would have a different outcome when we fell in love—the still-sensitive wounds that we had bandaged over with our defenses are reopened. If, when our partner fails us as our parents did, our childhood reactions don't produce the desired effect, we (having no other model of dealing with life than the example our parents provided) turn the tables and treat our partner the way our parents treated us. Responding to our behavior, our partner's childhood wounds are reopened and they then respond to us much as they reacted to their parents when they were a child.

Say, for instance, your parents criticized you for your bad grades or your sloppy room, and you felt guilty and cried and had the recurring thought that you "couldn't do anything right." You will tend to react the same way if your partner finds fault with you for dropping your clothes on the floor or not making enough money. On the other hand, when your partner makes a mess or performs at a lower level than you expect, you will tend to criticize your partner as your parents criticized you.

❧ *Repeat the task from yesterday, substituting, one by one, any other influential caretakers in your life—a grandparent, sibling, teacher, etc., noting your frustrations and responses. On the same notebook pages, list in column one all your frustrations you had with your other caretakers, in column two the negative feelings you had about each frustration, in column three your responses to each frustration, and in column four your deepest fear.*

As the complexity of my childhood unfolds, I feel even more deeply a light illumining the mystery of my life. In my silent time today, I relax and receive the truth as a gift, knowing that facing my past enables me to avoid repeating it.

I talk and talk and talk, and I haven't taught people in fifty years what my father taught me by example in one week.

— MARIO CUOMO

Can you remember what it was like as a child? We were forever being told what to do and what to say, and rewarded or punished to reinforce the message. But no amount of words, bribes, threats, or rewards can match the power of what we saw and learned with our own eyes and ears. We had front-row seats to the live action drama titled "What It Is Like to Be a Partner and a Parent," with our caretakers playing the starring roles.

The admonition to "Do as I say, not as I do" falls on deaf ears, or rather a deaf unconscious. Our primitive old brain takes in everything. It does not pick and choose among the information to which it is an eyewitness. Nor can it judge; whatever comes in is taken at face value: this is the way that it is.

The only way to escape the tyranny of our past is to unmask it. Often just seeing its devastating influence in our present life is enough to jolt us into taking action to unlearn the habits of the past that are causing so much heartache in the present.

❧ *Again turn to the "Childhood Frustrations" pages of the past three days. In each column, circle the frustration and the responses that were the most influential, or synthesize the information from each column into one response, and complete the following sentence:*
When I didn't get [fill in your core frustration, or a phrase that combines all the frustrations, from column one]
I felt [your negative feelings from column two]
and responded by [your responses from column three].
My deepest fear was [your fear from column four].
In dialogue tonight, share this information with your partner.

No longer afraid to know the truth about myself, I enter the silence today, rejoicing that I am becoming conscious.

Shared laughter is erotic too.

— MARGE PIERCY

We have such limited ideas about what is erotic in our culture—red lace negligees, candlelight, high heels, Ravel's *Bolero*.

We are so serious about sex, so uptight, so worried about whether we're doing it right, or doing it enough, and if our partner is satisfied. But when you think about it, sex is pretty funny. Look at the crazy positions we get into, the noises we make, the machinations we've gone through at times to get it.

Sex is supposed to be fun, you know. Laughter shared by lovers is a powerful aphrodisiac. It defuses nervousness or inhibition, it keeps the juices flowing. Why not dissolve into each other's arms in an ecstasy of giggles? How about a big laugh at your foibles, or because it tickles, or because it feels so good? Remember, this is nature's gift. Love and laughter are natural bed partners.

&❧ *Do something to create laughter in the bedroom with your partner today. Tell a racy joke, do some tickling, a little rough and tumble.*

In quiet today, I recognize that joy, laughter, orgasm, and ecstasy are deeply spiritual experiences. I feel the muscles in my body relax as I hold this thought: "Lovemaking and laughter make a joyous mix."

*Fortunately analysis is not the only way to resolve
inner conflicts. Life itself still remains a very effective
therapist.*

—KAREN HORNEY

Sometimes we try so hard to figure out what's wrong with us. We devour self-help books, attend workshops, go through years of therapy. We learn a great deal, we gain new insights into our personal histories and issues. Buoyed by hope and enthusiasm, we try to implement our new knowledge and skills in our lives. Yet our problems persist. It can be pretty discouraging.

But insight is not the same as cure. Experience itself is the real catalyst for change. Every day life presents us with problems to overcome—opportunities to turn the fruits of our insights into action. Resolution of our relationship conflicts and of our personal issues is the result of diligently acting on our insights, enacting new behaviors until they have become an integral part of our character. There is an enormous difference, for example, between first realizing that we have a hard time acknowledging our partner's point of view, then learning the skill of validation, and actually practicing that skill each and every day with our partner until one day we realize that we naturally, automatically make space for our partner's view without feeling threatened or displaced.

In a conscious relationship, learning the theory and skills of the Imago process, which leads to our spiritual wholeness, is only the homework for the journey we are undertaking. The relationship itself, the daily attention grounded in the meditative process, is the therapy that heals us.

❧ *Pick something you've learned from books or therapy and put it into practice today: acknowledge your partner's viewpoint; catch yourself before that criticism leaves your mouth; speak up instead of sulking.*

I visualize myself absorbing life's great lessons, not from some renowned teacher, famous therapist, or profound book but from the mundane interactions with my partner. My mind focuses on this spiritual truth: "The psychic healing I seek can be found in daily loving."

*Personal space refers to an area with invisible
boundaries surrounding a person's body into which
intruders may not come.*

— ROBERT SOMMER

When we claim we couldn't help overhearing our partner's phone conversation, when we have to know their every thought, when we feel it's our right to rummage through their drawers or call them five times a day, we've crossed the line between closeness and concern into intrusiveness.

We all have boundaries, physical and psychological, that define our personal space. These boundaries are defined in childhood as we separate from our caretakers and establish a personal identity. For many of us, unfortunately, those boundaries are fuzzy or practically nonexistent. Unsure of who we are, terrified of being abandoned, we have no clear idea of where we leave off and the next person begins. We're forever invading others' territory, then puzzled when we are treated as an intruder. In an intimate partnership, ill-defined boundaries can be a big problem.

We all need privacy, internal and external space that our partners can't invade without warning. We don't need to snoop in our partner's drawers if we trust them; we don't want to if we love them. If we want to know our partner's thoughts, it is far better simply to ask.

✌ *Think about the ways in which you invade your partner's boundaries. Is there enough open space in your relationship for you both to move around in freely? Are you afraid there are secrets you should know about? Do you fear your partner will escape? Then examine your own boundaries. Do you know where they are? Does your partner invade your space? Have a couples dialogue about all this; you may need to redefine the territory.*

In my time of quiet today, I recognize the importance of our having time apart from each other. I relax into the wisdom of this truth: "The time my partner and I spend apart can invite a certain closeness."

Sometimes what our partnership needs is not another discussion to work through problems, or another evening reading in bed, but a break from routine, a time-out from the usual. Life's too short, and too precious, to allow ourselves to be consumed with worry, to lose sight of the beautiful world we live in. When we find ourselves spiritually destitute, it's time to make specific plans on how to restore our souls. Time spent in nature, far from the cares of our everyday world, can be just the soothing balm we need to put life back into perspective.

How about a lazy afternoon, just you, your partner, and nature? If you can't go today, plan an outing before the end of the week. Set a date and decide what you'd like to do—a hike, a picnic, staring at the stars from your rooftop, a snuggle in the car watching the sunset?

I picture my partner and myself in a peaceful natural setting, drinking in the calm, reconnective energy of nature's bounty. Recognizing the sacred in such a moment, I meditate on this vision: "My partner and I are creating our own reality."

Returning to the source is serenity.

—LAO-TZU

When your relationship feels stressed, the natural response is to assign the source of stress to your partner, then try to control them so that they will conform to what you want them to be. But your partner is not the source of your stress, and control is not the answer. The stress lies within. When you blame and criticize, absolving yourself of responsibility, you are caught in your own self-righteousness. In that place you have little chance of doing your own inner work.

You can use the stress you feel in the relationship to learn more about yourself and to deepen your own spirituality. Spiritual growth occurs when you take responsibility for your own inner stress, recognizing that much of the conflict with your partner is an external version of the internal conflict between parts of yourself. When you accept another, you paradoxically experience an inner reconciliation as well, which ultimately leads to peace and joy, not only in yourself, but in your relationship. When, over time, you recover your inner serenity in this process, you will lose your inclination to disrupt the peace of others.

ᨕ *List your three biggest frustrations with your partner this week. Think about the time you've spent obsessing over these issues, and the pain they've caused. Bring your hurt and frustration with each one to mind, then release your feelings, simply letting go and experiencing the quietness and peace at your inner core.*

I go within to witness my inner war. I release my frustrations and absolve my partner of blame. I acknowledge in prayer: "When the artillery stops, serenity is found."

Some truths are especially hard to face, and this one shatters our romantic fantasies: Everyone lives with a wounded person.

In a conscious relationship, partners make it their intention to heal each other's childhood wounds. However, keeping our promise to fulfill this role is difficult, not least of all because our partner's behavior is attacking us where we are most tender and vulnerable. For all our good intentions, sometimes we cannot see beyond our partner's meanness and neglect to the pain that lies at their source. It is hard to have compassion for our partner when we are under attack.

In order to find the understanding to be motivated to give them help for healing, we need to be able to see that our partner's hurtful behavior arises out of their own wounding and pain. In this unit, you and your partner will be invited to tell each other about your wounds and begin to reimage each other as wounded rather than wounding.

❧ *Decide who will talk about their wounding today, and who will be the listener (you will switch roles tomorrow). The listener sits in a comfortable place (sofa, bed, or pillows on the floor) and holds their partner across their lap like a child. The speaker talks for as long as they want about what it was like when they were a child, how they were wounded, how they felt, how they responded. The listener says very little, just holding and comforting the partner, mirroring occasionally.*

Today in the stillness of my sacred place, I let myself fully acknowledge that my partner's childhood wound is the source of their frustrating behavior. I offer this truth in confession: "My partner is wounded and I am wounded too."

*Perfect love means to love the one through whom one
became unhappy.*

—SØREN KIERKEGAARD

When we are unhappy, it seems so logical to blame our unhappiness
on our partner. All the evidence seems to point in their direction. If
it weren't for *their* anger, *their* neglect, *their* insensitivity, we think,
we'd be fine.

In a way that's true. What we tend to forget is that we have chosen
our partner *because* of this pattern of anger, neglect, or insensitivity,
because it sets up a situation that we need to resolve. Our original
unhappiness dates back to childhood; we have merely found a reason-
able facsimile in our partner.

Now, in order to be happy, we have to learn to love our partner,
who is a stand-in for our inadequate parents and for the parts of
ourselves that we project onto them. That's hard to do when all we
can see is the misery they are causing us. When, through the holding
exercise we are able to see *their* misery, we can pull back from our
blaming and recrimination and renew our intention to nurture their
happiness.

❧ *Repeat the holding exercise described yesterday, switching
roles with your partner.*

**Opening myself to the continuing unfolding of truth, I recognize in
my time of stillness today that my unhappiness has its roots in my
childhood wounds, not in my partner's behavior. I meditate on this
thought: "It is in learning to heal the wounded spirit of my partner
that my own spirit becomes restored as well."**

*Trouble is part of your life, and if you don't share it,
you don't give the person who loves you a chance to love
you enough.*

                                                     — DINAH SHORE

A successful relationship is built on what we are willing to share with our partner. Sometimes couples get the idea that they should only share what is good or helpful or positive, that somehow a loving partner doesn't bother their mate with their petty worries and problems.

Wrong. Withholding our problems deprives our partner of the chance to show their love for us and to dig within themselves for the empathy and strength that is the fodder for their own growth.

🍃 *Title a new page in your notebook "My Partner's Childhood Wound." Write down your partner's wound as you understand it from their description during the holding exercise. When you have both finished writing, read your account of your childhood wounds to each other and confirm their accuracy, using the couples dialogue. Follow this with a big hug. The following meditation should be done whenever you lose sight of the wounding behind your partner's hurtful behavior.*

Breathing naturally, I imagine myself in a place where I am totally safe and relaxed. I look around with pleasure, noticing the calm beauty of my surroundings, the smells, the sounds, my own feelings of peace. I invite my partner to join me here, and I hold them in my arms as a wounded child, with compassion for their pain. Holding this hurt child in this sacred place, I imagine the energy of my love healing their wounds.

Age does not protect you from love. But love, to some extent, protects you from age.

> —JEANNE MOREAU

There are many people of tender years whose hearts are bolted closed from lack of love. Yet many an octogenarian feels as if life is just beginning because they love. Why does love keep us young? Because love requires activism: it demands that we keep growing and changing. It asks that our heart remain open to new experience, to the world, to others. Love makes us do great things; it does not tolerate a passive, wait-and-see attitude. We may fall in love at any age, at any stage of supposed decrepitude. But love will rattle our cage. And when we rise to the challenge, it will restore us to health. It's hard for the arteries to harden when fresh blood keeps pumping through.

ᖷ *Demonstrate that love keeps you young. Make a date with your partner to do something romantic together, even if just for half an hour: take a playful walk hand in hand, share an ice cream sundae, or go to a movie and neck in the back row.*

Today I feel connected to vitality and youth, and in quiet meditation, I ponder the timelessness of my love. When I take twenty minutes to surround myself in stillness, when I put that DO NOT DISTURB sign on the office door or go out and sit under a large shade tree in the park, I feel my own aliveness pulsating in my heart.

*To dream the person you would like your partner to be
is to waste the person your partner is.*

—ANONYMOUS

We all have fantasies of what we think our perfect partner would be like. But the one we end up with rarely matches our vision. It's amazing how much time and energy we can waste being upset, dwelling on our mate's shortcomings, or trying to make our partners match the dream. "If you'd just dress with a bit more sophistication," we complain, or "You could learn to play tennis too, like Anne's husband." We drop hints. We not-so-subtly show our disappointment.

But what about this real live partner you've got? Sometimes we are so lost in our daydreams that we cancel out the qualities our partner does have—their particular brand of warmth and charm, their sense of humor, their so-natural-you-almost-don't-notice-it sensuality, the compassion they can show for others. Bet you never dreamed you'd find a partner with such sterling traits.

So, get real. You're letting your partner's treasures go to waste. Put your fantasy aside and begin to explore the reality that is your partner. Who knows but that you'll unearth treasure beyond your wildest dreams.

&. *On a new page in your notebook, make a list of the qualities, large and small, that you have discovered in your partner in the past year. If there are fewer than five items on your list, it's time to pay more attention to your partner. By this time tomorrow, add three new things to your list that you hadn't noticed before.*

Today I let the tensions of the world roll off my shoulders during this time of quiet. I recognize the weight of all the negative processing I harbor, and I allow myself to relax into the peaceful reality of this moment. I prayerfully hold this thought: "I must let go of my fantasy so that I can love the reality of my partner."

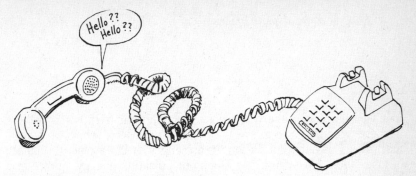

Ever feel as if you and your partner just aren't communicating? What you've got is a communications breakdown, usually the result of many small moments when you should have been talking but didn't.

Noncommunication all too easily becomes a habit. We're too preoccupied, or we find it risky or intimidating to express our feelings to an unresponsive mate. We feel that our remarks are twisted or misunderstood, so that simple conversations escalate into arguments. Eventually, we just give up and fall into a kind of incommunicado accommodation, an uneasy calm of silence and secrecy. We talk about the weather and ask our partner to change the television channel but avoid the openness that keeps life alive.

Silent partners are incapacitated in crisis. Years of small conversations may have to be condensed into one big one—and it still may seem too late to repair the damage. It's hard to be calm under pressure when we've lost the knack of clear conversation. And by the time we're in big trouble, we may no longer care to avoid disaster. So, speak up!

🍋 *Do something to improve the lines of communication in your relationship. Take time to talk about some subject you don't usually talk about—sex, money, spirituality, politics. Stick to the couples dialogue guidelines.*

In quiet contemplation today, I see the lines of communication between me and my partner humming with lively conversation. I recognize our communication as another form of spiritual unity and I vow: "I will be open with all of me and to all of my partner."

Love is a great beautifier.

—LOUISA MAY ALCOTT

We've seen it in ourselves, we've seen it in our friends: something happens when we are in love—or, more precisely, when we love—that makes us beautiful. When we are angry or in despair, the bloom of love fades. How can it be? Does our pulsating energy vibrate at a higher frequency when we love, do our cells reorganize at a higher level? Whether the explanation lies in biochemistry or psychology, loving another penetrates deeper than any beauty cream and is more effective than a week at the poshest spa.

❧ *Step up your beauty regimen. Do three things for your partner today. Be lavish with compliments and affection and small talk. Notice the difference in your mirror, and in the reflection of love in your partner's eyes.*

I take time today for the renewal of my spirit. Closing my eyes and breathing deeply and evenly, I let myself relax into a deeper psychic reality, a place usually beyond my awareness. This thought becomes my benediction: "Loving my partner creates beauty in myself, in my partner, and in the world."

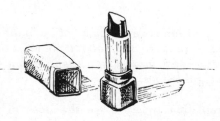

That the birds of worry and care fly about your head,
this you cannot change. But that they build nests in
your hair, this you can prevent.

— CHINESE PROVERB

Are you fuming because he forgot to put the toilet seat down again? Are you stomping around because she left her stockings to dry all over the bathroom? Beside yourself with worry about making the next mortgage payment? So worried, in fact, that you're not getting your work done and wake up each morning with a knot in the pit of your stomach?

We all have plenty to worry about. But the worry itself neither solves nor changes anything. Instead, the worries themselves can interfere so much with our clarity that they become part of the problem.

Life's troubles are ever with us; when one trouble goes away, another appears to take its place. Tension is to be expected in committed relationships. Only our attitude toward our troubles can be changed. And one way to change that attitude is to take time each day to detach ourselves from our worries and cares. In our time of contemplation, we can watch them fly about our head, without letting them come home to roost. Our inner spirit was meant for joy—not obsession.

Each time you come up against an irritation or worry today—
the cap off the toothpaste, the concern about the dentist's bill—
see if you can just notice it for a moment and let it pass from your
mind; move on to the next thought.

In meditation today I identify those things in my relationship and in my broader world that frustrate me. Rather than allow them to nest, I let these issues take flight. As the issues dissolve into nothingness, I begin to experience a greater sense of spiritual freedom. I admit with liberation: "I can control any given situation by the way I respond to it."

Anyone can become angry—that is easy; but to be
angry with the right person, and to the right degree,
and at the right time, and for the right purpose, and
in the right way—that is not easy.

—ARISTOTLE

Partners locked in a power struggle are plenty angry, but few couples know how to fight in a way that doesn't escalate the conflict. All they know is what they learned long ago—criticism, whining, rage, shaming, complaints, withdrawal—the usual clumsy weapons.

In this unit you will be introduced to a powerful relationship maintenance process that will allow you to communicate safely and release your everyday upset and anger so that it has a productive effect and does not get stored away until it escalates into a major conflagration. In the containment process, one partner acts as a safe and nonreactive receptacle, or container, for the frustration the other partner expresses. This receiving partner mirrors, validates, and expresses empathy for the sending partner, which creates safety for both. The sender needs the safety of knowing they can express their feelings of frustration without fear of retribution or backlash. The receiver needs to know they will not be attacked or harmed in any way. The containing effect of mirroring provides this two-way assurance, especially helping the receiver to stay fully and lovingly present.

🍂 *As a preliminary to doing the containment exercise with your partner, today's assignment is to identify the issues that currently anger you and write them down in a way that abides by the following two safety precautions:*
1. Use "I" language. *Own your experience by saying how you feel rather than blaming your partner. For example, "I feel bad when . . ." rather than "You make me feel bad when . . ."*
2. Describe the upsetting behavior. *Do not use abusive names or criticize your partner's character or motivation. For example, "I'm angry that you forgot . . ." rather than "You are unreliable . . ."*

In quiet today, I tap into that powerful place inside of me that houses my anger. I allow the heat of this anger to flow through my veins and meditate on this prayer: "The sharing of my anger is to help, not hurt, my partner."

A safe and healthy container for our charged feelings involves appropriate expression and appropriate reception within agreed-upon parameters. The container exercise that you are learning this week is essentially a one-way transaction in which one partner (the sender) gets to express a frustration—about their partner or anything else—to the receiving partner without a rebuttal or deflection. Only mirroring, validation, and empathy are allowed in response. It is *not* designed to solve the problem but to reinforce the habit of expressing frustrations in an understanding and tolerant atmosphere.

The container exercise is meant to be a brief exchange—typically three to ten minutes—for the immediate discharge of negative feelings before they build up. In order to assure a safe container for your anger, the following agreements are first made:

—All expressions of angry feelings are done by appointment only. The partner says, "I am feeling upset . . . [or angry or irritated]. Can we do the containment process?" Requests for appointments are granted as soon as possible, preferably immediately. Making an appointment allows the receiving partner to prepare and go into the containment mode described below.

- *Both partners stay fully present until the process is complete. (The containment process is over when the sender has completed their communication, not when a particular amount of time has passed.)*
- *Neither partner causes any bodily harm to themselves or their partner, and neither partner destroys any property.*

🏖 *Using the couples dialogue, discuss with your partner the idea of changing the way you deal with anger. Share your understanding of the three agreements above, and consider whether you are willing to assent to them.*

Today I enter the sanctuary of safety deep within and summon my courage and empathy to become a safe container for my partner's hurt.

Things do not change; we change.

—HENRY DAVID THOREAU

Few of us are skillful at either expressing or receiving anger—understandably, for its energy can be frightening, even overwhelming. But anger is only an expression of the life force—the same energy that operates in laughter or passion—gone on the defensive in response to hurt or a sense of helplessness. It is our primitive response to a real or perceived threat to our survival. Anger is like a fire. If we let it rage out of control, it damages or destroys us. If we suffocate it or stamp it out, eventually the cold and the dark seep into our bones and we become numb. But if we contain fire properly and allow it to burn safely, its energy becomes available for joy and passion.

🍃 *Today will also be a practice run, and you and your partner are invited to work together. One of you will be the sender, the other the receiver. Here are the guidelines for the receiver:*

- *Relax and take a few deep breaths. Feel yourself firmly grounded, anchored, and secure.*
- *Visualize your partner as a wounded child.*
- *Remember that your partner's feelings are rooted in their childhood. Your actions may have triggered their frustration, but you are not the original cause of the hurt and therefore not the target.*
- *Listen to what your partner says with empathy, care, compassion, and unconditional love. Mirror, validate, and empathize.*
- *Receive your partner's communication. Do not rebut or deflect it.*

I enter my safe place today, aware that anger, like fire, has creative and destructive power. As I relax more deeply, grounding myself in my breathing, I imagine coverting the fire of anger into joy and bonding. I anchor myself in this thought: "Anger is a protest against the loss of joy."

Never go to bed mad. Stay up and fight.

—PHYLLIS DILLER

The idea that we would be happier and healthier if we were fully in touch with our anger, fear, and pain goes against some powerful directives. We have been strongly conditioned by our parents and society to judge, repress, and deny strong feelings, our anger in particular. In childhood, our expressions of anger (and sometimes even fear of pain) usually met with negative response—punishment, being ignored, being yelled at, being shamed. Our experience on the receiving end of anger or rage also probably proved what we had been taught about its destructive power.

But the appropriate expression of anger is the key to regaining our joyful aliveness. In learning to express our anger in the container process, we find that we can release all our feelings without either devastating or losing our partner, and we realize that we can receive our partner's frustrations without feeling that they don't love us.

❧ *Today's task is to reverse roles, so that yesterday's receiver voices their frustrations (about topics other than the partner), and yesterday's sender contains them.*

Remember, acknowledging your partner's anger does not mean that you agree with them or that you accept blame, only that you understand that they are angry and that you affirm their emotional state.

Today I recognize that I can only be of help to my partner if I stay grounded and calm. I hold this wisdom in my heart: "Keeping myself centered will better enable me to contain my partner's frustrations."

Let our scars fall in love.

—GALWAY KINNELL

Over time, unexpressed anger becomes depression. When we suppress our anger, the rest of our life force gets blocked. Our capacity to love suffocates, along with everything else. Appropriate expression of anger is the key to regaining the joyful aliveness that filled us as children. Releasing anger allows all of our other feelings to flow—fear, pain, sadness, joy, love, all of them. Such feelings are our natural, appropriate, and necessary response to life.

🗫 *Today you and your partner will do your first containment exercise, using a frustration in your relationship. Decide who will be the sender and who will be the receiver. Follow this procedure:*

The sender picks a minor real-life frustration with the partner and asks their partner for an appointment.

The receiver agrees to receive the communication in a container transaction right away (for the purposes of this practice exercise). The receiver goes into containment mode and tells the sender when they are ready.

The sender then states their frustration as briefly, simply, and directly as possible.

The receiver mirrors, validates, and empathizes, then asks if the sender feels complete for now. Lovingly use the question: "Is there more?" If the sender has more to say about the original frustration, continue the process until they feel complete. When the sender is complete, they respond affirmatively and thank the receiver. The process ends with the receiver thanking the sender for openly communicating their feelings.

Tomorrow, switch roles, but before you finish for today, have a brief couples dialogue sharing your feelings and thoughts about the container transaction.

During this time of self-restoration, I allow today's frustrations to ebb. This thought becomes my prayer: "Containment and care for my partner's reality are essential parts of my own spiritual growth."

Nothing is settled until it is settled right.

—ABRAHAM LINCOLN

There is no such thing as a person who never gets angry. There are people who repress and deny their rage, but there is no one living who doesn't have it. Often we cover or deny our anger out of fear that what is inside of us is dark, ugly, and overpowering. Yet once we gain the courage to wrestle with this fear and fully express our feelings, we learn an astonishing thing: what is hiding inside us is our own blocked life energy. It is love, it is light, and releasing this energy is the ultimate purpose of love relationships.

As containment replaces all other forms of disagreement or fighting, we develop a clearer sense of boundaries and learn that we don't have to be entwined in or take on our partner's emotional state. We find we have less negative response to our partner's upset or angry feelings. We begin to allow ourselves and our partner fuller expression of emotions. Our acceptance of each other's feelings, combined with stretching to meet each other's needs, heals our deepest wounds.

🍂 *Repeat the containment exercise from yesterday, this time switching the roles of sender and receiver. Finish with a brief couples dialogue sharing your feelings and thoughts about the container process.*

Through working on anger, I keep in mind that I hold my partner's heart in my hand. Moving into a place of deeper inner peace, I pray for the knowledge to guard my partner's well-being throughout the process of self-declaration.

Didn't it feel good to get those frustrations off your chest? Congratulations for persevering through this difficult process—having the courage to face your anger and learn how to express it. There is no shortcut to dealing effectively with anger; the only way through it is direct and appropriate expression, which opens the way for more loving, good feelings.

Now that you've learned this new skill, use the containment process to express all your frustrations and highly charged feelings, instead of allowing spontaneous fights to erupt. Continue to practice the containment process as frustrations arise, so you will be comfortable with it. Learning to use this anger management skill to express frustrations is necessary preparation for the problem-solving skills of the behavior-change request process you will be learning in a future unit.

❧ Give yourselves a treat, something extra special—you deserve it! Get out of the house and do something playful together. Go to a baseball game, see a happy musical, take turns on the swing. Celebrate learning how to convert your anger into bonding and passion.

I celebrate having learned skills to maneuver through such a difficult part of my relationship. Going inward today, I acknowledge how hard it's been for my partner and me to carry our frustration alone. I focus on this thought: "We have found a way for our anger to unite us rather than divide us."

Ceremony is the smoke of friendship.

—CHINESE PROVERB

We usually associate ritual with holidays and religious observances, or the practices of tribal societies. But we all engage in rituals every day—our morning shower, that first cup of coffee, the morning TV or radio show we never miss. Though we don't think of them as rituals, we use certain repetitive routines to give structure and meaning to our lives. Rituals are powerful; the systematic repetition of any act or words has the effect of charging them with meaning. Just as we have cultural and family rituals, our partnership has evolved rituals of its own.

Without realizing what we are doing, we can ritualize with negative or destructive behavior—our typical surly reply to our mate's request, the coffee we fix for ourselves but not our partner, the habit of secluding ourselves in the basement workshop or the sewing room every evening. These acts send powerful messages to the unconscious. When we begin to identify the rituals that punctuate our daily lives, and assess whether their energy is positive or negative, we can begin to shape them to advance our goals, to accrue affirmative power and meaning in our lives. In this way, ordinary acts are thus transformed into extraordinary and powerful symbols of our interconnectedness.

Make a list of your daily habits, both at home and at work. Choose one that you feel has the potential to be shaped into the kind of ritual which would enhance your life. Perhaps you'll choose to use your lunch break to sit in the park and connect with nature. The evening cup of tea with your partner could be understood as a time to talk about your day before getting ready for bed.

During this time of stillness, I value the ritual of taking twenty minutes simply to focus on my inner world, opening me to a deeper interconnectedness. I open to this thought: "It is the simple, ordinary acts that endow my life with meaning."

✳ *My divorce came as a complete surprise to me. That will happen when you haven't been home in eighteen years.*

—LEE TREVINO

Did you hear the one about the traveling salesman—the one where the husband is away for weeks at a time? Or the commuter marriage? These are arrangements, not relationships.

No couple can expect to sustain a relationship if they're not actually together most of the time. Some couples think they can blithely pursue their separate interests, spending their evenings hanging out with friends or taking courses, and their mates will be patiently waiting for them when they return. Such arrangements often work out, for a while, but eventually the gap widens. The partners have little idea, and less interest, in what their mate is up to and who they really are. The setup that once seemed unfettered and convenient comes to feel boring and stagnant; something vital is missing. What they have is a parallel marriage: they're side by side but far apart.

It is the daily contact, the rubbing and jostling and bantering, that polishes and refines a relationship. Our yearning to feel alive and joyful will not be satisfied by the freedom to spend time apart.

🍃 *Have a couples dialogue with your partner about the balance in your relationship between time spent together and time spent on personal pursuits. Are you neglecting the relationship for other activities or escaping from a level of intimacy that feels uncomfortable? What needs to change so that you can be together in order to stay together? Decide on an exit you can close today.*

Today as I close my eyes and block out the world's frantic pace, I take quiet inventory of the balance between involvement and separateness in our relationship. Viewing the tally sheet, I let my feelings come up about our level of intimacy. I focus my heart and mind on these words: "Togetherness is necessary for intimacy."

Learn true joy, and you will meet God.

— SRI AUROBINDO

Many religions depict God as some abstract entity in heaven, a disembodied being who lives in the sky, cut off from our daily existence. This archaic view of God severs us from the God within.

Within each one of us is a state of pulsating aliveness, a God-essence that is inherent in us from the time of birth. But it is difficult to protect this essence from religious rhetoric and societal conditioning. Trained to believe in an objective, externalized god, we became amnesiac to our essential, internal divinity. Shaped to conform to society's mold, we forget our original state.

Whatever our circumstances, our relationship offers us a way— perhaps the best way—to reclaim our inner joy. Each time we sit quietly together, or make love, we can feel the pulse within. When we walk hand in hand in nature we can feel our connection with each other and with the environment in which we are embedded. Giving our partner a hug, drying their tears, or making them laugh clears space in our hearts where true joy can reside. Stretching to meet our partner's needs stirs our love, activating the divine within. We are that which we seek, and when we find and restore all of ourselves, yearning will end, joy will abound, for God is met.

❧ *Do something on your fun list today with your partner. Give yourself the sense of well-being that comes from a heartfelt belly laugh, revel in the afterglow of an orgasm. Allow the joy of being and union to flow through you.*

I allow my time of meditation and prayer to move me into a state of deep connection to the vibrancy of the universe. I hold this thought: "Learn true joy, and you will meet God."

Sometimes we make it hard for our partner to tell us what's on their minds. Though we say that we want to hear what's troubling them, our attitude or body language tells a different story. Maybe we become distracted or insist that they're exaggerating. Perhaps we react to their disclosure with angry silence or threats. Whatever the tactic, the result is that we intimidate our partner into being less than honest with us. Hardly a recipe for the intimacy and security we say we want.

It's worthwhile to look at the ways in which we deflect or short-circuit our partner's communications. Direct and honest dialogue is a gift we should welcome with open arms and ears.

❧ Notice throughout the day whether you create a welcoming space for your partner's thoughts or disclosures, or whether you put up subtle defenses that keep your partner from being fully honest with you. See if you can begin to let down one of those defenses today. If it's your habit to act offended or disbelieving, or to counter when your mate tries to say what's on their mind, see if you can stop yourself in time, and just listen, mirroring back what is said.

Moving to the calm still place at my core. I identify the subtle ways I deflect my partner. Breathing deeply, I say good-bye to each one of the evasion tactics I unconsciously use in my relationship. I hold this wisdom in my heart: "Open communication incubates the soul of a relationship."

*Among those I like or admire, I can find no common
denominator; but among those I love, I can: All of
them make me laugh.*

—W. H. AUDEN

Laughter is potent stuff. It can immediately change the mood, raise
the spirits, quell fear, stop tears. With its ability to mitigate pain, it
acts as a buffer against hard times. But it's all too often in short
supply in our relationships, even among partners who love and value
each other.

The ability to keep each other's spirits up, to bring laughter into
the house and have fun in the face of whatever is troubling us, is a
priceless asset in a relationship. You don't have to be a stand-up comic
delivering a rapid-fire stream of one-liners. What's called for is the
ability to recognize the humor in life and in ourselves, to be both
amused and amusing.

❧ *During the day today, make an effort to see the humor in life:
allow yourself to be amused by life's ups and downs, by human
foibles—yours and others. Tonight, make your partner laugh,
even if just by reading something funny from the comics or
tickling their feet.*

**Today I relax deeply into my sacred place and meditate on the fact
that I belong to the only species that can laugh. Suspending all other
thoughts, I tap into the wellspring of inner joy and smile at the
absurdity, the mystery, and the humor of life.**

Once a woman has forgiven a man, she must not reheat his sins for breakfast.

—MARLENE DIETRICH

It's that narrowing of your eyes . . . that hint of hurt in your voice . . . and your partner is once again reminded of their transgression. "I want you to know how you've hurt me," we're saying. What makes us think that guilt will motivate our partner to love us more?

Forgiving and forgetting is easier said than done. But constantly rehashing old hurts is destructive and produces nothing of value. So what if your partner forgot to pick up the cleaning, or made a pot roast that you hate, or made fun of your friend? It's not the end of the world; you've made your point, you've asked for a change. Let it go!

There are deep hurts that may seem unforgivable. This kind of absolution doesn't happen overnight; it may take years. But how will your relationship go forward if you're mired in the past? Release as much of the old hurt as you can, and take it one day at a time.

&❧ *Take out your notebook and jot down the things you find most difficult to forgive in your partner. Are you still holding on to that kiss he gave his old girlfriend at the reunion, or the time she was off on a business trip on your birthday? When you finish your list, rip the page out of the book and tear it up into little pieces or burn it—releasing those outdated grudges and letting in forgiveness.*

I open my heart to forgiveness and release my partner from responsibility for all past hurts. Recognizing forgiveness as a precondition of love, I prayerfully honor this reality: "In forgiveness is freedom."

Do candlelight dinners and nights of passion still punctuate your relationship? Do you still make a fuss over your partner's birthday, freely bestow a compliment, still listen together to your favorite songs? When couples get mired in routines and problems, when they cohabit in a soup of conflict and criticism, when years of unintentional neglect transmute into boredom, romance leaks from the relationship until it becomes but a dry framework on which to hang their lives.

Over the next several days you and your partner will be invited to *reromanticize* your relationship. At first what you are doing may seem artificial, and perhaps contradictory to the current state of your feelings for each other. But you'll be surprised to find that *acting* in a romantic and caring way toward your partner will actually make you *feel* more romantic; it will break the impasse. Through daily repetition of positive behaviors, the old brain repatterns its image of our partners, and we again become a source of pleasure for each other.

🐚 *Make a list of all the things that your partner currently does that please you. Complete this sentence in as many ways as you can think of: "I feel loved and cared about when you . . ." Be positive and specific. Examples: "when you call me at work just to talk," "when you come up behind me in the kitchen and kiss me," "when you walk the dog on nights when I'm tired."*

As I relax and breathe deeply, I let all feelings of irritation or ill will toward my partner fall away, and I bring to mind an especially loving thing my partner has done for me recently. With thanksgiving, I hold this thought: "My partner is a source of pleasure for me."

It isn't the great big pleasures that count the most;
it's making a great deal out of the little ones.

—JEAN WEBSTER

It's discouraging to see the signs of romance and passion fade. Without realizing it is happening, we slip into habits of indifference or exhaustion or neglect. The active pursuit of mutual pleasure that characterized our dating days is all but abandoned. No wonder we complain of boredom or of feeling unloved. Because we don't feel cared for, we may come to assume that each is purposely depriving the other of pleasure, setting off a downward spiral of withholding and recrimination.

That delectable mixture of excitement and caring is never dropped in a neatly wrapped package on our doorstep. We must create it— just as we did during our dating days, when we'd spend hours planning what to wear, what to say, thinking of special things to do for our beloved. If our relationships are pleasure starved, we must fatten them up with daily tidbits of caring, concern, fun, and affection.

☙ *Make a list of all the caring and romantic things your partner used to do. Complete this sentence in as many ways as you can think of: "I used to feel loved and cared about when you . . ." Examples: "left love notes around the house," "wanted to meet in the afternoon to make love," "peeled my orange at breakfast," "brought me silly surprise gifts."*

In deep meditation, I recall in detail a romantic occasion when my partner and I were first dating. I savor every detail, remembering where we were and what we said to each other, especially my partner's romantic and caring behavior. Bathed in this memory, I proclaim: "Remember joy."

Love thrives on trivial kindnesses.

—THEODOR FONTANE

In the course of a long relationship, we're sometimes called upon to make extraordinary efforts in support of our partners. Looking back, we can pinpoint those milestones—the months of working two jobs, the weeks spent in the hospital with a sick child, the year of scrimping when there was no work. But it's the little, daily acts of caring—the kiss, the cup of tea, the words of reassurance, the errand run—that lay the foundation of safety and nurturance that enable us to give our all in the hard times. Trivial though they may seem, the personal attention and effort that they draw from us, the subtle reframing of our ideas of partnership induced by such seemingly unimportant acts are the stuff of bedrock.

❧ *Make a list today of the caring or romantic behaviors that you have never asked your partner for. Complete this sentence in as many specific ways as you can think of: "I would like you to . . ." "make love to me outdoors next time we go camping," "run my bath and then soap my back," "read poetry to me," "buy me some silk boxer shorts."*

When you have finished, take all three lists that you've made and rate each caring behavior on the lists according to how important it is to you, with 1 indicating that it is "very important" and 5 "not so important."

I let my imagination soar today, dreaming of the kinds of caring, romantic behaviors I have been afraid to ask for from my partner. Cultivating the spirit of receiving, I affirm: "I ask for and welcome my partner's care."

Each of us has our own idea about what constitutes caring behavior in a relationship. For one person, it's gifts or flowers or dinners in fancy restaurants. For another, it's loving words, a compliment, a bedtime story, or a foot rub. What one person thinks is romantic, another finds corny. Often we expect our partners to mind read exactly what it is that we want. When they don't, when they give us flowers instead of a foot rub, we take it as evidence of their insensitivity or inattention.

Infants who can't talk need to be mind read. Adults say what they want. That's why, when we make our lists of caring behaviors, we specify to our partners *exactly* what will make us feel loved and cared about. There's no mind reading, so there's no disappointment.

&. *Exchange lists with your partner. Put an X next to any items on your partner's list that you are not willing to do at this time. All the remaining behaviors should be conflict free. (Note: at any point in the future, feel free to add new behaviors to your list.)*

Today I think about the caring behaviors that my partner has asked of me. I visualize myself giving each of those gifts to my partner, one by one, and notice that each gift is received with love and appreciation. I offer this prayer with an open heart: "It is in the giving that I receive."

Today you are invited to begin exchanging caring behaviors with your partner. It may feel awkward at first, but stick with it, regardless of how you are feeling at the moment about your partner. By repeatedly play-acting the kind of romantic behavior that you once felt, you will actually change the chemistry between you. What at first seems artificial will soon feel natural. You will begin to see your partner as a bringer of pleasure, and your partner will again perceive you as nurturing and loving. You will be allies rather than enemies.

Remember that these behaviors are to be given as gifts, with no strings attached. They are not to be bartered for behavior of equal value, and there is to be no scorekeeping of who is giving what—and how much—to whom. Only gifts that are given unconditionally are perceived by our unconscious as having value.

❧ *Beginning today, give your partner at least one of the behaviors on their list every day this week. When your partner does a caring behavior for you, acknowledge it with a comment of thanks or appreciation. Keep on giving the behaviors in spite of any resistance you may feel.*

As I relax, breathing deeply, I picture each act of caring that my partner and I give to each other as a drop of solvent which dissolves the anger between us. This thought radiates from my heart: "Small acts of love are redemptive."

If we come to this living water, which is contemplation, we will never thirst for anything more in this life.

—SAINT TERESA OF AVILA

Though many religions codify and regulate prayer, there is no correct protocol or procedure for prayer. The act of prayer is simply a way of tapping into an energy deep within ourselves. It need not be labeled or ritualized. It is enough to recognize that as a river taps into a larger body of water, we too must replenish our resources from a larger source. The center of our being intersects with the center of the universe that many call God.

Our lives can indeed be exhausting. At times we fear collapsing, losing control, failing to meet our obligations and self-imposed demands. When we push ourselves too far, for too long, illness and collapse are inevitable. The mind and body retaliate against our neglect.

Our ability to care for others begins with self-care. The twenty minutes a day we take for quiet rest or introspection, is the place where self-restoration can happen. Others' needs and our own responsibilities are set aside as we focus on our own thoughts and feelings—or on nothing at all! We replenish the storehouse in which our energies are recharged.

Commit to at least twenty minutes for yourself today. Sit outside and write in your journal; lock yourself in a room with a DO NOT DISTURB *sign on the door; take a walk where you won't run into anyone you know.*

I allow myself to tap into the energy that is available within, and recognize it as the source of my empowerment. In this place of prayer, I celebrate the wonder of life.

There are so many ways in which we subtly sabotage our partners. "C'mon, honey, one little bite of this chocolate cheesecake won't spoil your diet; it's soooo good." "You'll never work up the nerve to ask for a raise; you chickened out last time." If you asked us, we'd say we were only trying to help.

What's behind such undermining behavior? Perhaps fear of change. When one partner moves ahead, the other may fear the results—abandonment, a shift in the balance of power, loss of status. However, when we can see our partner as having equal value to us, we can applaud the way their accomplishments enhance our life.

🐾 *What goal or project is your mate currently working on? Finding more free time to relax or meditate? Writing the Great American Novel? Think of three ways you can lend your support and do them this week.*

Today I picture my partner's endeavors, and I allow my deepest feelings to surface. Are there traces of envy? Competition? Anger? I confess these feelings and look for the inner strength to shift to a genuinely supportive attitude. I commit instead: "My partner's accomplishments bring life to my relationship."

Ultimately, I just have to believe and Kevin has to tell me once in a while that ours is the greatest love story. That's kind of what you live on.

—CINDY COSTNER

Picture your relationship as a movie, a detective story in which two people come together to solve a puzzle to which you each hold half the pieces. You and your Imago partner struggle to fit the pieces together. It's hard work.

Each Imago match is a love story unlike any other, with its own twists and turns of plot, its hair-raising scenes and tender moments. In hard times, in particular, a dramatic shift can occur when we are reminded by our partners that we are supremely loved. Take time to sprinkle your relationship with this extra attention. See what a superlative or two a day can do to transform your detective story into a hot romance.

Create your own love story by flooding your partner with praise. Make plans to enact a love scene from your movie. It may feel forced at first, but go ahead, have fun with it. Select a romantic spot, and tell your partner they're greater than the greatest movie star.

Shifting to a broader perspective, I let go of the petty frustrations I harbor about my partner, and relax deeply into the care of the universe. I make this vow: "I will surround my partner with safety and praise today."

Ah, doesn't it feel good to kiss and make up? Then why is it so hard to do? Why do we sulk around the house grumbling, refusing to say a simple "I'm sorry" or accept our mate's apology? Are we afraid of losing face or admitting we were wrong? Nothing is gained by holding on to grudges, by adamantly staying mad. Ironically, we are convinced that our anger and righteousness somehow protect us.

Our grudges are leftovers from childhood, a feeble way of holding our ground when we feel insecure. We've been indoctrinated to think that if we've done something bad, *we* are bad; to admit fault is to admit we're unworthy of our partner's love. The more grounded we feel in our partner's love, the less likely we are to fight about stupid and inconsequential issues in the first place, and the less desperate we feel about having the last word. Our desperate struggle to keep our ego intact is a barrier to moving on to more important topics— like kissing and making up.

   Apologize to your partner for a grudge you've been holding on to, some little unresolved issue that has been creating distance between you. Go ahead: kiss and make up.

In quiet contemplation, I visualize myself sitting cross-legged in a forest. I see the anger inside me as a red dye coursing throughout my body. At my command, all the anger in my body flows through my veins into my spine, and runs down into the earth, leaving me free from anger and filled with love.

Time wounds all heels.

—JANE ACE

We've all seen those relationships in which one partner seems to be a saint. No matter what their partner says or does, they understand. Sometimes it goes on for years, the abusive partner smugly certain that they can use their mate's good nature to their advantage forever. Then one day, of course, the saintly partner walks out, leaving behind a shocked and devastated mate.

We can all get away with acting like a heel for a while—for an hour or a day, maybe for a month if we're lucky. Our partners love us, they're aware of the extenuating circumstances, and they try to understand. But taking advantage of our partner's compassion is a dangerous game. The time will come, without fail, when what we dish out boomerangs right back to us. We cannot inflict pain on our partners without hurting ourselves. Eventually, love untended dies, our own self-hatred solidifies, our own growth is stunted. Who is wounded now?

❧ *Today, watch for signs that you are acting like a heel—when you don't listen or when you interrupt, when you yell or criticize, when you undermine your partner. Catch yourself, and try to replace each wounding behavior with one that is healing.*

I resolve to be a healer rather than a heel. Sometimes I know I'm callous, wounding my partner while trying to get them to meet my needs. Today I confess my mistakes, knowing that forgiveness can be mine.

*The flesh is suffused by the spirit, and it is forgetting
this in the act of lovemaking that creates cynicism and
despair.*

—MAY SARTON

How does it happen that sex falls with a thud to the bottom of the
list of things we do together? Wasn't it once at the top—intimate,
spontaneous, all-consuming? Sex has a hard time surviving budget
conflicts, in-laws, exhausting schedules, the demands of children, and
life's innumerable mundane realities. All too often, sex becomes a
currency of exchange, a source of discomfort, something to avoid.
The job of sex.

Any deterioration of union in a relationship is serious. Keeping
passion alive in a long-term relationship is a matter of safety, intentionality, and attention. The next four days will focus on the area of
sexuality in your partnership, and your commitment to its power and
beauty in your life.

*Do one specific thing today to rekindle passion in your relation-
ship. Satin sheets on the bed? A tape of mood music? A candle
on the bedside table? Even if you don't make love, cuddle with
your partner and talk about ways to enhance passion in your
relationship.*

**I pause for a moment, and let life's busy-ness slip away. Sitting
quietly, with my eyes closed, I allow my innate calm to surface and
permeate my body. Deeply relaxed, I savor a favorite memory of my
partner and me making love.**

You mustn't force sex to do the work of love or love to do the work of sex.

— MARY MCCARTHY

Love and sex are partners in a healthy relationship. In an intimate partnership, sex without love, or love without sex, is an incomplete, one-dimensional experience. But in many relationships sex and love become separated, usually because each partner is more comfortable in one or the other compartment. One partner feels anxious expressing love except through the act of sex, while the other expects expressions of caring to substitute for sexual involvement.

It's not as unusual as it might seem for partners to be divided on this issue, since we seek to annex in our mates what is missing in ourselves. But just proximity to what is missing does not solve our problem; in fact it makes things worse at first, as our sexual—or affectional—inhibitions are stirred up by our partners.

Neither sex nor love can fully flourish if they are isolated; each nourishes the other. In a conscious relationship, sex and love are intertwined. Where there is discomfort, the partners stretch into the unfamiliar territory with each other's support. Intercourse is constant; it just changes its focus from body to mind to heart. All three are involved, no matter the point of contact.

❧ *Have a conversation with your partner about how sex and love commingle in your relationship. Is one side your territory and the other your partner's? Come up with one way you might each stretch to meet in the middle: the affection-aversive partner might make it a point to look their partner in the eyes and whisper endearments while making love; the sex-aversive partner might initiate sex, or a new position, or share an unexpressed desire.*

Moving into my inner sanctuary, I recognize the ways in which I compartmentalize love and sex, and let the boundaries between them dissolve. I celebrate this truth: "True passion is the union of sex, heart, and mind."

*The instinct of fidelity is perhaps the deepest instinct
in the great complex we call sex. Where there is good
sex, there is an underlying passion for fidelity.*

—D. H. LAWRENCE

Couples in passionate relationships know a secret—that great sex,
the kind that lasts, is the product of emotional commitment. Fidelity
to another results in a fidelity to the self that is essential to the
strengthening of one's personhood and wholeness.

Fidelity challenges us to overcome fear, reticence, and the shame
of lifelong taboos. How much easier to buy into the illusion that there
is a better sexual relationship out there with some new partner, new
position, or new context than to face the terror of facing our partner
in all our nakedness. But serial-partner sex can't hold a candle to the
passion that evolves in a relationship that has endured and grown
through commitment, openness, and safety. This passion begins with
talking to your partner about your sexual desires, and sharing your
vision of a loving sexual partnership.

 Have a conversation about sex today in which you tell your
partner three fantasies or desires. Be specific. Ask your partner
to identify one of the three that they feel could become a reality,
and talk about how to make it happen.

In my period of quiet today, I imagine sharing my desires with my
partner. Then I turn my attention to the fantasies my partner voiced.
I use this time to ground my commitment to meeting my partner's
desires. I contemplate this truth: "True passion is born of fidelity."

When a man and a woman practice their mutual wiles on one another they are imitating the way God works on us; and to the extent that these wiles draw them both out of their mundane narrowness, they are literally cooperating with God's gentle seductions. The more the lover excites the partner into a frenzy of passion, the more godlike he is.

—ANDREW GREELEY

In our culture, we have no models for the merger of spirituality and sexuality, no permission for them to coexist. Certainly in many religious contexts sexuality is a major taboo; in others it is openly celebrated. How important it is to unite them. In a conscious relationship we bring all of ourselves to our partner, including the full spectrum of our sexuality. Sexuality is a basic impulse of aliveness; to express this impulse fully in the context of a committed relationship is a spiritual act that restores our sense of connectedness to all others. Bringing the sexual and the spiritual together in partnership not only unites us at our most vulnerable point but restores the innate sexual aliveness lost in childhood. This merger deserves our full attention.

❧ *Make an appointment with your partner today for a couples dialogue about the relationship between your upbringing and your sexual experiences. Share with each other the teachings — religious or secular — that shamed you about your sexuality.*

In quiet contemplation, I allow any feelings of sexual inhibition or discomfort to come up, recognizing that I can let them go. I hold in mind this thought: "In a committed partnership, sexuality and spirituality are merged."

*Sex is play. You begin to win in your sex life when
you come from this position.*

—MARGO WOODS

Most of us grew up in a home and a society that put work and industry above fun and pleasure. The sexual and bodily taboos that were passed on to us as children have had the effect of imprisoning, rather than liberating, our innate nature. We view life through the bars of the many "thou shalt nots" that were driven into our psychic landscape. If this is what we absorbed from our religious upbringing, we've missed the whole point.

During our teen years, with hormones surging, some of us broke out of prison for a while to explore the sexual landscape. But most of us scurried back inside when we became adults, still without a clue as to how to integrate intimacy and sexuality.

Sexual play unites intimacy and sexuality. When we're fully exploring the "thou shalts" of our sexual essence, we are in sync with core instincts that deserve to blossom. So put some wild and crazy fun back into your partnership, where it belongs. Couldn't you use a little diversion? Where's that old spark? Don't forget, adults are just recycled teenagers.

🍂 *Do something to inject playfulness into your sex life today: feel each other up at the dinner table; have a shaving cream fight; tickle each others' toes; slather each other with oil and have a wrestling match.*

I call upon the reservoir of pulsating energy at my core and picture myself romping playful and joyful as a young colt, jumping society's fences with unfettered energy. I take pleasure in knowing that this frisky colt roams freely deep within, and I befriend it.

Experience is not what happens to you; it is what you do with what happens to you.

—ALDOUS HUXLEY

Every couple meets, falls madly in love, falls out of love, fights and makes up, goes through crises and periods of smooth sailing. We can't eliminate periods of difficulty from our lives any more than we can eliminate rain from the cycle of the seasons. Nor would we want to, for both rain and difficulties bring new growth.

Our only choice is in how we respond to our experience. We can remain ignorant of the forces that shaped us as children. We can refuse to learn new behaviors and change the outcome of our unhappy lives. Or we can open our eyes to the truth about ourselves and our past, and, with our partner's support and compassion, learn new and effective ways of coping with our experience. This is what adults choose to do in a conscious relationship.

☙ *Today, think about a common pattern or occurrence in your relationship, perhaps a recurring core argument to which you have a knee-jerk response—to complain, to withdraw, to blow up in anger, to sabotage. Try to recall where you first encountered this behavior and when you first started to use this tactic. What one thing can you do differently today that might get a different response from your partner and might break this old pattern of stimulus and response?*

Sometimes I feel as if I am in prison, with no choice but to follow the rules. Moving to a place of inner calm, I reach deep within to my freedom and see myself walking out of my prison into the light, breathing deeply the fresh air of choice.

If you want to read about love and marriage, you've got to buy separate books.

— ALAN KING

It wasn't so long ago that marriage was little more than an economic and social institution that served as a framework for the maintenance of family and society. Love and marriage were only occasionally often coincidentally or serendipitously, connected.

All that began to change in the eighteenth century when people became free to marry the person they fell in love with. So now, as the song goes, love and marriage are supposed to go together like a horse and carriage. And with that freedom, marriage—like religion and psychotherapy—became a path to healing and wholeness, a way to go beyond our wounds and limitations to experience real love. What a blessing this is! Partners in a conscious marriage take advantage of this opportunity every day and claim, through their awareness and intention, the gift of love.

❧ Today, be aware of what is really important in marriage—not convenience or status or economic security, but real love. Read your relationship vision aloud with your partner as a reminder.

I take twenty minutes to go within today and contemplate the marvel of my relationship as a union of structure and passion. This insight is mine: "Love is the life of marriage."

Challenges make you discover things about yourself that you never really knew. They're what make the instrument stretch—what make you go beyond the norm.

—CICELY TYSON

Some of us want to live the American dream of the easy life—no work, no conflict, no effort; just sit by the pool in the sun, drinking iced tea, watching attractive, scantily clad, bronzed bodies walk by. So it's a big disappointment when we realize that life is not an endless vacation and our love is not always like a red, red rose.

Challenges, difficulties, hard times: they all go with the territory of the conscious relationship. The intimacy of partnership, and the self-examination it brings, require us to plumb the depths of our souls. We learn things about ourselves that we wouldn't ever have had to face otherwise. It's not as pleasant as a month on the beach in Waikiki, but what a gift! So much of what we spend our time on, so much of what we wish for, is intended to keep us from having to face our demons, to keep us from knowing ourselves. It is through meeting life's challenges that we unearth pleasures that we would never find at the beach.

ɞ *On a new page in your notebook, write down three challenges you currently face as a result of your relationship. Instead of experiencing them as difficulties, think of them as gifts. Write your partner a thank-you love note in appreciation for giving you these opportunities to grow.*

I quietly visualize myself sitting with three gaily wrapped gift boxes in front of me. Each is a challenge given to me by my partner. One by one, as I untie the ribbons and open the boxes, I find a new opportunity to become my true self.

Is your partner so boring that reading the newspaper is really more interesting than chatting over breakfast? It's good to know what's going on in the world, but what is going on with your partner should be the headline news. Why bother to be in a relationship unless we make a real investment of ourselves? Remember, we need time together as much as we need time alone. *And that alone time shouldn't be taken when we're together.*

There's much to know about our partners that is far more fascinating than the latest ball scores or fashion breakthrough. Breakfast is a good time to talk and touch for even a few minutes, to report a dream, or to check in on each other's moods and plans before going off to work or to pursue separate interests. Start your day fortified with a hearty helping of togetherness!

~ *Start the day right. Put down your paper and make small talk with your partner, find out what's going on in the world across the table from you. Share a laugh, make a plan, complain about the weather.*

As I shed the frustrations of the day and retreat into a time of calm, I focus on honoring my partner's reality. I pray for the ability to acknowledge that my partner's news should come first.

The greater part of our happiness . . . depends on our dispositions and not on our circumstances.

—MARTHA WASHINGTON

Have you ever noticed how some people are unhappy in what seem to be the most glorious and fortunate circumstances? The wine isn't dry enough, they want a bigger house, a faster computer. Then there are others who seem more than content with very little; they savor each sunset, get a chuckle from their neighbor's tall tales. Testimony to the old saying that it's not the cards that you're dealt but the way that you play them.

When we're struggling in our relationships we sometimes feel overwhelmed, powerless to change things. We feel as if our life is happening *to* us, that our partner is doing things *to* us. Feeling powerless—and therefore blameless—for our plight, we feel helpless as well to change it.

We all have the power to make ourselves miserable; some of us do it extremely well. We are inclined to think the worst about our partner and to sink into despair at the slightest downturn of events. We're so absorbed in our version of events that we are oblivious to the possibility of playing our cards another way. But it is within our power to choose to view the same circumstances more positively. Remember, we can elect to look on the bright side, not to feel overwhelmed but challenged by difficulties, to see the positive in our mates.

❧ *Turn a negative into a positive today. On a new page in your notebook, write five negative thoughts you hold about your partner and your relationship. Then try looking at the bright side. If you "never have enough money," do you have "enough money for food and our basic needs?" Be happy about that. If your partner is a few pounds overweight, what part of their character means a lot to you? Their loyalty? Their humor? Give that your focus today.*

In a time of prayer, I confess that it is up to me to decide how to play the cards in my life. I hold in focus this liberating reality: "The attitude I carry today is a choice. Today, I choose happiness."

*People say that what we are all seeking is a meaning
for life. I don't think that's what we are really
seeking. . . . I think what we are seeking is an
experience of being alive.*

—JOSEPH CAMPBELL

We all seek meaning in our lives, explanations for the workings of
our complex, sometimes overwhelming world. We want clear-cut
definitions, the security of knowing who, what, when, where, and
why. We seek answers to the puzzles of life and love, to the riddles
of the universe, the neighborhood, and our partners. Science and
technology foster the illusion that we can find answers to the essentially mysterious. But when we do find answers, they only lead to
other questions, and the emptiness at our core remains.

Many of us with a keen interest in understanding ourselves and our
world become complusive seekers, our lives a continual round of
books, seminars, and retreats. We endlessly discuss our process and
worry about our path. But it can be argued that this search for facts,
for enlightenment as to life's meaning, is but a pale, desperate
substitute for the actual experience—and expression of—the innate
aliveness that we have lost.

In opening ourselves to the full range of feeling in the course of our
partnership journey, we awaken the dormant core of our aliveness.
When we *are* alive, when we *feel* alive, when we are able to *express*
our aliveness, we no longer have to seek the meaning of life. We
know it with certainty in our bodies, hearts, and minds.

ᘐ *Let today be a day of* being *rather than* doing. *Don't think
about the meaning of love, or life; be* loving, *be* alive.

Experiencing release in my time of quiet, I recognize that my dogged
search for answers to life's questions can eclipse my actual experience
of aliveness. In joy, I hold this thought: "Surrendering to being ignites
my true aliveness."

Have you ever noticed the made-to-order match-ups that couples make? One partner logical and unemotional, the other exuberant or inclined to hysteria; your easily excitable friend fell in love with someone who never raises his voice above a whisper. This pairing of opposites happens so frequently it would seem to be a natural match, another of nature's clever symmetries.

Each of us has a tendency to either minimize or exaggerate the way we express our energy. Those of us who minimize can be called "minimizers" and those who exaggerate can be called "maximizers." Diminishing or exaggerating our affect seems to be an evolutionary expression of the survival instinct to fight or flee in response to danger. The maximizer is the active one, sort of like a hailstorm, often expressive and explosive, making no secret of their feelings, fighting to get what they need. The minimizer is contained, passive, fleeing inward like a turtle to avoid being hailed upon, afraid of emotional or physical injury.

Today you'll look at the characteristics of the minimizer to see if the description fits you; tomorrow the maximizer. You'll find out if you are the turtle or the hailstorm!

᠕ *Here is a list of traits that describe the minimizer. Circle the phrases that describe you.* ♥ *Implodes feelings inward* ♥ *Diminishes affect* ♥ *Denies dependency (counterdependent)* ♥ *Generally denies needs* ♥ *Shares little of their inner world* ♥ *Tends to exclude others from their psychic space* ♥ *Withholds feelings, thoughts, behaviors* ♥ *Has rigid self-boundaries* ♥ *Takes direction mainly from themselves* ♥ *Mainly thinks about themselves* ♥ *Acts and thinks compulsively* ♥ *Tries to dominate others* ♥ *Tends to be passive-aggressive*

During twenty minutes of stillness, away from the whirling world around me, I look to discover how I have protected myself. Recognizing that I don't have to be one way, I celebrate my true nature, free from all defenses.

*In love you find the oddest combinations. . . . If it
weren't so serious, we could laugh at it.*

—GEORGE DAVIS

Opposites *do* attract! Some of us always exaggerate our responses,
and the rest of us tend to diminish them. But the extremity of our
response will depend on the timing and extent of our wounding.
Though we all sustained injury at every stage of childhood, usually
there was one age at which our wounding was most profound. As
you've probably noticed, some people are more hysterical than
others, and there are many levels of detachment or intrusiveness or
enthusiasm. The earlier our wounds were inflicted, the more devastating their effect, impairing our ability to meet the challenges of the
next stage of childhood. Thus, a wound sustained during infancy will
have a far more lasting effect than injury sustained at nursery school
or during the shift from child to young adult.

*❧ Here is a list of traits that describe the maximizer. Circle the
phrases that describe you:* ♥ *Explodes feelings outward* ♥
Exaggerates affect ♥ *Tends to depend on others* ♥ *Generally
exaggerates needs* ♥ *Is compulsively open, subjective* ♥ *Tends to
be overly inclusive of others in psychic space* ♥ *Tends toward
clinging and excessive generosity* ♥ *Has diffuse self-boundaries*
♥ *Generally asks for direction from others, distrusts own direc-
tions* ♥ *Focuses on others* ♥ *Acts impulsively* ♥ *Usually submis-
sive, manipulative* ♥ *Alternates between aggressiveness and pas-
sivity*
*Compare the number of circled traits on this maximizer list
with the number of circled traits on yesterday's minimizer list.
Whichever list has the greater number of circled traits describes
your habitual response pattern.*
So, are you the turtle or the hailstorm?

**Today I see how my partner is different from me, and I release my
frustration that we are not the same. Rather, I give thanks that my
partner's distinct nature balances my own, and is to be celebrated. I
let myself begin to feel traces of joy.**

The greater the contrast, the greater the potential.
Great energy only comes from a correspondingly great
tension between opposites.

—CARL JUNG

Now that you know whether you are a minimizer or a maximizer, you've probably figured out that your partner is the opposite. Not only that; there's another piece to this puzzle. In all likelihood, your partner was wounded at the same stage of childhood as you, and thus the depth and degree of their wounding is similar to yours. In other words, we choose partners at our own level of psychic development. Our partners are no more or less emotionally healthy than ourselves, it's just that they reacted to their wounding very differently. Ah, nature.

Knowledge of the minimizer/maximizer dynamic in a conscious relationship is useful in understanding the roots of our conflict with our partners. In understanding this pattern, the extremes of our maximizing or minimizing behavior can be tempered as each partner stretches beyond their fears and limitations to meet the other's needs: a clinging spouse can overcome her fear of abandonment to allow her partner more independence; the aloof partner overcomes his fear of smothering to be more available and affectionate.

❧ *Have a couples dialogue with your partner about your mini-mizer/maximizer pattern, and how your respective adaptations affect the relationship. Discuss how you might each change your behavior to temper your habitual patterns. For instance: "I'll really make an effort to spend some time just talking and cuddling after the kids are in bed, if I can then read for a while without more interruptions, and without you making me feel bad about it. Would that work for you?*

Today, in quiet, I accept the mystery of opposite attraction as necessary poles of a suspension bridge. I summon the courage and strength to span our differences and connect the opposites in our relationship. These words become a prayerful vow: "I commit to ending all the blame about my partner's nature and accepting, even appreciating, the balancing pole it offers me."

It's so easy to love our pets—they're so responsive, so grateful for our attention; they make no demands. Our partners are another story. They expect to be treated as equals, they want understanding and attention, they bore and anger us, they have the power to cause us pain. Why can't they just be as loving and grateful as the dog?

The wish for an uncomplicated, stress-free relationship is understandable, but it is a childish wish. Intimacy with a real, flesh-and-blood person is the product of intention and hard work. In the long run, it is only through mutually responding to each other's need for understanding and attention, only through resolving boredom and anger that we win our partner's love and gratitude. It is only through meeting each other's demands for time, and alleviating each other's pain through changing our hurtful behavior, that we can truly be best friends.

ᨃ *Pet your partner today; feed them something yummy; be best friends. Go for a walk together.*

In my time of quiet today, I keep in mind that real love with a real person is achieved only through hard work. I give thanks that I have a loving partner who is on this journey with me.

*Love requires respect and friendship as well as passion.
Because there comes a time when you have to get out
of bed.*

—ERICA JONG

Couples are often shocked when the passion of romantic love fades. Without the emotional and sexual free-for-all, it doesn't seem like much is happening. They've fallen out of love, as they define it. So maybe it's time to move on.

Well, yes. It's time to move on to the cultivation of respect and friendship and the many other ingredients of real love. This can be done in or out of the sack. But it has to happen, and the earlier it starts the better.

Intimate relationships operate on many levels, and each enriches and sustains the others. The passion of courtship only hints at the complex love that blends sex with concern, humor, faith, acceptance, and myriad other factors. It is a way of teasing you into a committed partnership. Rest assured that the passion will return, a hundredfold, in the course of the journey. But you have to make the bed before you can lie in it.

🍂 *What ingredient is in shortest supply in your relationship? Empathy, honesty, laughter, generosity? Do one specific thing to sprinkle a handful of it around today.*

I recognize my yearning to feel in love, to wanting ecstasy to last forever. Taking time for inner solitude, I move from this simple notion and ponder the richness and complexity of mature love.

*Knowing is the most profound kind of love, giving
someone the gift of knowledge about yourself.*

—MARSHA NORMAN

Can you recall a time when you deeply listened to your partner,
when the way you responded brought a deeper level of intimacy and
gave them the security of feeling understood and known at a profound
level?

This kind of understanding is the natural by-product of mastering
and using the couples dialogue. When we mirror our partner's
communications, we give them the experience of really being heard.
When we validate, we let them know that what they say makes sense,
whether or not we agree with it. When we respond with empathy,
we let them know that we share their feelings.

Partners in a conscious relationship go far beyond small talk and
daily trivia. They want to know all about each other. They hunger for
details of their partner's wildest imaginings and deepest longings.

&♥ *Have a dialogue with your partner about the meaning of life,
spiritual beliefs, or an unexpressed desire. Mirror, validate, and
empathize.*

**In quiet today I imagine that I am a miner with a light on my hat,
descending deeper and deeper underground into the core of my being.
As I bring light into this darkness, I find treasures that I can share
with my partner.**

Pay close attention now. Our couple here is demonstrating a key Imago process skill: the belly laughing exercise. This is no joke. Belly laughing ranks right up there alongside the couples dialogue and the containment process in importance. It's a one-minute miracle, guaranteed to get those endorphins pumping, cast out boredom, and deactivate anger. Okay, are you ready for your instructions?

❧ Today's task is to learn and practice the belly laughing exercise.
- *Stand facing each other, about a foot apart.*
- *Take a few deep, easy breaths. Relax your shoulders and neck; let your arms hang loose; unlock your knees. Make eye contact with your partner.*
- *Standing in place, begin an easy bouncing motion from the knees. Once you get into a rhythm, say "Ha" with each bounce, until you have a nice, rhythmic "Ha-ha-ha-ha-ha-ha-ha" going.*
- *Allow the body to relax, the jaw and muscles to loosen. Maintain for one full minute.*

Try it and see what happens. You'll enjoy it!

Suggested dosage: once daily for one minute.

Allowing my spirit to open, I find within me a joyous child running through a field, sloshing along a creek bed, spinning in circles, laughing and giggling. I join this child in play during a time of visualization and recognize that this vital aliveness is my God-essence within.

Marriage is a mistake every man should make.

—GEORGE JESSEL

We all feel at some point that our relationship was a mistake. How could we ever have thought we loved this insensitive, small-minded creep? We're so diametrically opposite in every way, so incompatible—whatever made us think we had anything in common? Every conversation is so difficult, every decision so contentious. To top it off, we're bored.

There's really only one alternative to subjecting ourselves to the trials of partnership. We can play it safe and remain single, avoiding entirely the problems and pitfalls of intimacy. But then how will we learn the lessons of love? How will we recover our lost self? How will we experience the intense joy of spiritual union that is the reward of a lifetime commitment to our partner's happiness? Deep down inside, we know that there is a purpose to our struggles. Many of those who have been through the most bitter and painful divorce often find themselves soon enough wanting what they know they can only find in partnership with another.

When things look bleak, remind yourself that if you and your partner work through the Imago process, your deepest needs will be met.

No matter how troubled your relationship is today, make a list of five reasons why you are glad you are in a committed relationship. Share them with your partner tonight.

Although I have not always been sure our relationship was right, as I relax into a time of peace today, I prayerfully absorb this truth: "What I mistake for a mistake may be my path to healing and wholeness."

There is no fear in love, but perfect love casts out fear.

—I JOHN 4:18

The root of all human problems is the fear of the other. That's a big assertion; how could it be so? Because if we recognize and accept another as equal in value to ourselves, we have to recognize that we are not the center of the universe. In a relationship, this universal fear takes personal form in the shape of our partner. Our fear is aroused by our partner's demand for equality—for equal space, equal treatment, equal validity. And so we struggle for primacy and power, disguising our own fear of our partner by making our partner afraid of us. We devaluate them and invalidate their truth in order to feel an illusory centrality.

The secret to love is letting go of fear. But you must not only surrender your own fear. You must cease being an object of fear for your partner and become instead a symbol of safety in your partner's mind. Real love surrenders the need for primacy, the drive for absoluteness, the need to diminish others to enhance oneself. In a conscious relationship, partners willingly share the center and forswear the weapons of fear—withdrawal, anger, criticism, threats of abandonment. They drive our fear with their love.

❧ *For a few minutes, consider the ways in which your behavior inspires fear in your partner. Do something different today that will inspire safety. If your habit, for example, is to say in times of crisis, "I don't know why I'm in this relationship. You're a nut case!" and start packing your suitcase, resolve to say instead, "I love you and I'm committed to this marriage. However, I'd like to do a mini-container exercise now so I can tell you why I'm upset. I want us to be able to work through this."*

In meditation today, I name and release the ways in which I create fear in my partner. I then shift in my attitude and claim this truth: "My partner is safe in my presence."

*It isn't until you come to a spiritual understanding of
who you are — not necessarily a religious feeling, but
deep down, the spirit within — that you can begin to
take control.*

— OPRAH WINFREY

How would you answer this question: Who, or what, am I? On the deepest level we are essentially spiritual beings. The term "spiritual" is often used interchangeably with "religious," but they are not the same. "Religion," the root meaning of which is "to tie back or reconnect to," has come to refer to institutions, belief systems, and rituals that attempt to activate the spiritual, the source from which they come. Unfortunately, in the attempt to capture the spiritual, religion freezes it in time and space, and it all too often becomes dogmatic, thus widening the gap between the seeker and his goal. When religion loses contact with its source, the spiritual gets reduced, distorted, or even obliterated—as witness the slaughter of thousands around the globe in wars fought over religious beliefs.

But the spiritual is present whether we choose to cultivate it or not. It is our essence, our innate drive toward wholeness. It is not something we acquire from the outside, but it can be developed within each of us. We can tap into it by choosing to live consciously in our relationships. In this process, we experience oneness and joy, an acceptance of differences, and a deeper level of love. We experience God, a code word for this deeper, more whole level of the self.

🍂 *Think today about using your relationship to develop your spirituality. Identify a part of yourself that is underdeveloped, perhaps your inability to express emotion, your discomfort with touching your body, your lack of confidence in your ability to think clearly. Consider how you can develop this aspect of your innate nature in your relationship. Ask for your partner's help.*

In quiet today, I contemplate the reality that I am essentially a spiritual being seeking wholeness. I hold this thought: "God is that within me which seeks to become whole. Love is the path."

> *As so often happens in marriage, roles that had begun almost playfully, to give line and shape to our lives, had hardened like suits of armor and taken us prisoner.*
>
> —MOLLY HASKELL

Like most other things in life, gender traits are distributed along a continuum, on which the macho male and the femme fatale are at either extreme. Most of us fall somewhere in the middle by nature, but our culture does not easily accommodate ambiguity, and we are socialized toward gender certainty at either end of the spectrum. We acquire the trappings of our gender and become practiced in the ways of our sex.

When we meet our partner, we want to show off what we've learned. Before long, without much conscious planning, we've filled up all the partnership job descriptions pretty much along traditional gender lines. Alice = cooking. Fred = lion's share of wage earning. Alice = handles feelings. Fred = does the thinking. Ten years down the line, Fred can't boil an egg and Alice has no wage-earning potential. They're trapped by their roles yet dependent on each other to provide what they lack. They'd be lost without each other's services.

We forget that in our home, and in our relationship, we do not have to play by society's rules. In fact, we must not, if we are to be more than partial selves. No one should have to earn all the money or boil all the eggs.

&❧ *Today's task is to begin, with your partner, to break down the artificial role definitions that are imprisoning you and your relationship. Identify a role-defined chore that each of you now assumes total responsibility for and work out a way of sharing that duty. This might be a simple matter of taking turns servicing the car or setting the table, or learning what's involved in fixing the kids' lunches, or filling out the health insurance claims.*

I envision standing before the wall that separates men and women. As I enter into my deep place of courage and strength, the wall collapses, allowing the energies on both sides to flow together. I recognize that this is necessary for my innate spiritual wholeness to emerge.

When we fall in love, we believe our deepest, most fundamental yearnings are going to be satisfied.

But when we commit to our partner, our anticipation of having our needs fulfilled turns into an expectation. We both pull back from the active giving and caretaking that characterized the early days of romance. We regress to that childhood place where we expect to have our needs met, period. That's highly unlikely, since we've chosen a partner with the same shortcomings as our childhood caretakers, a partner who is bound to fail us in the same devastating ways. Welcome to real life: this rude awakening is the beginning of the power struggle.

🏵 *At the top of a double-page spread in your notebook, write "Partner Profile" and divide each of the two pages into two vertical columns. At the top of column one write "Positive Traits." Stop for a moment and think back to when you first met your partner, about what attracted you to them, and what you liked about them. In column one list those traits, using simple adjectives or phrases: "good listener," "remembers special occasions," "wild dancer," "generous with time," "terrible puns." Circle the three traits that you liked the most.*

Today I access deeper spiritual courage and acknowledge the fact that I am full of expectations. Breathing deeply, I slowly release an expectation with each exhalation, and notice myself becoming more open—less angry with each breath.

*Marriage is, of all transactions, the one in which
people expect the most from others, and are least
honest themselves.*

—JANE AUSTEN

The transition from romantic love to the power struggle may be
abrupt or gradual. But at some point partners discover that their
feelings for each other are less intense, and there is a pulling back.
Now there are fewer love nibbles, a dropoff in favors and flowers.
There are longer hours at work, more reading or TV, more time with
hobbies or friends.

The partners have figured out that not only are their own expectations not being fulfilled but their partner has a stash of expectations
as well. Many of these expectations have never been expressed as
such. They are so much a part of the unconscious picture we have of
partnership that we *assume* they will be met. One will do the cooking,
and one the dishes; one will be the social secretary, and the other
the handyman. One will assume that Sunday mornings are for going
to church and calling the family, while the other expects to hang out
in bed and read the paper. All of this on top of the primary assumption
that drew them together—that they would love each other as their
parents never did. What they are forgetting is that people don't seek
intimate relationships to take care of their partner's needs but to have
their own needs taken care of. This is the fundamental sticking point
of the power struggle. This is where the shift must occur.

☙ *Label column two of the "Partner Profile" you began yesterday
"Negative Traits," and list the traits that your partner has exhib-
ited that you don't like, again using simple adjectives or phrases:
"messy," "secretive," "easily upset," "workaholic," "makes ex-
cuses." Circle the three traits that you most dislike.*

**In a reverential stillness, I acknowledge my disappointments with my
relationship. Turning to the divine within, I confess that I have looked
for perfection without seeing my own limitations.**

*We are more together than we know, how else could we
keep on discovering we are more together than we
thought?*

—WENDELL BERRY

We are sometimes taken aback by the uncanny resemblance between our partners and our caretakers. We haven't wanted to look
too closely at the signs, so we are startled by the double-take déjà vu
moments that come up from time to time, when the ghost of our
mother or father seems to superimpose itself over the image of our
partner across the dinner table.

Yes, we are more together than we know. It is with our Imago
partners that our unfinished business with our caretakers becomes
visible, that the potential to rewrite our history becomes a tangible
reality. Each time you realize that you and your partner are more
together than you thought, you are acknowledging that this seemingly
diabolical situation has the benevolent purpose of bringing the impasse
of childhood to a happy resolution.

🍃 *Compare your partner's positive and negative traits with the
positive and negative traits of your Imago, Day 58. Place a star
(★) next to the ones that are similar. See the connection?*

**Knowing that I must face the truth in order to be free, I move into a
time of wordless prayer and experience the decoding of the mystery
of my relationship. I celebrate each new insight about the choices I
have made.**

When you've exhausted all possibilities, remember this: you haven't!

—ROBERT SCHULLER

When we are up to our ears in the power struggle, it's hard to make sense of how it all started, or how it will resolve itself. If we could step back and get a broader view of the situation, we would see that the power struggle goes through predictable stages, not unlike the stages of grief identified by Elizabeth Kübler-Ross in her well-known book *On Death and Dying.* The stages look like this:

Shock: You're not the person I thought you were.

Denial: You're the person I always thought you were, but you're just having a bad day.

Anger: I'll make you be who I want you to be and coerce you into giving me what I want.

Bargaining: I'll give you what you need if you give me what I need.

Resignation and Despair: I give up. I resign myself to our failure to work things out and despair of finding real love. Let's just make the best of a bad deal or go our own ways.

Acceptance: I accept you as wounded and defended, and commit to the healing process. *This is where real love begins.*

🔊 *Spend a few minutes today thinking about three behaviors you would like from your partner and how you would feel and react if you got those behaviors from your partner. Example: "She massages my back without asking, and it makes me feel cared for; I react by being more understanding of her needs." "He calls me from work each day, which makes me feel secure; I react by being more accepting of his long hours."*

Seeking a broader perspective today, I admit that I have been shocked and disappointed, and out of fear and pain, I have responded to my partner with coercion. Breathing deeply, I release frustrations with this hope: "Conflict is the chemistry of change."

*I do not love strife, because I have always found that
in the end, each remains of the same opinion.*

— KATHARINE ANTHONY

Many couples spend years in the anger stage of the power struggle. They manage to hold the relationship together through bargaining, with each partner trying to get what they want through negotiation: "You do this for me, and I'll do that for you." "If you spend more time kissing and caressing me, I'll agree to have sex more often." "I'll go to the church picnic if you don't nag me about mowing the lawn."

Traditional couples therapy often colludes in prolonging the agony by teaching partners bargaining skills and urging them to forge behavioral agreements without understanding or addressing the hidden agenda that fuels their anger. This "quid pro quo" arrangement works to some extent for some couples, but it is only a palliative, not a cure.

❧ *Spend a few minutes thinking of three behaviors that your partner gives you that you especially like. Write them down, adding how they make you feel and how you react to them. For example: "She never leaves the house without kissing me good-bye; it makes me feel loved, and I react by wanting to show her how much I love her." "He picks wildflowers for me on his morning walks, and I feel happy that he thinks about me, and I react by showering him with extra affection."*

Today in my time of quiet reflection, I see myself as a merchant trading one thing for another. Knowing that such trades bring no healing, I release this image and see myself offering gifts of unconditional love to my partner.

The truly sensuous takes time and a feeling for the deliberate, undulating rhythms of the body and of nature.

—GEORGE LEONARD

Has it been a while since you and your partner spent a languid evening in sensual exploration? Since you stayed in bed all morning making love? Sometimes it seems that life conspires to relegate sex to the bottom of our priorities list. We're too busy with important concerns, too estranged by anger and disappointment, or too uncomfortable with our partner for the intense intimacy of heartfelt lovemaking. When we get to this point, making love comes to feel like an unnatural act.

Engaging with each other sexually can be difficult after a long day at work, or dealing with the children. Neither partner feels rested, much less sexually turned on; their desires run more to television or a good book. But maintaining our sexual connection with our partner is important for sustaining the vitality and deepening of intimacy. It won't happen instantly, and it will require initiative, a conscientious setting aside of time, and talking through concerns and fears that have been swept under the rug.

One place to start is to put some effort into making your bedroom a special place conducive to making love, a space where you can have a memorably sensual evening with your partner. Go out and buy eight or ten candles, and have them lit as you and your partner get ready for bed. Turn off the overhead light. Burn some incense, play music that reminds you of a special time spent together. Perhaps an X-rated movie would inspire new creativity. Like every aspect of your relationship, sexuality requires thought, care, and intentionality.

Do one thing today to make your bedroom a place where it feels natural to make love.

I take time to anticipate the coming evening, when my partner and I can speak of love through our bodies. I recognize that the union we celebrate is an expression of the holy.

"**I** know you'd look for a new job if you had more confidence."
"Remember when you could still fit into that dress?" "I guess I can't
expect to win a tennis match when you're my partner."

There's a kind of low-voltage criticism that partners seem to slip
into after years of disappointment and disillusionment. It barely has
the power to hurt or shock anymore. The partners are immune to it.

It takes work to keep a relationship alive and well, to air and resolve
our grievances, so that they don't go underground. If they're left to
fester, the unaddressed disappointments and irritations pile up.
Growth slows, boredom sets in; we stagnate. We're not unhappy,
perhaps not even lonely. But life is dull and predictable, and somewhere beneath the surface—beneath the thinly veiled barbs—simmer
unassuaged pains and near-forgotten longings. Their hidden message
is "I may not be miserable, but I'm not happy, and it's your fault."
How quickly those criticisms would evaporate if we felt safe and
appreciated by our partners.

*&. Notice how many remarks you make today that are veiled
criticisms. Write them down; it's a way of measuring the meanness
in your relationship.*

**As I move into the place within where greater insight becomes
possible, I become aware that all my partner's criticisms are veiled
hurts. I vow today to respond to the hurt and transcend the form in
which it was communicated.**

The greatest revelation is stillness.

—LAO-TZU

If you're like many people, you have an active mind. You're always thinking, analyzing, computing. A cacophony of voices vies for attention in your head. We are experts on action and activity. We feel guilty if we're not beginning a new project or tying up the loose ends of an old one. Masters of the external, we are novices when it comes to our inner life. When it comes to stilling the inner chatter, we don't know how to turn down the volume.

It takes practice to cultivate the potential for stillness and receptivity, but there is nothing complicated to learn or analyze. All you need to do is sit—quietly, alone, and experience the holy for at least a few minutes each day. There's little we can do to change our fast and furious world, except to learn to access the inner world where God is often found.

🍂 *Take a break today from all that hectic activity. Do something to nurture your inner life and still all that internal chatter. Listen to music, meditate, take a silent walk at sunset.*

For twenty minutes today, I focus on breathing deeply, relaxing more with each exhalation. I allow an animal to come to mind, and getting to know this animal, I become aware that it is a symbol of my inner, instinctual wisdom. This animal has a message for me, and I listen. What does it say?

Be yourself, that's all there is of you.

—RALPH WALDO EMERSON

If we hope to be known and accepted by our partners, it's counter-productive to try and keep a smile on our face all the time, to stoically keep silent about our hurts and disappointments, to pretend that we just *love* golf, or that we're comfortable at large parties. If we are to grow closer to our partners, and to feel secure and safe with them, we must risk exposing ourselves. We must let them know who we really are.

The simplest way of letting our partners in on who we really are is to tell them. That way there are no mistakes. Unfortunately, many couples' conversations revolve around life's logistics: "What time should I pick you up from work?" "Where should we eat dinner tonight?" When our lives are busy, we don't often find time to share our real selves.

☙ *Let your hair down. Find time for some nonessential talk with your partner today—over dinner, or while you take a walk together. Tell the simple truth about something that's been on your mind: about what happened at work, your childhood, what you had for lunch. Describe what happened, how you felt about it, how it reminded you of another incident—share with your partner your full experience.*

In quiet today I open myself to the courage to be all of myself with my partner. In the spirit of healing, I commit to these words: "I will share all there is of me."

Couples who stay together without working through their conflicts, without nurturing intimacy, wake up one day and find they're in a rut. They're stuck in their lives and stuck with each other. Where would they go, for one thing? Who would have them? Their marriage becomes a test of their endurance and their tolerance for boredom.

Be warned: the future will be pretty much like the past as long as you continue to let things slide or do things the same way in your relationship.

To have a brighter future, you must learn to do things differently. You must replace the behaviors that aren't working in your relationship with effective new ones. Are you ready to climb out of your rut? Then it's time to start doing things a little differently.

List three ways in which you feel stuck in a rut with your partner, in patterns and habits that inhibit love and growth. Pick one rut and step out of it today. Do something different with your partner today—anything. Switch places at the dinner table, make love in a different room, go to a new restaurant . . . or just say "I love you" with a huge, unexpected hug.

Today I contemplate the ways in which my partner and I are stuck. I visualize the rut we are in. I visualize an emotional lifeline tossed to me, which I use for my daring escape. I climb out of the rut, allowing myself to feel the freedom of doing something new, bold, and exciting. Suddenly I visualize myself dancing with my partner.

*In a successful marriage, there is no such thing as
one's way. There is only the way of both, only the
bumpy, dusty, difficult, but always mutual path!*

          —PHYLLIS MCGINLEY

In our partnerships, we're so anxious to stake out our territory, so wary of being taken advantage of or dominated. We had to do this as children, in order to be sure that we got our share of the limited love. Still remembering how hard we had to fight for what we needed, afraid of being hurt again, we protect ourselves by trying to have things our way. "You and I are one," we say; but inside we think, "and I am the one."

We end up making deals with our partner, negotiating for space and love and chores. We use our anger or wiles. We trade favors. Then we add up the score, happy when we get our way, defeated when we seem to have lost ground. But when partners get their way through coercion or connivance, they have no confidence that they've gotten what they want because they are loved. They assume it was because they were tough and strong. So they continue to treat each other as adversaries.

As you and your partner move through the Imago process, a shift will occur over time that ushers the two of you gently onto the same path. In learning to hear each other out, in increasing your willingness to see the other's point of view, you'll make a surprising discovery. Many times your partner's expressed need turns out to be an undiscovered need in yourself. You will find that your desires are not mutually exclusive. You can both have your way.

 Have a couples dialogue with your partner about the value of working things out in a way that is satisfactory to both of you. Then pick a disagreement you have—one of your turf wars—and find a mutually satisfying solution.

In the quiet of prayer today, I summon the courage to let go of the need to always have my way. I visualize my partner and me walking on parallel paths, which soon converge into one. It is here we both can walk, hand in hand.

> *All men should strive to learn before they die, what*
> *they are running from and to and why.*
>
> — JAMES THURBER

The power struggle, that long stretch of pain and frustration between the end of romantic love and the beginning of real love, is made up in great part of ignorance. Ignorance of its purpose and procedures, and ignorance about our partners.

The purpose of the power struggle is identical to the purpose of romantic love—to finish childhood and get the needs met by our partners that were not met by our parents. The procedure—the only procedure—for getting those needs met is the resolution of the tangled web of frustrations that partners find themselves caught in.

In order to dissolve the frustrations, couples need to know what those frustrations are—their own and their partner's. During the next week you will be invited to identify your frustrations with your partner, and the feelings and reactions associated with them. Your knowledge of the source of your frustrations with your partner is a powerful weapon in your battle to get what you need in your relationship.

&. *Before doing the following exercise, think for a few minutes about your partner's frustrating behaviors. Then label two facing pages in your notebook, "Frustrations with My Partner." Draw a vertical line down the center of each page to make four columns. Today, label the first column "Frustration," and list all of your partner's behaviors that you don't like. "He stares out the window and won't reply when I'm talking to him." "She lies in bed watching soap operas when the house is dirty." "She gets hysterical over the slightest things." "He gets furious when I ask him to tell me when he is coming home."*

Going within today, I shed my fear of my partner's frustrations and draw upon my core strength to understand them, knowing that this is the path to deep spiritual growth.

Our ignorance about the power struggle extends to a series of false
assumptions that seriously compromise our ability to cope with the
realities of our conflict:

1. *You know what I want, so I don't have to ask.* Our partners are
   not mind readers. Even if they don't ask, we have to tell them
   what we want and what's on our mind.

2. *If I cause you enough pain, you will meet my needs.* Well, it's
   true enough that, in the short term, our partners will do things
   to get us off their backs, or shut us up—just as children do. But
   eventually your partner will retaliate against the source of pain.

3. *You exist only for me.* Your partner is not only a separate and
   different person, but of equal worth, with equal rights. You're
   just going to have to share the center of the universe with your
   partner.

4. *You could meet my needs if you wanted to.* Only if you tell your
   partner clearly what they are, and only if they're not forced to.

❧ *With yesterday's list of your partner's undesirable behaviors in
front of you, relax, and think about a specific time that you
experienced the first behavior. Recall exactly what your partner
did and anything else about the incident that seems meaningful to
you. Then notice what your feelings were at the time, and ask
yourself for a single word or phrase that describes them. Label
the second column "Feelings" and note these there. Repeat the
process until you have identified the feeling associated with each
behavior.*

In my twenty minutes of stillness today, I draw upon the courage to
become aware that I am controlled by assumptions left over from
childhood. Choosing to free myself from the past for a future I desire,
I breathe deeply and release one assumption with each exhalation. I
hold this liberating thought: "Assumptions are prisons of the mind."

*"We must resemble each other a little in order to
understand each other, but we must be a little different
to love each other."*

—PAUL GÉRALDY

Another irritant of the power struggle is that at some point partners
make the disturbing discovery that traits in their partners that
attracted them are beginning to drive them crazy. The husband's
rational approach to problems is stirring up the thinking capacities
that she had long buried under an avalanche of bright chatter. Her
desire for frequent sex, which once helped him to overcome his
inhibitions, now brings him to a fever pitch of anxiety. They are
uncovering what was in each other all along—their missing parts—
and they don't like it one bit.

The mistake that partners make at this point is to believe that
conflict means that they are married to the wrong person. On the
contrary, they are married to the right person for maximum personal
growth. The power struggle is growth trying to happen.

*Label column three "Reaction." Then take a minute to relax.
Again review your partner's frustraing behaviors, but this time
take note of your typical reaction (you may have more than one).
Write down all the common reactions that you have identified for
each of these behaviors. "I blow my top and stomp around the
house in a fury." "I sulk until my partner apologizes." "I get
revenge by coming home late without explanation."*

**Relaxing, I allow myself to see that most of what I dislike in my
partner is a mirror image of myself. I recall in prayer: "The truth
shall make you free."**

Rancor is an outpouring of a feeling of inferiority.

—JOSÉ ORTEGA Y GASSET

According to psychological theory, most of what is inside us came from outside. We create our subjective inner world through a process called internalization. Taking what is outside—knowledge about trees, the universe, other people—and setting it up inside is the basis of all learning.

What is interesting is the way we accept or reject our introjections of outside persons in whole or in part, which is what we inevitably do with our caretakers. If the quality that we take in is confluent with our self-image, it becomes an integral part of our identity. But the parts of ourselves that we cannot accept are projected onto others. This is an act of self-protection.

The logical target is our partner, to whom we relate as though they possess the trait we cannot bear in ourselves. Our rancor toward our partner for having the trait we deny is a measure of the unconscious inferiority we feel for having that trait.

❧ *Label column four "Fear." Now, for the last time, relax and again review your frustrations with your partner. This time be aware of the fear that gets triggered by each behavior, the fear that you are protecting by acting in the way you do in column three. Write down the fear associated with each frustration: "That she will leave me." "That I'm not loved." "That they think I'm boring."*

In quiet contemplation today, I reflect upon my needs, seeing their roots in my childhood, rejoicing that my relationship is a resource for all that I missed. I honor this reality: "My future can be different from my past."

*Childhood is less clear to me than to many people;
when it ended I turned my face away from it for no
reason that I know about.*

—LILLIAN HELLMAN

Many of us block out our childhood, or at least the painful parts. But
though we turn our face away from it, we cannot leave it behind.
Having no other model for our behavior, we act out our childhood
pain using childhood tactics.

When we identify our childhood wound, our partner's traits, and
the ways in which they frustrate us, the truth of the Imago is revealed.
We are horrified: Am I really doomed to be with a partner who will
wound me again? Have I really repressed the traits that my partner
needs from me? Am I accusing my partner of having traits that I deny
in myself?

The truth of the Imago is hard to take, but it will also set you free.
It maps the territory of your growth and healing. Such detailed
knowledge redeems us from the pain of ignorance and repetition and
brings our problems into the light where we can work on them with
intention and consciousness.

What you have learned this week about the ways in which your
partner frustrates you tells you exactly the childhood needs your
partner must meet for your healing.

🐚 *Today, review your insights of the last four days and add any
additional information that might come to you now. Circle the
frustrations, feelings, fears, and reactions that seem to affect you
the most. Take a minute to compare your partner frustrations
with your childhood frustrations from days 105–108; there are
likely to be similarities.*

**Today I open myself to the conjunction of my past and present
relationships, seeing that needs I bring to our partnership come from
my past. I honor this reality: "I am a composite of all my experiences."**

"The love of truth has its reward in heaven, and even on earth."

—NIETZSCHE

We have our subtle ways of communicating with our partners. There's the sidelong glance that translates as "You don't really mean that, do you?" The groan under our breath says "That's the stupidest thing I ever heard." Then there are the prolonged sigh, the burned dinner, the overlooked hug at the door.

All of the above are roundabout ways of saying what is on our minds, but this sort of sign language is a kind of chimp-level communication compared to the precision of words. Since each of these gestures is open to all sorts of interpretation, we have no way of being sure that our message is properly received.

Plain, direct conversation is such an effective, efficient way of speaking the truth that it's a shame we don't make more use of it. When we use the couples dialogue to speak our mind, we avoid misunderstanding and miscommunication and bypass the elaborate charades that often contort our meaning.

🍂 *Speak the truth today. Whenever you catch yourself in one of your habits of indirection, articulate your communication in words. Translate that glance, that curt reply, that frosty embrace into something that your partner can more clearly understand. Use the couples dialogue.*

Although it scares me to think of telling my partner all that is on my mind, I relax into that place of inner courage and visualize myself on a stage speaking from my heart all that I think and feel. I make this prayerful vow: "I surrender all forms of indirect communication."

Remember how you went out of your way during your courtship to stay in shape, to dress up, to find new places to go, to have something to say about the news? What has changed? Do you no longer care whether your mate finds you attractive and fascinating?

There's certainly something to be said for not having to put up a false front with our partners, always smiling or holding in our tummy. But there's a big difference between becoming comfortable with each other and letting ourselves go completely, not making the effort to be alluring, interesting, or fun to be with. Big mistake!

In a conscious relationship, we make the effort to attract and fascinate our mate every day. We take responsibility for being our best selves.

&❧ *Do something today to clean up your act, something that will get your partner's attention. Wear something smashing, initiate a conversation on a new subject, make a nice dinner, get a haircut. (Show your partner how interesting and attractive you still are.)*

In my time of quiet today, I relax all stored tensions and give room for spontaneity to surface. I rejoice in this hope: "Romance and attraction can take life once again in my relationship."

*I neglect God . . . for the noise of a fly, for the
rattling of a coach, for the whining of a door.*

— JOHN DONNE

Our spiritual journey is not defined by the twenty minutes of quiet
we set aside each day, not confined to the time we spend in church
or working on our relationship with our partners. These activities
are spiritual muscle builders, evidence of our intention to enrich
our spiritual life, but they are not the measure and breadth of our
spirituality.

Our spirituality is not separable from the secularity of our acts. It
is that which binds all things together, informing the quality of the
time we spend with our partner and the tenor of our words and
gestures. Simply being with our partner, reading side by side,
laughing at the dog, baking a birthday cake together can, with
awareness, be the continuing evolution of our spiritual path.

&. *Spend time simply being with your partner today. Go for a
drive, sprawl on your backs in the yard and stare at the stars,
snuggle up together with your books. Recognize the divinity
present in those moments.*

Closing my eyes in stillness today, I contemplate the spiritual quality
of simply being together, reveling in the joy of mundane moments. I
allow these memories to cascade over me, washing away any current
frustrations. I hold this thought: "The presence of the sacred in the
ordinary is a matter of perception."

*Just as sexual energy has helped man out of his
spiritual state into the body, so it can help him to
return in full awareness to his divine primal state of
wholeness.*

—ELIZABETH HAICH

Perhaps nothing has been subjected to as much religious persecution
in Western culture as the human body. Spiritual and sexual ecstasy
have been seen as mutually exclusive—to have one, we must forgo
the other. This persistent prejudice against bodily ecstasy has de-
prived both sexual and spiritual life of their potential richness and
transformative potential.

Yet how similiar are the impulses behind both the spiritual and
sexual drives—to find union with another, to surrender to something
larger than our isolated selves, to transcend this earthbound existence, to fill our existential emptiness. In surrendering to deep sexual
union with our partners, we experience our divinity.

&. *Merge with your partner tonight, body to body. Later, use the
couples dialogue to discuss with your partner the idea that sexual
love can be an experience of spiritual union.*

**In my time of quiet, I breathe deeply, relaxing my body, releasing
my sexual inhibitions, and I allow a deeper sense of surrender into
my sexual feelings. I focus on this thought: "Sexual union with my
partner is a form of spiritual communion."**

I like living. I have sometimes been wildly, despairingly, acutely miserable, racked with sorrow, but through it all I still know quite certainly that just to be alive is a grand thing.

—AGATHA CHRISTIE

When we are enmeshed in the power struggle, we feel miserable. We keep having the same fights, over and over. The same buttons get pushed, time and again. And it hurts afresh each time. Sometimes we apologize and patch things together. Things seem to be all right for a while. But then one of us says or does something amiss, and we're off and running again. We wonder if our relationship will ever get any better. It seems pretty hopeless.

But just to be in a relationship that offers the potential for true love is a great boon that we often overlook in the midst of our travails. The misery, the unhappiness, contain hidden clues to what *will* make us happy. Our despair is a wake-up call to plunge into the depths, with the support of our partner, and unearth its causes. The opportunity to do this, however frightening or painful, is a grand thing. It is the path to feeling fully alive.

๛ Talk with your partner today about any discouragement you feel about working through your problems, and renew your efforts to stay with the process, making sure to validate and empathize with each other's feelings.

I confess the utter weariness I feel with my relationship, and let the tears come. Relieving this inner pressure, I can better move to my inner source of strength. I commit to holding this resolve in my heart: "Commitment, both rational and spiritual, is my path for wholeness and healing."

When you make a world tolerable for yourself, you make a world tolerable for others.

—ANAÏS NIN

Learning to love our partner may overshadow the importance of learning to love ourselves. But until we overcome our self-hatred, we cannot love another. Self-love is not about indulgences that feel great in the moment but about true acceptance of ourselves as we are. That's not so easy, because most of us are burdened by self-loathing that we don't even recognize—a self-rejection rooted in childhood that we deflect with alcohol, overachievement, shopping sprees, braggadocio. Yet we can become enraged when our partner is insensitive or uncaring to the very feelings we trample on ourselves.

We dread laying aside our masks and learning to love what's inside—fears, failures, and all. In loving what our caretakers and others rejected in us, we are breaking powerful taboos. But isn't it unfair to ask our partner to do the job alone? You must do your part to heal your self-hatred. Until you do, you will not trust your partner's love.

❧ *Recall an experience in which you were complimented by your partner and you felt unworthy of receiving the compliment or rejected it. This is an instance of self-rejection. Give yourself the compliment—"You look so nice tonight"—and say back to yourself, "Thank you!" Take a deep breath and say aloud, "This is true of me."*

As I sit in sacred stillness today, I hold a picture in my mind of myself, with all my problems, being embraced by a larger, more forgiving energy of the universe. As I accept and love my own brokenness, I make it easier for my partner's love to touch me.

Most marriages stall in the power struggle. But marriage doesn't have to stay stuck. The power struggle is supposed to happen, for it is a necessary prelude to recovering the potential hinted at in the romantic stage. It is not even a negative indicator but a sure sign that we are with the right person for our maximum potential growth.

Understanding the particular dynamics of your struggle with your partner goes a long way to being able to resolve it. This will be a challenging exercise and will take some time to think through. But it is, in a sense, the key to the kingdom.

&. *Title a new page in your notebook "My Power Struggle with My Partner," and complete the following sentences:*

I am attracted to you and have chosen you because you are . . . [*fill in the key positive and negative traits of both your partner and your caretakers*] and because you . . . [*fill in the most important behaviors you liked and the negative behaviors that hurt you, from both your partner and your caretakers*].

I wish you would always be . . . [*positive traits*] and would always . . . [*positive behaviors*] and especially would . . . [*behavior you like most from partner*]
so that I would always feel . . . [*feelings you have when partner gives you desired behavior*].

When you . . . [*main frustrations with partner*] I feel . . . [*feelings as a result of frustrations*] and I react by . . . [*reaction to frustrating behavior*] to hide my fear of . . . [*fear aroused by frustrating behavior*].

When I . . . [*reaction to frustration mentioned above*]
I cause you to react by . . . [*partner's response*]
and being . . . [*partner's negative traits from first phrase above*].

Reminding myself that freedom lies in knowing the truth, I move into a place of inner courage and allow myself to see the unfolding of the deeper pattern that has controlled my life. As its shape becomes more clear, I see an opening in the darkness.

*You are the known way leading always to the
unknown, and you are the known place to which the
unknown is always leading me back.*

—WENDELL BERRY

The power struggle is not supposed to last any more than romantic
love is supposed to last. It is a transient phenomenon, a conduit to
the creation of selfhood in each partner. To stay stuck in the stage of
romance or the power struggle is to abort nature's process of
attempting to finish the creation of a self that cares for others.

Here again is the grand design of nature: that while the focus on
the self may be a prerequisite for personal survival, moving beyond the self to the concern for, and intimacy with another is essential
to the spiritual evolution and survival of our species. The creation of
real love is nature's way of repairing and completing itself—through
you.

🕭 *Today read out loud to each other the power struggle statements that you wrote yesterday. Acknowledge each other's communication by saying, "Thank you for telling me that." As you
share these agendas with each other, keep in mind that this
information is only for the purpose of educating each other. The
information may affect your behavior toward each other in the
future as you use it to construct new ways of being together, but
there is no obligation to change your behavior right now. Share
the information in a loving and helpful manner.*

In quiet prayer I allow myself to feel a deeper vitality and life energy
flowing through my body. I focus on these words: "The power struggle
is just a stop on the way to real love."

How are the terms of endearment in your relationship? Are you practicing your billing and cooing? Our pet names for our partners are our little secret; heaven knows we'd be embarrassed if anyone else heard us cooing at each other this way. But our private love language is a way of feeling close as a couple. After all, it's hard to be angry at someone you call Pookie.

❧ *Whisper sweet words to your partner today, the words you know they love to hear.*

In my quiet time today, I dip into my inner well of youthful aliveness and bring the spirit of fun to my relationship today.

To burn always with this hard, gemlike flame, to maintain this ecstasy, is success in life.

—WALTER PATER

We are innately sexual beings. Our sexuality is part of the pulsating energy of the life force, which we express through body, mind, and psyche. Our yearning for sexual union with a partner is a core manifestation of our drive to achieve union with the cosmos.

While sexual expression should come naturally, it is more often an area of shame and frustration in our lives. For the truth is that ours is a sex-negative culture. That may seem hard to believe when sex is used to sell everything from toothpaste to life insurance, but the particular *in flagrante* way in which sexuality is outwardly expressed in our culture is to some degree a measure of its repression below the level of consciousness.

Our ignorance about sex, which in large measure is the result of the lifetime disinformation campaign that our culture wages in our homes, in church and school, and in the media, needs to be overcome if we are to reclaim our innate sexuality. The best reeducation and training program is the one we devise with our partner in the privacy of our home. We have the equipment, but it is just out of tune. We need to oil the instrument and practice, practice, practice. We could make beautiful music together.

❧ *Begin a sex education class with your partner today. This could be a discussion of what pleasures you, about where and how you like to be touched, about what you are afraid of or curious about. Or it could be a practice session.*

Moving to a place of inner calm today, I visualize myself imprisoned by my sexual beliefs. Having served my time, I see myself escaping from these cultural bonds and returning sex to its place in the natural and sacred order of things.

*What do we live for, if it is not to make life less
difficult for each other?*

—GEORGE ELIOT

How is it that we so easily end up in a contest with our partners to
see how miserable we can make each other's lives—how much we
can criticize, reject, or ignore our partners, how much blame we can
put off on each other? And who wins—the partner who criticizes the
most? The one who feels less bad about themselves after a brawl?
The one who's still standing when the relationship is reduced to
rubble? The idea that making life difficult for our partner will have the
effect of making life easier for ourselves is ludicrously illogical.

Because, really, isn't this what we're all after in our relationships—
for life to be a little easier, safer, and more loving? And isn't this
what we're unconsciously trying to get from our partners—and just
as unconsciously punishing them for not providing.

Our relationship should be a haven from the sometimes harsh and
unpredictable world outside our door, a place where safety is guaranteed. If we cannot make each other's lives easier, after all, what's
the point?

&❧ *On a new page in your notebook, make a list of five ways you
make your partner's life difficult: "I tease him about his bald
spot." "I act hurt when she doesn't have time to walk the dog with
me." "I continue to complain about my mother-in-law." Then list
one thing you could do to make your partner's life easier with
regard to each item above, and do one of them each day for the
next five days.*

**Today I visualize myself bathing my partner in love, and holding this
thought in my heart: "With love I can stretch beyond my own comfort
zone to meet my partner's needs."**

It may seem like a virtue to avoid conflict, to smile about a frustration, to go for a walk to cool off. But conflict doesn't disappear just because we refuse to engage ourselves. Even if we don't rock the boat, it will sink unless we plug up the leaks.

Many people avoid conflict because their only experiences with trying to speak their mind in childhood were painful and demeaning. They have no idea how to turn an argument into a healing experience. For others, avoiding conflict is just a way of avoiding contact. But conflict can lead to intimacy and understanding when you regularly use the containment process to air your conflicts in a fair and nondestructive manner. You can't win the game if you refuse to play. In a conscious relationship the outcome is always win-win.

🍃 *Confront your aversion to conflict. Ask your partner to do a containment exercise about something that has been bothering you that you've been keeping to yourself. Speak up!*

I hold this thought in a time of stillness today: "I have the courage to confront conflict in my relationship and turn it into a healing experience."

Loved people are loving people.

— KATHARINE HEPBURN

Children need to be loved. To the degree that they are loved, they grow up healthy and happy and able to love others. Many of us, as adults, spend our lives looking for someone who will give us the love we never got as children. But what we really need is not someone to love us; we need someone to love. To get the love we need as adults, we must give it. Unfortunately, many of us don't know how.

A conscious relationship is an ongoing lesson in becoming a lover, of developing a spirit of an in-dwelling God. We stretch outselves to give love daily to our partners, without expectation of return. We find that genuine love attracts love. Once shared it comes back to you with interest.

❧ Think of one way that you know your partner needs to be loved and make a point of expressing that love today in an intense, unforgettable way. If your partner needs to be told that they are loved, say so ten times. If they need to be listened to, be all ears. If they need to cry unabashedly, tenderly dry their tears.

As I relax today and enter my deep quiet place, I see my partner as a whole, spiritual being who has been wounded as a child. I see my love healing my partner's wounds, then coming back to me and healing my wounds. I see our love flowing back and forth between us in a continuous oscillation of healing.

We express our individuality through our clothes, our home, our taste in art and wine and sports. It's a way of telling others who we are. So when our partner's style contradicts our own image of what is tasteful, we find it difficult to accommodate them. But in the world we share, we have to find a way for our personal styles to live together, for mutual self-expression to flourish. Our styles may clash, but we should not.

We're all entitled to our ideas about personal taste. But criticizing our partner's choices is a sure sign that we're too reliant on our image, too dependent on what others think. In a conscious relationship, partners approach matters of personal style with an attitude of cooperation and peaceful coexistence. They learn to live with their partner's cowboy boots or fake fingernails. They may even learn to like them. Moreover, they may be relieved to find that their furniture and what they wear has little to do with who they really are.

🍃 *Go shopping (or flip through some magazines) with your partner and point out to each other things you particularly like and dislike. Be honest with your opinions—it's all right to disagree. Validate your partner's choices unconditionally.*

Taking time for reflection today, I cherish this thought: "I may not love what my partner loves, but that does not change my love for my partner."

A man usually marries because he wants to "cure" his mother.

—CARY GRANT

When we meet our Imago partner, we are unconsciously drawn to their similarities to our parents, in hopes of fixing our painful childhoods. But as we get to know our partner better, we find that *because* they possess the negative traits of our caretakers, what we want most from them is what they are most unable to give.

For instance, if your caretakers frequently left you alone, you have probably been attracted to an Imago partner who is also physically absent, perhaps working late at the office every night. What you need in order to counteract your childhood experience and heal your deepest wounds is to have your partner spend more time with you. If you ask and your partner responds, you will get the attention you've always craved and your childhood wound will be healed. You will have cured your parents.

The key to cure is *change*. In a conscious relationship, each partner changes to respond to the needs expressed by their mate. Over the next several days, you'll be invited to learn the skill of behavior-change requests, a process in which you identify the embedded desires behind your frustrations and communicate those desires to your partner, minus the criticism. If you both are able to change in the specific ways each of you needs, you will grow in the process, and you will get your needs met.

&❧ *Divide a page in your notebook into two vertical columns. Label column one "Frustration" and make a comprehensive list of all your chronic frustrations with your partner, the ones you constantly complain about: "You don't clean up after yourself," "You spend too much money," "You drive too fast," "You don't follow through when you say you are going to do something for me." Phrase your frustration as if you were completing the sentence, "I don't like it when . . ."*

I offer a benediction today, that through my frustrations I will be able to understand my needs better. I put aside my self-sacrificing attitudes, and decide: "It is important to spend time identifying my needs."

When you love someone, all your saved-up wishes start coming out.

—ELIZABETH BOWEN

All of us carry our secret needs through life, waiting for someone to come along to fill those empty places and make us feel whole. When we meet our Imago partner, we think we've hit pay dirt: Here is the one that can give us what we desire.

The agenda of our unconscious is to get our original caretakers to change to meet our needs. But childhood is over, and that didn't happen. So the next-best thing is to find someone to meet our needs who is so like those who originally wounded us that our old brain can't tell the difference. In other words, for us to heal, we need our perfect Imago partner to change in specific ways to become like the good parents we never had. (Of course, our partner has the same unconscious agenda for us, and wants *us* to change so *they* can be healed.) When our partner doesn't live up to our expectations, we end up frustrated and disappointed.

But our conscious frustrations contain valuable information; they hold the key to our unconscious childhood wounds. A deep, unmet need—something we didn't get from our caretakers that we desperately want from our partners—lies hidden behind every frustration. Identifying the desire embedded in the frustration is the next step in identifying the exact behavior we need to fulfill it.

🍃 *Take your list of frustrations from yesterday and label column two "Desire." Write down the desire or desires behind your first frustration. Phrase each of your desires positively. Write what you do want rather than what you don't want: "I want to feel safe and relaxed when you're driving," rather than "I don't want to feel scared when you drive."*

Relaxing into a time of reverence, I enter the place of strength within. I hold this thought: "Taking care of my needs will better enable me to care for my partner."

Ask, and it shall be given you.

—MATTHEW 7:7

"**Y**ou never . . ." "You don't . . ." "You won't . . ." That's what we are most familiar with, frustrations expressed as complaints and criticisms. We do it to our partner; they do it to us. There's a better way, and that is to simply ask for what we want rather than blaming. That's how you convert a frustration into a behavior-change request.

A behavior-change request is a positively phrased, very specific, measurable, doable behavior that we would like from our partner. For example, if your frustration is: "You always withdraw when I am upset," your desire might be: "I would like you to comfort me when I'm upset." You can then translate this general desire into a specific request for a behavior change, complete with all the information your partner needs to effectively give you what you want: "When I'm upset, I would like you to comfort me by putting your arms around me and stroking my hair."

Giving your partner information about what you want or need in no way obliges them to do what you ask. But when in response to a behavior-change request we overcome our resistance and *stretch* our limitations, both partners benefit from the healing. The receiving partner heals their childhood wound, and the giving partner reclaims their wholeness.

❤ *Title a new page in your notebook "Behavior-Change Requests." Make a list of behavior-change requests that would satisfy the desire you identified yesterday that is at the root of your frustration. For example, if your desire is "I want you to be more reliable about meeting me on time," your behavior-change request could be, "When you are going to be more than fifteen minutes late I would like you to call. There may be several specific behavior-change requests connected to one desire; write them all down. Indicate the relative importance to you of each behavior-change request with a number 1 (very important) to 5 (not so important).*

Taking time for a period of renewal, I focus my mind and heart on this truth: "Sharing from a place of love will enable my partner to respond with love."

Come to the edge, he said. They said: we are afraid.
Come to the edge he said. They came. He pushed
them . . . and they flew.

—GUILLAUME APOLLINAIRE

The traditional wisdom about relationships is that people don't change, so we should accept our partners as they are. But that leaves us in a dilemma. Since we lost our wholeness in childhood, no growth can take place *unless* we change. We are forever doomed to being a partial person, and our partner will always have unmet needs.

Recognizing this dilemma, nature paired us with a partner whose demands and frustrations constantly challenge us to grow beyond our limitations—to walk to the edge and fly—so we can give them what they need. It is in this stretching beyond our comfort zone that we reclaim the parts of ourselves lost through childhood wounding and social conditioning.

❧ *With your partner, decide which one of you will ask for, and which will grant, a behavior-change request. Using the couples dialogue, the partner making the behavior-change request chooses one frustration from the list made yesterday, and expresses first the desire behind the frustration, and then at least three changes in behavior that would satisfy that desire. For example: "I would like to feel safe when you are driving. I would like you to stay within five miles of the speed limit; not to drink when you're going to be driving; not to tailgate and try to pass every car; to leave enough time that we don't have to rush to our destination." Use mirroring and validation as needed until three desired behaviors are so clearly described that the partner knows exactly what is wanted. From the list of requests, the receiver chooses a request or requests to grant right away.*

In my time alone today, I honor this new skill I am learning, aware that as I take care of my partner in targeted ways, and my partner takes care of me, we have the opportunity to engage in core healing with one another. While some of these behaviors may seem superficial, they are offering me a chance to transcend myself.

*It is one of the most beautiful compensations in life
that no man can sincerely try to help another without
helping himself.*

— RALPH WALDO EMERSON

The biblical saying that it is more blessed to give than to receive is true. Granting our partner's behavior-change requests results in a two-way healing. It's rather elegant: the partner who grants the request stretches into an undeveloped part of himself and changes a dysfunctional trait that has been part of their character. The partner receiving the behavior change gets childhood needs met and heals old wounds.

Here's an example of how that two-way healing works. Say your partner was an only child and felt suffocated by their mother's constant attention. You grew up in a very large family where there was constant group activity—sisters and brothers were always around and you were never alone. Your partner needs much more space and time alone than you are accustomed to. By granting your partner's behavior-change request to give them more space and time alone, you not only help heal your partner's childhood wound by giving them what they want, but you also benefit by discovering, perhaps for the first time, your own essential joy in having time and space for yourself.

❧ *Switch roles today, with the recipient of yesterday's behavior-change request becoming the granter today.*

Remember, behavior changes are gifts. Once you have said you will grant them, do so regardless of how you feel about your partner and regardless of how many changes your partner is making.

I celebrate in my time alone the elegant ironies of nature! So much healing will occur if I stop resisting and simply trust the process.

Changing to give our partners what they need is a fearsome challenge. We have to let go of our old, entrenched behavior, which makes us feel vulnerable and unrecognizable to ourselves. We have to overcome our anxieties about stretching into unfamiliar territory. Sometimes a behavior change involves admitting that we were wrong and risking being seen by our partners in an unflattering light.

But there is no faster route to self-reclamation, to the tearing down of the barriers that hide us from our lost self, no surer way to build up our own heart muscles. Granting your partner's behavior-change request is heavy lifting, proof of your strength and of your ability to be a whole and loving person. You should be right proud of yourself today!

🍃 *Think about the behavior change that you have granted your partner during these last days. What part of yourself is being healed and strengthened in the process? Congratulate yourself for your commitment and fortitude. Give yourself a treat today—time to yourself, a nap, a new book or music or shirt, a massage or manicure.*

In the quietness of my inner sanctuary today, I see myself exercising the atrophied parts of myself. As I continue, the original muscles of my true self become toned and I feel myself capable of great feats of strength.

You'd think by now that evolution could have at least evolved into the place that we could change ourselves.

—LILY TOMLIN

Why all this effort? At this point, you're probably exhausted. One day, you're expected to contain your instinctual response to your partner (like throwing this book at them), and respond from a place of understanding. The next, you're asked to unearth deep unconscious motivations that are the ghosts come to life in your current life. (And taking on ghosts is no easy matter.) Some days, you really get with the program beautifully. Other days, all your efforts are in vain. "Is something wrong with me that I can't change myself?" you wonder. "Did evolution pass me by?"

Such doubt and discouragement are only natural as you engage in this process. This is extremely difficult, intense work you've undertaken. It gets overwhelming and frustrating even for those who have been using the material for a long time.

But hang in there. The process has its ups and downs. Recognize it as a part of the natural rhythm of the psyche; accept the limits on how much you can integrate at a time. Like our physical bodies, the psyche also needs its time to rest.

❧ *Suggest a day of time-out between you and your partner. For this one twenty-four-hour period, use avoidance tactics wherever possible. The rest is going to do you good!*

In renewal today, I give myself permission to be easy on myself. Bathing my spirit with a gentle acceptance, I recognize that a self-forgiving attitude will make it easier for me to forgive my partner as well. I honor this truth: "The role of gentleness—on both myself and my partner—should not be underrated."

Let me not to the marriage of true minds
Admit impediments. Love is not love
Which alters when it alteration finds,
Or bends with the remover to remove:
O, no! it is an ever-fixéd mark,
That looks on tempests and is never shaken . . .

                                   —WILLIAM SHAKESPEARE

Shakespeare's flowery words may sound archaic or stilted in our tell-it-like-it-is times. Yet their message remains timely. We are immersed in a culture that worships newness, that endorses change. We are trained to bolt at the first sign of trouble, without giving much consideration to what we're bolting *to,* or just what it is we are leaving behind.

Commitment is the essential condition, the ground zero of a conscious relationship. Our love for our partner is not circumstantial and does not waver in times of trouble, when things change, when the unexpected happens. The problems—the tempests—that inevitably arise are not to be avoided, or to be wished away, but to be met headon and worked through together. Thus does our love become strong and tempered. Therein lies the poetry.

❧ *Read your relationship vision aloud to each other today, to remind you of your unshakable commitment.*

In my time of solitude, I acknowledge how often the storms of life have darkened my world. I pause, giving thanks that my partner and I are protected by the shelter of our mutual commitment.

I am at two with nature.

—WOODY ALLEN

It's not hard to get the impression that we humans are somehow apart from, rather than a part of, nature. Our technological wizardry and polyvinyl paraphernalia seem convincing enough evidence that our world is man-made and that we are well in control of nature.

If we could only step back far enough, we'd see that all of nature is a complex, teeming organism, of which we are an integral part. We are embedded in a matrix of purposive consciousness. We influence and are influenced by this grand context. We are the apex of nature, the part that is *self-conscious,* that can study itself and change itself. However, having distanced ourselves from nature, we are at the same time nature's most wounded part. But it is through our higher consciousness that nature intervenes and corrects itself. Our relationships are the vehicle for that correction. In healing ourselves through our relationships, in breaking down the barriers that separate us from our partners, we restore our spiritual wholeness and reestablish our awareness of our connection with all of nature.

🍃 *Take a walk in nature today; connect with the other inhabitants of this planet. Hug a tree, frolic in the rain, pet rocks, feel up the earth, hug a baby. If you wish, share this walk with your partner.*

While in a place of natural beauty, I allow myself to absorb the smells and sounds of nature, overcoming my sense of separation. I draw sustenance from this insight: "I am an essential part of the wondrous universe."

Do you provide reliable, regular information and feedback for your partner? In a conscious relationship our partners need us to mirror, in a loving way, who they are. They need to hear from us what we think of them and how we react to their choices and behaviors. They need to feel reflected and verified by us. This is part of the ongoing dialogue of partnership.

But sometimes we are so withdrawn, so tuned out that we haven't the foggiest idea what they're up to. We are shocked to learn that they are unhappy, that they've been studying Italian for three years, that they no longer have asthma attacks, or that they have taken their lives elsewhere and found other friends who care what's going on in their lives.

❧ *Be especially aware of your partner today, taking in information, noticing details and nuances. Give your partner feedback about your research. Reflect what you see back to them. "You seem to be less nervous about your new boss." "I notice that you like to wear that dark green hat I gave you." "You've been so affectionate this week."*

In a time of quiet today, I imagine myself truly seeing and reflecting my partner's truth in love. I make this vow: "My partner's news is my first priority."

Husbands are chiefly good lovers when they are
betraying their wives.

— MARILYN MONROE

As lovers we typically slack off in our attention to our mate over time, giving the best of ourselves to others. We put our best foot forward at work, demonstrating our loyalty and attentiveness and can-do attitude. We save our best stories and jokes for our friends. We're the stalwart of the PTA, the friend in need.

It's as though we gave our best effort to close the deal. But now that we've snared our mate and gotten them to promise that they will love us, we can concentrate our efforts elsewhere. Besides, our friends and coworkers don't seem to complain as our partners do, and don't make unreasonable demands. They appreciate us.

An affair is not the only way to betray our commitment to our partner. That is only one form of infidelity that can sabotage the relationship. Any other person or thing that exceeds our partner as a priority is a form of unfaithfulness. In a conscious relationship, we give our partner the best we have to offer. Just think how all that love and attention, charm and loyalty we dispense so freely elsewhere could transform our relationship.

🍃 *On a page in your notebook labeled "Exits," list five ways you have given to others the energy that belongs to your partner. Reaffirm your commitment to keeping the passion alive in your relationship, to sharpening your amatory skills and your knowledge of your partner's desires. Begin with a little lovin' today. A foot rub, a back rub, sweet whispered words, an unexpected kiss? Show your partner you're still an interested lover.*

As I make time for a period of solitude today, I see it as an opportunity to deepen my fidelity to my partner, to create the loving attitude I want to carry in my heart. I ponder the truth of this paradox: "In putting my partner first, I receive the gift I give."

Virgin birth is the birth of the spiritual in man out of the animal man. When you are awakened at the level of the heart to compassion and suffering with the other person, that is the beginning of humanity. Love, you might say, is the burning point of life.

—JOSEPH CAMPBELL

As we fight for our psychic survival as children, our natural empathic connection to others is disrupted. We become preoccupied with self-preservation, and our interactions with others become self-centered, focused on what we need to get, and how to get it. We become more and more self-absorbed. Our interest and knowledge center on our own small world; our perpetual emotional static disrupts clear input from others.

In order for things to change, we must face the fearsome task of extricating ourselves from the center of our own tiny universe. We must go through a spiritual rebirth. That happens when we open ourselves to our partner's pain and empathize with their wounding, when we transcend the self-absorption that isolates us. This opening to the wounds of the partner, and the commitment to their healing, is the core agenda of the conscious relationship. In this emergent compassion for the pain of another a spiritual transformation takes place. To relinquish our self-centered worldview, to share the center of the universe with our partner, opens the heart and calms the inner static. Then we begin to experience our interconnectedness with all things. We are no longer alone. We have been "born again."

🎕 *Once again today, visualize your partner as a wounded child. Hold in mind one story in particular that they have told you—an incident of shame or abandonment or abject sorrow. As you focus on this pained child, allow yourself to feel compassion for your partner.*

In reverential quiet today, I allow my self-absorption to fade as I direct my energy toward the needs of my beloved. I allow myself to feel their pain as if it were my own.

Unable are the Loved to die/For Love is Immortality.

—EMILY DICKINSON

The Greeks were brilliant military strategists, and one of their great discoveries about war contains a valuable lesson about love. The Greeks recognized that the best way to keep peace was to guarantee to their enemies that they would be treated like one of their own— like a friend—while they were on Greek territory. This is the basis of *agape* love.

To those of us who have been wounded before, such a tactic perhaps seems foolhardy. Wary, watchful, defensive, we've been hurt by those we loved before, and we have no reason to suspect it won't happen again. But you cannot intimately love someone you do not know, someone you keep at a distance and regard as a potential enemy. It's a conundrum, for openness is possible only where there is no fear.

When you think about it, love is the most practical of behaviors. The greatest guarantee of our own safety and welfare is to treat our partners as equal in value to ourselves, to guarantee their physical, emotional, and spiritual welfare while in our presence. This making of equals creates *philia*, love between friends, which is the goal of a conscious relationship. This strategy, which is new for most of us, moves us in the direction of an evolved spiritual state.

&. *Identify a recent way in which you have made your partner feel unsafe with you: a threat of leaving, an angry response to a simple request, withdrawing from time together. Think about how you would like to be treated in this same circumstance, and amend your behavior to treat your partner in this way.*

In quiet contemplation today, I visualize a land in which there is no crime and no war, where people are able to walk the streets at night. And within such surroundings, I am so attuned to my partner's needs that our relationship becomes a virtual fortress. I hold this thought: "In order to live in a land of safety, I must guarantee my partner's safety."

Someday, after we have mastered the winds, the waves,
the tides and gravity, we shall harness for God the
energies of love. Then for the second time in the
history of the world, man will have discovered fire.

—PIERRE TEILHARD DE CHARDIN

Did you ever see a couple sitting in a restaurant, looking bored to tears, waiting for their food to arrive so they have something to do? You can tell just by watching them that they are pretty miserable.

They are sadly missing the boat. So often couples in routine, humdrum marriages fail to recognize the transformative potential of their relationships. They resign themselves to the status quo. They haven't a clue that a committed relationship, with all its tension and struggles, if managed properly, can be the incubator of powerful forces of love.

Just as fire can melt and merge two substances, filtering out impurities, so too can the fires of the power struggle ultimately transform your relationship into a deep and powerful union, capable of impact even on the world beyond the doors of your home. The love created by a healed relationship is a force of nature, a force for good in the world that becomes more powerful with each transformed relationship. Can you envision a world that harnessed the energy of countless loving relationships? A world in which there were no miserable couples polluting the air in restaurants?

❧ *Recall a situation in which you and your partner experienced the power of your love for each other. Perhaps there was a time when one of you nurtured the other through a serious illness, for example. Harness that event, imprint it in your mind, by sharing your memory with your partner. Together, commit to finding a way to re-create that powerful love in the near future.*

Today I contemplate those areas—however few they may be at the moment—of real love between myself and my partner. They are simmering coals, glowing, however faintly, beneath a damped fire. But they have the potential to ignite and expand until they become a powerful force for transformation, first within my own hearth and home, and then spreading out to warm the world.

We should be able to resolve our differences without resorting to full battle regalia. But unless we know *how* to fight, we may need armored protection to ensure our emotional survival.

For many of us, conflict is synonymous with battle. We never learned as children how to fight fair, asking for what we want directly and without accusation. Punished or shamed or belittled, we learned only how to avoid pain, not how to prevent or resolve it. All we have to show for our efforts are our battle scars and a hodgepodge of childish ploys. Now our own home is a war zone and we have no idea how to deescalate the fighting.

Imago skills can help here. When we master the couples dialogue and learn to use the containment process to air our differences, we are instituting disarmament policies.

ɜ. *Time to call a truce. Use the containment process to resolve one conflict that arises today—your upset about the unfinished laundry, the television show you want to watch, your anger over your partner's bossiness.*

Seeking the power of the sacred today, I summon the inner courage to take off my armor and end the fighting. This truth has profound meaning for me: "Love and self-protection are incompatible."

Perform random acts of kindness and senseless acts of beauty.

—ANNE HERBERT

Isn't this a wonderful idea? No more you-do-this-for-me-and-I'll-do-that-for-you. No more gifts with strings attached. No anticipated payoff. No obligation. No reward. Kindness for the sake of kindness. Beauty for beauty's sake.

We can become so absorbed in the daily struggles of life, and so indoctrinated with the mean-spirited buy-and-sell mentality that is practically a matter of policy in our world, that we forget that kindness and beauty exist in the world because people—like us—make it happen. Kindness costs nothing and need only take a moment—a smile, a helping hand, a compliment, a thoughtful gesture. Beauty is in the art, inspiration, and care we bring to the little things in life—a simple bowl of apples on a clean table, a whitewashed fence, a freshly scrubbed copper pot, flowers from the garden. Through such subversive acts we change the world. And we wake up to a natural spirituality that surrounds us. Let's hear it for free love—and beauty!

❧ Perform random acts of kindness and senseless acts of beauty today—at least one of each. Leave acts of kindness in your wake— send money anonymously to charity, help a stranger across the street. Don't look back. Do something senselessly beautiful— strew rose petals in your bed, make ketchup hearts on the dinner hamburgers, recite a poem on the bus.

During this time of prayerful reflection, I become aware of my power to have impact in the world through unfettered goodness, with free gifts, and visualize myself acting lovingly without restraint.

We live by encouragement and die without it—slowly, sadly, angrily.

—CELESTE HOLM

We all have memories of slights and criticism from our parents, our teachers, our schoolmates. Some of them were devastating, weren't they? Because of these experiences, we got rid of the unacceptable parts ourselves, editing what we were willing to show to the world. Despite these painful memories—and in a way because of them—we visit the same tortures on our partner. But really, does it do any good? Does it get the reaction we want? Does it add to the storehouse of love in our relationship? When we criticize our partner, we're just replaying old scripts, persisting in using the ineffective ploys of childhood.

How much more effective to swamp our partner with words of love, to inundate them with validation and praise. Today you will gather the raw material for tomorrow's positive flooding exercise.

❦ *Spend a few minutes reflecting on your partner's good qualities: all the reasons you find your partner lovable, what you like about their looks or their way of doing things. Recall the kindnesses your partner does for you and others; call to mind every talent and ability and sensitivity, every endearing quirk. Write each one down, phrasing it as a compliment, as if you were speaking directly to your partner. For example: "You have great taste in ties." "I love the way you listen so patiently to the kids." "You always seem to know when I could use a good joke."*

I visualize myself as a light shining on my partner, warming them with praise for all their positive traits. This truth is mine today: "I strengthen my heart as I nourish my partner with unconditional, outrageous praise."

Today you'll be invited to do the positive flooding exercise. This may not be easy at first. Some couples are embarrassed to give—or receive—this kind of unbounded validation. Others' difficulty can be traced to their timidity or inhibitions. Still others find it hard to set aside animosity and grudges; they are far more in touch with the content of their criticisms than what they might find to compliment.

These are exactly the barriers that the positive flooding exercise is designed to break down. We open the floodgates, to wash all away in a tidal wave of praise.

❧ *In the positive flooding exercise one partner sits while the other walks around their chair, delivering an endless stream of praise and compliments. Take turns as praiser and praisee. As the praiser, you should tell your partner all the good things that you wrote down yesterday—and any new material that comes to mind. Circle around and around your partner, letting your voice rise and your enthusiasm build as you go. Don't hold anything back. And don't forget to have fun yourself in the process.*

During a prayerful interlude, I turn within to convert the anger and frustration I harbor against my partner into a river of praise. I consider this paradox: "Flooding my partner with praise fills me with joy."

God respects me when I work; but God loves me when I sing.

—TAGORE

Have you been working hard on your relationship? Learning all about the Imago process, practicing the couples dialogue, taking responsibility for your actions and feelings? Many of us bring a dogged sense of duty to the work we are doing, especially when we are feeling unsure of the terrain that we are covering. We approach each task— be it shopping at the supermarket or dealing with conflict within our relationship—with a highly responsible sense of what is appropriate. Sometimes we're so diligent and responsible that our spirits sag under the weight of it all.

All that effort is commendable, but when it becomes a wet blanket over our high spirits, it's time to lighten up. Today, throw the work out the window and focus on ways of channeling joy into your relationship. Connecting with your partner from a joyful place can revive the relationship, making difficulties seem less difficult somehow. Suddenly you are not in this alone. And slowly, you can begin to reconnect with the wonderful person you married.

❧ *Sing something today—old rock tunes in the shower, a rousing hymn as you exercise. Sing your partner a love song, whistle while you work.*

In quiet reflection I begin to identify how I use responsibility to keep myself from pleasure and joy. Letting go of all my lists of things to do and the responsibilities that I carry, I relax my spirit, along with my tense muscles, and give voice to a cheerful song.

Intelligence is not to make no mistakes
But quickly to see how to make them good.

— BERTOLT BRECHT

Admitting we're wrong is so hard! But it can work wonders. A simple "You're right, honey, I was wrong" can instantly deflate an argument. Anger and mistrust ebb away, and our partner feels respected and listened to. We feel so much better for having told the truth. Admitting we're wrong contributes to the fund of trust in the relationship—nobody's perfect, after all. In a conscious relationship we recognize that it's more important to be truthful than to be right.

ِ♣ *'Fess up. Admit to your partner that you were wrong about some conflict or event that occurred recently. "You were right about the amount of topsoil we need for the yard." "I spent too much money on clothes last month." "I was wrong to accuse you of ignoring me at the party."*

Drawing strength from a time of contemplation, I absorb the idea that the outcome of confessing my mistakes is another step on my journey to wholeness.

What happens to the promises we make in the throes of romance? We vow eternal love, our undivided attention, fidelity, companionship, financial support, lots of sex, and to always feed the dog. We meant these promises at the time, didn't we?

A promise is a sacred trust, and when it is broken we feel betrayed. Though our childhood may have been strewn with broken promises, we must overcome our hurt and mistrust to change that in our partnership. It's vital to keep our promises—the big ones included in our wedding vows, and the little agreements we make every day. Which means we should only make promises we intend to keep. It's much better to say, "No, I can't promise to go away for the weekend with you because I might have to work," than to say yes to keep the peace or deflect your partner's disappointment for the moment. Honesty is the best policy in a conscious relationship.

ਨਿ *What promises have you and your partner made to each other—last week, last year, at your wedding? Have you been true to your word? Renew one promise to your partner today, and take a step to fulfill it.*

Moving into a deep, relaxed state during my time of meditation, I offer this prayerful vow: "My word is gold where my partner is concerned."

*A person in love sometimes mistakes a pimple for a
dimple.*

—ANONYMOUS

Oh, the rose-colored glasses through which we see our partners
when we fall in love! Were we drunk, were we sleeping? How could
we ever have thought that this selfish creep was generous? That this
cold fish was sexy?

Romantic love is a kind of temporary insanity. Our unconscious is
so determined to find someone to make us whole again that it
overrules our rational mind. We see only what we want to see, and
censor any incoming data that conflict with what our rational mind
would call better judgment. The negative aspects of our Imago
partner (which our unconscious has judged desirable) are invisible to
us until we have bonded to them for healing—until it is too late. Until
the veil of illusion has fallen, until we give up our denial and rationali-
zation of our partner's faults, all we can see is the dimple.

The end of romantic love, when the truth about our Imago partner
is all too apparent, is often followed by an equally irrational period in
which all we can see is the pimple, as we slog through the power
struggle. *Neither vision is complete or accurate.* When, through our
efforts and understanding, we emerge from the valley of conflict with
love and acceptance of our partner's dimples *and* pimples, we have
the whole picture.

🍂 *Tell your partner today how much you love them—citing both
one dimple and one pimple specifically.*

**As I enter my meditative state today, I relax my need for perfection
in my partner and in myself. Instead I offer thanksgiving for dimples,
pimples, their all. I honor this truth: "Our uniqueness is our divinity."**

*It is not for the love of a husband that a husband is
dear; but for the love of the Soul of the husband that a
husband is dear. It is not for the love of a wife that a
wife is dear; but for the love of the Soul of the wife
that a wife is dear.*

— THE UPANISHADS

One of the most important aspects of a conscious relationship
happens when we move into the deeper level of relatedness where
we can discover each other's woundedness from the past. Even as
adults, the wounds of childhood remain sensitized—raw, easily
bruised or reactivated; they are not within our control. When touched
by current circumstance, they trigger instinctual, reactionary responses that may even be chemical in nature. These wounds (yours
as well as your partner's) are the probable source of the majority of
frustrations you experience in your relationship.

A marriage has a chance to realize its potential only when we
commit at the deepest level to embracing the childhood wounding in
one another. The very act of commitment is healing for our partner,
and paradoxically, for ourselves. This is the work of reality love in a
relationship, the stuff of soul making—becoming whole, recovering
our original self.

❧ *In your notebook, write down your understanding of your
partner's most painful past experiences, using the words and
phrases your partner has used. If you do not already know this
information, make time to ask today. Even though your partner
may speak of these matters in a cool and detached manner, be
aware that your partner is most vulnerable when talking about
these issues.*

**I take the information about my partner's deepest hurt and move into
an inner sanctuary. There I visualize my partner in their struggle,
overwhelmed by forces beyond their control. In prayer, I imagine
love radiating from my being, encircling and protecting the soul of
my partner.**

It all comes down to who does the dishes.

—NORMAN MAILER

This is not as frivolous a remark as it seems. Couples often become mired in power plays over chores. Wars are fought over garbage, battle lines drawn over who vacuums what room how often. Sulking and resentment accumulate like dustballs.

These are all legitimate concerns. The tenor of a marriage is revealed in the day-to-day details of how we live our lives, in the sense of fairness, the willing division of labor. You can pretty well gauge the success of a marriage not so much by who does the dishes but by how partners arrive at that decision.

In a conscious relationship, these issues are slowly dissolved through the couples dialogue, not because deals are struck, but because partners learn to value each other as equal to themselves. Chores transcend roles, gender issues become irrelevant. Doing the dishes becomes an act of love, rather than an act of surrender or rebellion against control.

❧ *Use the couples dialogue today to talk with your partner about how the chores of your relationship are apportioned. If you need to, reapportion responsibilities in a way that reflects your love.*

In my time of quiet today, I embrace this revelation: "Inequality breeds discontent; sharing creates bonding."

*For one human being to love another: That is perhaps
the most difficult of all our tasks; the ultimate, the
last test and proof, the work for which all other work
is but preparation.*

—RAINER MARIA RILKE

Nothing in life is as difficult as the journey to real love that you have
undertaken with your partner. There will be times when the next
step seems impossible, when fear and anger seem like an uncrossable
chasm. Few of us have had sufficient preparation and training for this
journey. It's kind of ironic and sad, somehow, that we manage to
learn Italian, or the intricate rules of baseball, or how to make
hollandaise sauce, but are stymied when it comes to the art of loving
our partner. We are miseducated.

But there is hope for the relationship-impaired. Our ability to work
and to learn, honed from years of practice, can be applied to our
partnership. The energy we spend on our tennis game, the diligence
with which we research the buying of a new car or the market for our
company's new product can be diverted to our relationship, where it
really counts. All that we have learned about love and human nature
is an investment in our future. Every act of caring, every effort at
self-awareness, every attempt made to deepen our spiritual nature
makes this most difficult of journeys easier. And, as everyone who
has made the journey knows, it is well worth the effort.

*Make a point to touch your partner when you talk to them
today—take their hand, fondle their arm, put a hand on their
shoulder, put your arm around them, give them a hug, give them
a friendly poke or a love pat.*

**Today I visualize myself entering the School of Love, open to learning
the secrets of committed love. On the blackboard is a sentence I
commit to memory: "If I fail at love, I fail at all else."**

*We have what we seek. It is there all the time, and if
we give it time, it will make itself known to us.*

—THOMAS MERTON

Why are we so reactive when our partner requests a behavior
change? Is it because we fear some loss of power over our own lives,
or is it that we fear we are losing our own identity in the relationship?

We cling so doggedly to our ideas of who we are, that ragtag
assemblage of quirks and gestures with which we've learned to
identify. In reality, the self you fear losing is not your real self
anyway. Your essence is buried under a crust of habits and defenses.

What your partner asks of you is not something that doesn't belong
to you. It is with you now but hidden and atrophied from disuse.
Every time you overcome your resistance to changing your behavior
to meet your partner's requests, you'll be moving closer to becoming
who you really are.

🍂 *Grant a behavior-change request your partner has been asking
for. See if you can identify the buried part of yourself that has to
emerge to make that change.*

**During my time of quiet contemplation today, I marvel at this
thought: "In changing to meet my partner's needs, I become myself."**

Do you ever have the feeling that your partner came from another planet, perhaps another galaxy? That their emotional responses to life are so completely different from yours that you can't even talk with them? This is a function of the minimizer/maximizer matchups that most couples make. One is calm, cool, and collected. The other bounces off walls. But while their reactions are vastly different, partners usually share a pretty similar emotional intensity—one is as volatile as the other is unflappable. Contrary to what we might believe, there is not a gap between the emotional level of ourselves and our partners. It's just that we operate on opposite sides of the feeling spectrum.

As hard as it is for the minimizer and the maximizer to cope with each other, they each have something to learn from the other. The controlled, unemotional minimizer can learn from their mate how to get in touch with their buried feelings and express them. The overreactive maximizer learns ways to bring their intellect into the picture, so they are not always at the mercy of their feelings. Using the couples dialogue and the tools of the Imago process, you can meet in the middle, where heart and mind join, and both raise your level of emotional health.

❮ *Spend a few minutes in dialogue about a minor conflict in your relationship, noticing how your responses, and those of your partner, reflect your minimizer or maximizer tendencies. Then talk with your partner about the insight you've gained by seeing the underlying dynamic between you.*

Drawing hope from a place of solitude, I amplify the insights I've gained today by focusing on this truth: "Growth can come from our incompatibility."

*Cherish forever what makes you unique, 'cuz you're
really a yawn if it goes!*

— BETTE MIDLER

Our choice of an Imago partner and the way we respond to them is
a product not only of the nurturing we received from our caretakers
but of the messages they gave us about the world we live in. The
process by which we were indoctrinated with the cultural rules and
customs we were expected to obey is called *socialization*.

Ostensibly, this was *for our own good*, so that we could live in the
world without fear of rejection. The premise of socialization is that
society is dangerous to you until you understand its ways, and *you*
are a danger to society until you learn to fit in.

While socialization is necessary, no society has figured out how to
have its children fit into the world without injuring them. The rules
and regulations of most societies tend to focus more on what is *not*
permitted, and what is forbidden or taboo, than on what is acceptable.
And our caretakers—representatives of society, already hobbled by
their own conformity to the rules, demand that we repress essential
aspects of our true nature. By the time we meet our partner, most of
us have long buried what makes us unique.

In this next week, you will be assisted in tracking down your lost
self, the forgotten aspects of your innate nature that were sacrificed
in the name of social acceptance, and see how they influenced your
choice of partner.

🕊 *In your mind's eye, take a trip today back to your childhood
home. Walk around your house; check out the neighborhood and
visit your school. Notice books and magazines and television
shows and movies. What did people say to you? To each other?
What did you say to yourself? What were your childhood dreams
and impulses? Listen—with your ears and eyes and all your
senses—for the messages you received about how to live in your
world.*

**As I move into peaceful quiet, I become aware of the aspirations and
impulses I felt as a child that are now missing. Knowing that these
feelings are the key to my inner wholeness, I celebrate them in joyful
prayer today.**

Shape up or ship out.

—U.S. NAVY

We are socialized in both direct and indirect ways. Direct messages come in the form of "dos" and "don'ts," "shoulds" and "shouldn'ts." Right and wrong are conveyed with a steady barrage of admonitions: "Don't touch yourself 'there,'" "No running with that dress on," or "We don't do that in our family." How about the subtle character assassinations, such as "Nobody likes you when you are sad," or "You're too smart for your own good"?

Messages come in via friends, teachers, even from television and movies. But for the most part, the messages of socialization are transmitted more subtly. We absorb them like invisible radio waves from everything that we hear and see—everywhere. We learn what works—what wins us friends and special treatment, what turns people off, what is ignored or laughed at—in other words, what we need to change about ourselves.

Certain limits are, of course, necessary. But most of us had to alter ourselves so much to fit in that we have forgotten that we ever had a raucous laugh or wanted to write poetry. Having to curb our anger *and* our enthusiasms, our innate, pulsating energy no longer flows freely. The spiritual essence at our core was shut down as we selectively closed off forbidden areas, and our channels to the outside world became limited. Parts of us are now inaccessible, not only to ourselves, but to our partners.

❧ *Title a new page in your notebook "My Lost Self." Write down the messages of socialization you found yesterday in your memories of your childhood.*

I recognize my time in quiet today as critical to my own self-discovery, to identifying the essential parts of my nature that society's regulations have squelched. I allow my thoughts and feelings to surface, and embrace every one. I ponder this wisdom: "Self-acceptance is a prerequisite to acceptance of another."

> *I'd the upbringing a nun would envy and that's the truth. Until I was fifteen I was more familiar with Africa than my own body.*
>
> —JOE ORTON

Socialization differs from family to family, community to community, by region and by country. What's acceptable for a kid growing up in Manhattan doesn't play in Peoria. The demure coyness that girls learn the value of does not go over on the football team. As we learn the rules, we tend to censor ourselves more in some areas than in others. Since our society values thinking, this area is validated and encouraged. Feelings are more heavily censored, although women are given some leeway here. In the realm of the senses, well, you could write a whole book about sexual and bodily taboos. In the process of becoming a social creature, acceptable in society, a lot of what we are gets lost.

Our lost self reveals itself every time we identify some missing ability, some message we have taken to heart: "I can't dance," "I can't draw a straight line," "I can't have an orgasm," "I can't figure it out." When we examine the messages we grew up with and break them down by categories, we can begin to see where our energies are constricted and where to begin the long process of opening up the channels that block the expression of our true spiritual wholeness.

❧ Go back over yesterday's list of socialization messages, and label each one by category. Indicate with the appropriate letter whether each one pertains to T=thinking, F=feeling, A=acting, or S=sensing.

Today I give myself time to grieve for some of the unlived parts of myself, the impulses I had to abandon in order to survive. Quietly, I allow the tears to come for the parts of me that died young.

No partner in a love relationship should feel that he has to give up an essential part of himself to make it viable.

—MAY SARTON

When you got together, you chose your partner in part because they possessed traits you lacked—your partner's wholehearted guffaw compensates for your quiet laugh; your partner's enjoyment of sex helps you to overcome your inhibitions; your partner was attracted to your efficiency and your ability to remain calm under pressure.

But two half-people don't make a whole. Eventually your partner wants you to let down your hair and have fun, and is irritated by your sexual inhibitions. And you're tired of having to organize the whole household. Many of your partner's criticisms of you, and their expressed desires, are clues to your lost self. Instead of requiring you to give up a part of yourself, they call undeveloped aspects of yourself into being.

Our expectations for our partner, and our beliefs that we have to be a certain way in order to be loved, have disastrous consequences in an intimate relationship. Whatever our preconceived ideas, what we need for ourselves and our mate is to be spiritually whole. We have already given up parts of ourselves in order to find and secure a mate. Now we have to reclaim those parts to make the relationship whole.

☙ *Turn to "My Lost Self" in your notebook. Sit quietly for a few minutes with your eyes closed and think about your partner's criticisms of you and their requests for changes in your behavior: "Don't bother me when I'm reading." "You shouldn't act like that in front of the neighbors." "Stop giggling like a child." List each of your partner's comments on a separate line, and label them according to category: T= thinking, F= feeling, A= acting, or S= sensing.*

In quiet today, I recall that mot ancient traditions allow for life after death. Accessing that hope in my deep self, I allow the resurrection of the lost parts of myself, the phoenix rising from the ashes of repression. This thought becomes mine: "The parts of me that are dead shall live again."

> *I was as a gem concealed:*
> *Me my burning ray revealed.*

— THE KORAN

Ironically, the lost self traits that we annex by joining with our partner to make up for what we lack end up making us uncomfortable. Our mate's enjoyment of sex, which we at first welcomed, now makes us squirm. When our partner asks us to loosen up, we get defensive, and accuse them of being frivolous, and reproach them for not accepting us as we are.

It's not surprising that we resist agitating those still waters within ourselves. The stretching required to recover our lost self is often uncomfortable, even painful. But still waters lead to stagnation. Reclaiming the parts of ourselves that we were told were undesirable, unacceptable, or unattractive is like treasure hunting; we are repossessing valuable assets long buried.

❧ *Take some time today to tune in to the areas of resistance and discomfort that you are aware of, especially those you try and shield from your friends and partner. A partial list might include: showing your feelings, dancing, making love with the lights on, answering personal questions, asking for advice or help, enjoying time off, speaking in public, asking people for money even if you've earned it. Write down those that come to mind under the appropriate heading: T = thinking, F = feeling, A = acting, or S = sensing.*

In a wordless prayer I acknowledge the hidden glow of my inner gem, and appreciate my partner giving me the feedback that will enable it to shine.

When a person is unhappy at home, they spin fantasies of the life they could have if it weren't for their partner, if only they were free. . . . But maybe you don't need to be footloose and single again to live out your dream. A fantasy may be just what your relationship needs. In fact, your partner probably has a few fantasies of their own. Perhaps if you shared them, you could agree on a dream you both could pursue: a river-rafting vacation, new adventures in the bedroom, free-lance work that would free you from the daily grind, a garden of earthly delights. If you're going to escape your day-to-day doldrums, take your partner with you!

‽ *Share a special dream with your partner. Embellish your fantasies about how you would like your relationship to be or something you would like to do together. Then agree on a first step you both can take toward making your dream come true.*

In a quiet interlude, I allow my dream to come fully to mind. I offer a prayer of thanksgiving today that in some ways my fantasy is already reality.

*Though I speak with the tongues of men and of
angels, but have not love, I am become as sounding
brass or a tinkling cymbal.*
                                        —1 CORINTHIANS 13:1

In an ever-progressing, over-achieving society, we're all caught up
with developing expertise. We become intent at putting our best foot
forward with shoes well shined. We meticulously research wording,
so that the achievements on our résumés are described in most
glowing terms. We research wine lists so that we can order the best
chardonnay at our next social evening with just the right air. And we
ooze tact and diplomacy when meeting someone we want to impress.
All this effort has its place, as long as we can hear the cymbal tinkling.
    The real job of becoming human is in the development of deep
connection. For it is here that universal love is born. Easy to talk
about. Much harder to achieve. It takes heart. For most of us, our
hearts are indeed brassy, having been hardened by past wounding.
The work of a conscious relationship gives warmth and flesh where
once the heart grew cold and hard. Recognize that the time you spend
in quiet each day is helping your heart to soften, your feeling state to
open, and your connection to universal love to strengthen.

*❧ Commit to using the couples dialogue in each interaction with
your partner over the next twenty-four-hour period. Recognize
this as real love being cultivated within your relationship, within
your heart.*

**This truth becomes a balm for my soul: "Love beareth all things,
hopeth all things, endureth all things."**

*And the trouble is, if you don't risk anything, you
risk even more.*

—ERICA JONG

We are all prey at times to the temptation to play it safe, in life and
in our relationship. We may not be deliriously happy or successful,
but we've survived this far. The sad truth is that we're afraid to
change; we remain stuck in our old behaviors and ineffectual childhood
defenses because they are familiar. As much as we might want things
to be different, we can't bear to risk any further loss. Better to stick
with what we've got.

By now we know how our partner will react, for example, when we
come home late from work: they'll act hurt and all but refuse to talk
during dinner. Later on, we'll blow up at them for some small thing—
changing the TV channel, leaving the door unlocked—to show them
that they're not perfect either. It works somehow. We love each
other, we understand the pattern; it's just a habit.

This is high-risk behavior. In our hearts we know that our love will
erode just a little each day. That we'll get to the point where we don't
talk at all, where we'll just be kind of mildly miserable. A part of us
knows that if we don't take the risk of looking beneath our behavior
to see where our patterns originated, we are doomed to stay stuck in
them.

If we don't risk losing it all, we will never win it all, either. If we do
not risk taking the extra step, telling the hard truth, asking for what
we want, we risk missing a far richer life. Paralyzed by our fear, we
risk losing the opportunity for great love, for the restoration of our
whole, fully alive selves.

ã *Today, face down your fear. Take a risk in your relationship.
Tell your partner what you really feel. Ask for what you want.
Try a new tactic.*

**Knowing my fear of taking risks, I commit to a period of quiet today,
taking the time to get in touch with the bravery at my core. This
becomes my pledge: "I will risk authenticity to birth the creative and
divine in my relationship."**

*When marrying, one should ask oneself this question:
Do you believe that you will be able to converse well
with this woman into your old age?*

— NIETZSCHE

In the beginning, we had plenty to talk about with our partners. We exchanged life stories in garish detail, pored over family photo albums, giggled over our baby pictures. Secure in our partner's love, we divulged our dreams, and couldn't wait to tell them what had happened at work.

So what happened? Why has the talk around the dinner table degenerated to "Pass the milk"? Why do we dread our partner's reaction if we tell them about something that is upsetting us? Isn't there anything interesting in the news? What happened to our scintillating opinions? When was the last time we shared a secret longing? Why does our attention flag when our mate starts telling us about their day?

You cannot really love someone unless you know them deeply. And you certainly can't know someone unless you can talk to them. The couples dialogue is the core tool of a conscious relationship. Couples who plan to be able to talk to each other into their old age would do well to master it. It feels awkward and stilted at first to follow the rules, but as you practice the skills of mirroring, validation, and empathy, they will become second nature.

Practice the art of conversation over dinner tonight; make sure you have something of interest to say. Pay special attention to mirroring what your partner says, listening carefully and paraphrasing what is said until your partner confirms that they have been fully understood.

As I shut out the world and enter a time of quiet prayer, I look at my surface, perfunctory relationship with my partner. I decide to restore the energy and excitement to our partnership by nurturing the art of conversation, and am encouraged by this truth: "I have the power to animate new life and energy within my partnership."

*The absolute yearning of one human body for another
particular one and its indifference to substitutes is one
of life's major mysteries.*

—IRIS MURDOCH

Every couple has to find its own way. Society provides guidelines
and our families provided models. But often they are inadequate and
don't address our deepest needs.

Happiness doesn't come from squeezing yourselves into society's
vision of a relationship or from meeting your parents' expectations.
Your partnership offers a powerful and supportive framework for
creating a union customized to fit your unique and specific needs, a
relationship that is perfectly suited to the two of you. It is the product
of minutely and intimately knowing each other, and committing
unstintingly to meeting each other's needs—whatever form it takes.

Going against the images and rules of society is not easy. We are
all so steeped in our culture's messages that it's sometimes hard to
know our own minds. And nonconformity often meets resistance. But
don't miss the opportunity. What you and your partner do together is
your own little secret; it's nobody else's business. Remember, the
life you live should be your own.

🙠 *With your partner, look at your relationship vision with new
eyes. Does it exactly reflect what the two of you want? Are there
items on the list that you feel should be there because that's what
a relationship is supposed to look like? Make any changes necessary to tailor it to your unique needs: "We each have red bicycles."
"We only sleep on satin sheets." "We don't eat anything that we
don't grow ourselves."*

I take time to go into a place of serenity today, shedding the pressures
of the outside world. With each deep breath I take, I release myself
from yet another "should" or "ought" that bombards our relationship.
I recognize that I'm free to be creative, to live out a relationship that
is unique, to express my own rich inner divinity.

Husbands are like fires. They go out when unattended.

—ZSA ZSA GABOR

Husbands and wives do go out when unattended; they go out to play somewhere else. Relationships need maintenance, a daily stoking of the fires—with conversation, affection, care and feeding. Otherwise the flame dies, passion smolders, and all that's left are ashes.

Too often we let our relationships burn down, not for lack of love, but for lack of attention. We become out of practice and out of touch, too tired or preoccupied to make the extra effort. Eventually our unattended partners start looking elsewhere for attention.

Are you playing with fire, letting your relationship cool down through neglecting to tend to it? It won't take much to begin to fan the flames—a kiss, a flower, an understanding ear, a funny story— *today.*

&. *You're both planning to take a shower today, aren't you? Do it together. It will give you a chance to talk . . . wash each other's back . . . whatever . . .*

In quiet prayer today, I allow myself to ponder any ways I may be neglecting my partner. I then visualize my relationship as smoldering coals. In my imagination, I begin to stoke the coals, adding attention until I see the flickering flames reignite.

> *Self-pity in its early stages is as snug as a feather mattress. Only when it hardens does it become uncomfortable.*
>
> —MAYA ANGELOU

"**O**h, poor me. My life is so hard, my partner is so cold and mean." "My partner just doesn't understand my childhood wounds." "Nobody will ever love me in the way that will really make me feel safe." "I'll never have the relationship I want." "There's nothing I can do!"

Well, not with that attitude, you won't. It's tempting to let ourselves drown in our own tears of woe, to let self-pity become an excuse for inaction. Feeling sorry for ourselves can seem comforting when we're feeling low. Certainly there are times when we need to allow ourselves to feel our own sorrow and console ourselves.

But self-pity in and of itself does nothing to improve the situation, and it can so easily cross that fine line into blame. When all our energy is focused on ourselves, it becomes rancid and we develop a disease called victimization. The best cure for self-pity is to wrestle one's attention away from oneself and find another focus for your concern. Our partner for example. What is troubling *them,* what wounds are still causing them pain, what sympathy can we offer for their suffering? The natural spiritual flow of energy is outward. Try it. Perhaps there is something that you can do for your partner that will make you both feel better.

🍃 *In your notebook, make a list of all your self-pitying thoughts about your relationship. Convert each item on your list by writing "I appreciate . . . ," filling in the blank with a way in which you have been blessed or fortunate. Share the appreciations with your partner.*

As I make a time of quiet today, I compassionately acknowledge the difficulties in my life and console myself over the hardships I face. Feeling my spirit strengthen, I accept the challenge of rising above these problems. I consider this illuminated idea: "Face my partner as lover, not victim."

Here is a bit of advice for every woman who wanted to take shop in school, for every man who harbors a secret wish to learn to make needlepoint pillows: Do it, and don't let anything or anyone stop you.

So many of the ways in which relationships become strained and boring have to do with the way we've been brainwashed into following the rules. And few rules are more personally devastating than the restrictions that define our boundaries as men and women.

It's never too late to satisfy the dormant rumblings of the lost self. So be all that you can be. Women, where's that wild-man energy? Men, worship your inner goddess!

🍃 *Name something that you've always wanted to do, or some quality that you wish you had more of, that you never explored because of your gender. Take one step today to learn that new skill or practice that trait. Enroll in an auto repair course. Buy a needlepoint kit. Make an assertive phone call. Volunteer to bottle-feed the injured animals at the ASPCA. Don't hesitate to enlist your partner's help.*

Today I look at the parts of myself that remain undeveloped, and the ways in which I have held on to the person I think I am. Entering my place of courage, I visualize myself using the resources of my relationship to evolve spiritually into the person I can be.

Do the thing, and you will have the power.

—RALPH WALDO EMERSON

You can probably name opportunities that have come up in your life that you passed up because you felt afraid or unsure, or incapable of meeting the challenge. Perhaps it was running for school office, or asking for a promotion, or skydiving, or inviting someone for a date. Whatever it was, and however it might have changed the course of your life, you missed out as well on the growth—the personal power—inherent in challenging your doubts and fears.

Your partner is offering you new opportunities to challenge your self-imposed limits, asking you to meet needs that will require you to confront entrenched character defenses, to stretch into unfamiliar territory. What your partner wants may feel unnatural to you, and practically impossible to accomplish. You may feel that granting your partner's request, which seems to require changing your very core, is a matter of capitulation, a giving in, losing ground in the turf wars you so tenaciously wage.

Quite the opposite is true. When we reach deep inside to bring out the part of ourselves that our partner demands, we are reclaiming our essence, the source of our power. We become who we are, instead of what we've been, which is someone else's idea of how we should be. It is the reclamation of that buried essence that we have been unconsciously yearning for. As we do the thing that is hardest, we restore our vitality and aliveness. This is the key to our personal and spiritual fulfillment.

❧ *Identify one of your partner's behavior-change requests that you have been resisting, one that sets your teeth on edge every time you even think about it. Take one small step to fulfilling that request today.*

In my place of inner peace, I work on responding to my partner's needs, moving away from my fear and concentrating on responding from a place of groundedness. In my safe place I acknowledge: "Stretching to love is the source of my deepest empowerment."

*I prefer to explore the most intimate moments, the
smaller, crystallized details we all hinge our lives on.*

—RITA DOVE

We're often exhorted to look at the big picture—the expanding
universe, the global economy, the national debt. We are fascinated by
massive undertakings—the race to build an international telecommun-
ications network, the colossal task of building the superconducting
supercollider, a megamovie about the return of the dinosaurs, a new
assault on Everest or Mars. What we often overlook is that every
major undertaking is a feat of attention to details—planning, schedules, scale models, teamwork, budgets, feasibility studies, training,
practice, simulations, paperwork.

The same is true of real love. Bouquets of long-stemmed roses
and anniversary vacations are wonderful, but they are the easily seen
hallmarks of love. It's the small gestures, not the grand ones, that
tell the tale, and contain the essential flavor of a relationship. The
errand run on the way home from work, the reassuring words in the
doctor's office, the look in the eyes, the unwavering reliability, are
what our relationship hinges on. These are the things that are most
profoundly affecting, or most painfully missed. This is what our
unconscious registers with crystal clarity.

🍂 *Pay attention to an easily overlooked detail in your relationship
today, something you might usually gloss over as being unimportant. Look over the list of caring behaviors requested by your
partner (Day 138) and choose the tiniest one, the one that seems
most insignificant to you—a gentle good-night kiss, the half-
teaspoon of honey they like drizzled over their grapefruit, bringing in the morning newspaper. Give your partner this target
behavior today.*

**Celebrating the sacred today, I visualize myself using a magnifying
glass to look at the beautiful intricacy of the details that make our
partnership work.**

Does any of this sound familiar: "Me? Stingy?" "Are you trying to tell me I'm jealous?" "I don't see myself as cold and cynical."

The negative qualities in ourselves that we are unaware of or don't acknowledge but that *others* know all about constitute our denied self. These denied traits, usually too painful to acknowledge, are sometimes introjected aspects of our parents that we particularly despise: an insistence that everything is fine when it isn't, a drive for perfection, compulsive eating in response to stress. To admit to these behaviors is to recognize that we *are* like our parents. Such a realization is too awful, so we refuse to see the truth.

Over the next three days, you will be invited to investigate your denied self.

🦫 *Title a new page in your notebook "My Denied Self." On each line, write down a negative trait that your partner has identified or criticized in you. For example: "You're too self-centered." "You have a subtle way of insulting people." "You can't take a joke."*

Now do the same with regard to comments from friends, family members, and coworkers. Put a check mark next to any criticisms you've heard from more than one source. Where there is overlap, there is likely to be truth.

I allow the quiet of meditation to help me relax my resistance and open my curiosity to the unknown in myself. I hold this thought in wonderment: "The pain of self-knowledge is the path to wholeness."

The delights of self discovery are always available.

—GAIL SHEEHY

Our denied self is revealed when we heatedly reject having negative character traits attributed to us by others. We don't recognize them and we feel we are being misunderstood. Our mate might accuse us of being a cheapskate, for example, when we would characterize ourselves as thrifty. A friend calls us high-strung when we feel we are just being enthusiastic. We may indeed be thrifty and enthusiastic, but in all likelihood we are also a high-strung cheapskate.

At other times, we reveal the hated traits of our denied self through our criticism of others, for what we dislike most in our partners and in others is often true of us. We complain that "you never want to make love" when the truth is that we don't initiate sex. This way we don't have to admit we are cold, or indifferent, or afraid, or shy. Or we scream in frustration, "You never tell me how you're feeling" to deflect our own inability to reveal our emotions. *Criticism is a form of exhibitionism;* what we deride in others is often a flagrant display of our own unsavory traits.

Such criticisms of our partner can serve a purpose: They actually enable us to see the traits we are blind to in ourselves. In learning to love in our partner the hated traits we project on them, we are able to love what we deny in ourselves as well, and mitigate our self-hatred.

❧ *On the same notebook page titled "My Denied Self," list the traits you hate most in your partner and in others. When you have finished, take a critical look through your list and see how each trait might actually describe you. Put a check mark next to those that do.*

In quiet prayer, I gently consider the traits I most disdain in my partner as hidden parts of my own character structure. I see acceptance of these qualities as an ultimate act of self-love. Today, this meditation is mine: "Loving the unlovable in my partner is the only path to true self-love."

It's so painful to hear our partner's criticisms, to see the less-than-savory behavior that surfaces in an intimate relationship. It's no wonder we try to distance ourselves from it, and try to lay the blame on our partners.

But accepting the awful truth about ourselves that we try so hard to deny can be tremendously liberating. For one thing, we find that our partners love us even with our flaws. After all, they've known all along about the qualities we've tried so hard to deny and to pin on them. More important, our partner's criticisms are like a map to buried treasure. In hunting down and accepting what we try so hard to keep under wraps, in stretching to change our damaging behavior, we become whole again.

🥄 *Think about a criticism you've made of your partner that you now recognize is true of you—your denied hostility or pettiness or overreacting. Tell your partner that you now understand that you have been projecting the quality onto them because it was too uncomfortable for you to see yourself as having this trait. Notice your relief and the closeness it creates between you.*

I move into a deeper contemplative state today, having released the tensions involved in deflecting criticisms and projecting negative traits on my partner. Embracing these traits as a fuller reality of myself, I bravely claim these words: "The truth will make me free!"

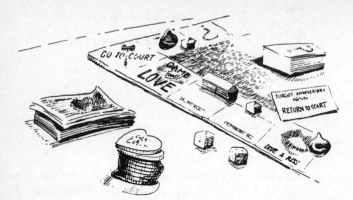

Maybe it's because we live in a consumer society in which we're bombarded with buy-and-sell messages that many people approach their relationship as though they were playing "Let's Make a Deal." They negotiate chores, make trades for favors, barter goods for services. "If you let me play golf this Saturday, I'll watch the kids on Sunday." "I'll come home from work earlier, if we can have sex." "I'm not going to take the car in for servicing unless you promise to be more careful about checking the oil regularly." Even therapists sometimes encourage this tit-for-tat bargaining, recommending to couples in conflict that they solve their problems by negotiating a contract that addresses their complaints.

All couples have to work out the division of life's labor and come to some agreement about who does the dishes and who the laundry. But relationships are not deals, and the caring we get because we've paid or traded for it never feels like the real thing—to either the giver or receiver.

🍃 *Give a caring behavior or a small gift to your partner today with no strings attached, and no expectation of something in return. Do it purely as an expression of love.*

Today I visualize the careful untying of each string with which I attach my partner to me. My deepest spirit acknowledges: "Gifts are free."

Divorce is defeat. . . . It's an adult failure.

—LUCILLE BALL

It's easy to get a divorce in our society. But though it may seem like a great escape from our problems and frustrations, it is hardly a victory.

When we learn how the Imago process works, it becomes clear that conflict is the grounds for a relationship, not, as we have been taught, for divorce. We are matched with our incompatible partners so that we can address old wounds and heal them. It is the conflicts we have with our partner, when squarely faced and worked through, that lead to growth and wholeness.

Staying in a relationship that seems riddled with insoluble problems is a hard choice when divorce seems the easy way out. But a conscious relationship also offers an escape from marital misery— skills and processes that lead to increased intimacy rather than separation. When both partners actively engage in the process and commit to working through our conflicts, we are on the road to healing.

🏖 *In your notebook today, under the heading "Frustrations," list your current grounds for divorce. Your partner's brutish (or nonexistent) lovemaking, their cold judgment, their refusal to help with the kids so you can take night courses? Instead of stewing and fantasizing about your escape, make an appointment for a mini-container exercise to express one frustration; then ask for a behavior-change request.*

Drawing strength from a centering prayer, I see myself as a long-distance runner, staying the course, reaching the goal of committed love. I affirm: "Success in my relationship is the result of facing up to conflicts."

Have you got your partner on a short leash? Do you ever feel like a trophy that your partner proudly displays? Our mates are not possessions, not trophies, not prize catches. Yet we are often tempted to exercise control over them in numerous—often unconscious—ways, fearful that they will escape. But the very act of holding tight will eventually make our partner want to pull away.

Possession may be nine-tenths of the law, but it's a much smaller fraction of love. Control is a tricky business. Once we start we have to be constantly vigilant to see that the fences are secure. It's far more effective to deal directly with our partner about matters of safety and insecurity, so that we can rest assured that our partner is with us by choice, rather than because of our threats or manipulation. Besides, everyone knows that a caged bird doesn't sing.

&♠ *Examine the ways you treat your mate as an object you think you possess. Write down any ways in which you schedule their time, screen their friends, budget their money, pass judgments on their clothes or activities. Or does your partner keep you on a short leash? Use the couples dialogue to discuss with your partner about allowing each other more freedom in a way that feels safe for you both.*

Closing my eyes in silence I breathe deeply. With each exhalation, I let go all forms of possessiveness and give my partner total freedom to be themselves. This thought comes in prayer: "Only in freedom can my partner truly be with me."

When you're learning, you're burning—putting out a lot of heat. When you're all burned up, then you become light.

—DA FREE JOHN

There's so much to learn, about ourselves, about our partner, about relationships. But we can't solve all our problems by reading books or attending discussions and workshops. There's no avoiding the hot crucible of conflict in which the deepest learning takes place. Though the learning that comes our way through our relationship is sometimes painful and difficult we should welcome it. In staying the course, dealing directly with our character defenses and conflicts—through trial and error, through the effort of years of struggle, we are burning away all that is dark, dysfunctional, and detrimental to real love. In learning to incubate the vital energy of love deep within our spirits, we break free into the light.

❧ *Learn something new about your partner today. Ask them to express a frustration with you that they have hesitated to share. Invite them to use the mini-container exercise, then respond with mirroring, validation, and especially empathy, so you can experience what it is like to enter into the experience of another.*

Taking time for the sacred today, I visualize all the troubles, worries, fears, and hurdles of our relationship being consumed in a fire of learning, until all that is left is the light of real love.

*If you do not worry about a misfortune for three
years, it will become a blessing.*

—HINDU PROVERB

Nothing can eclipse joyful feelings more effectively than worries.
Dark, tenacious, they block the sun. Some part of us knows that our
worries are screening out pleasure. Yet we can't seem to let go, as
though obsessing about our problems will somehow make them
disappear. Our minds become so wound up, like overfunctioning
machines, that our immune systems wear down. We take to bed with
a cold—it's a good excuse to relax. Yet we rail against the cold, upset
at the lost time, the work unfinished.

The things we worry about in our relationship—the continuing
fights, the scarcity of caring, the routinized sex—are unchanged by
chronic obsessing. Worry saps the energy that we need to do
something constructive about the problem. It robs life of its beauty
and vitality. If you were to spend the time that you now devote to
worrying about your problems to using the Imago process to do
something about them, you will find, three years from now, that
those very problems were the provocateurs of deep, pivotal change.
What you once labeled misfortunes can be transformed into blessings.

*At some point today, while on your lunch break or puttering
around the kitchen, set a timer for fifteen minutes. As the time
ticks by, indulge your worries to the fullest. This fifteen minutes
is carved out for them alone. After the fifteen minutes is up,
however, release them. The following meditation will help.*

**Today, in a period of quiet prayer, I visualize my worries as feathers
being tossed to the wind. I watch as they are whisked away. I trust
this process of releasing my worrisome issues, looking forward to the
day when I see them as blessings.**

If you continue to do what you have always done, you will continue to get what you have always gotten.

—ANONYMOUS

We get so stuck in our accustomed way of doing things, paralyzed by fear of rocking the boat, by lack of imagination, or by sheer inertia. But still we want things to be better: we want more love, more security, more fun. But how can we expect anything to be different if we keep acting in the same way, keep saying the same things? If a little yelling or a little withdrawal didn't get us what we want, will more of the same do the job?

It's a simple matter of cause and effect. If you want things to be different, you've got to start the ball rolling in a different direction. Doing something different does not require cataclysmic upheaval. Just a small behavior change—the insult withheld, the smile instead of the scathing glance, the simple act of caring or generosity—can have powerful repercussions.

❦ *Think about some way in which your relationship is in a rut, and about the repetitive behavior that created that rut. Do you eat the same thing for breakfast, go to sleep at the same time every night after you watch the eleven o'clock news, always respond angrily to your mate's request for help with the bills, patronize the same restaurant and movie theater every week for your Saturday night date? Today, make a small change in what you've always done: have blueberry pancakes for breakfast, make love while watching the news, go over the budget in a bubble bath, make dinner a picnic in the backyard.*

Today I summon joy and spontaneity from a place in my soul where God dwells to cocreate a richer relationship with my partner. I quietly utter this prayer: "With small changes come the promise of new beginnings."

Amazing grace! How sweet the sound
That saved a wretch like me!
I once was lost, but now am found,
Was blind, but now I see.

—JOHN NEWTON

Grace makes itself known in the amazing ways we've all experienced—someone synchronistically hands us the book that is just what we need at the moment; a vivid dream indicates the solution to a problem; an old trusted friend steps into our life just when we're in a crisis. Even our meeting with our Imago partner has a certain grace, because we are so perfect for each other's healing and spiritual journey.

When we are feeling wretched and overwhelmed by our troubles, we cannot see the grace in our lives, and we curse our fate. This is only the fault of our perception. Grace is as present when we are working through the process of healing our childhood wounds as it is when we are happy, but we are too blind to see it. When we feel stuck, it is hard to trust the universal web of love and order, nature's tendency to move toward healing and repair. We can indeed be saved by love, if we can but trust the unseen.

❧ *Open your eyes to the grace in your life today. Make a list of at least five amazing insights or experiences you've had with your partner. Share them in a couples dialogue tonight.*

Today I become aware that I can do many things to express love, but at some point I am no longer in control, and something larger than myself expresses itself. In peace, I surrender to the gift of grace that supports my conscious efforts.

Inside you there's an artist you don't know about.

— RUMI

Surprisingly, many of us have positive traits that we don't recognize but which others are aware of. When these traits are pointed out to us, we have been introduced to the disowned self. Even though the traits of our disowned self are not in themselves negative, we refuse to acknowledge them because they don't fit our self-image. If we see ourselves as being businesslike, for example, we may not want to acknowledge that we are also vulnerable.

Disowning of positive traits often relates to our gender conditioning. A man may downplay his love of cooking because he's been conditioned to think of it as women's work. A woman may reject her aggressive tendencies because they're unladylike.

Although people who know you well see your positive qualities, you may be embarrassed or fearful of possessing them. You might unconsciously suppress your nurturing instincts, for instance, if your environment stresses that having a career and being financially independent are more important than raising children. But those nurturing instincts will surface in other ways—taking care of friends, tending to sick animals, saving the whales. As part of reclaiming our true selves, we must own up to the sweet about ourselves as well as the bitter.

❧ *On a new page in your notebook labeled "My Disowned Self," list the positive traits others recognize and compliment you for but which you have a hard time believing or accepting. Look over this list of positive traits and see how each one might actually describe you.*

I confess my strength and beauty today and embrace this truth: "Pride is an expression of the divine."

When you do something you are proud of, dwell on it a little, praise yourself for it.

— MILDRED NEWMAN

How we admire—even envy—our partner sometimes: the magnetism that makes them the life of the party, the calm and collected way in which they respond in an emergency, their ability to articulate their thoughts and feelings. What we're often reacting to, however, is the disowned parts of ourselves that we've projected onto them.

What we adore in our partner is often undeveloped potential in ourselves, traits that were demeaned or discredited in the world in which we grew up. The love and care we needed seemed contingent on burying those parts of us, so we sacrificed our wholeness for acceptance. Now, when we might like to have those envied traits, it brings up conflict, and a feeling of disloyalty to those who said those very traits were not lovable.

Just as we must love in our partner what most frustrates us in order to accept those same qualities in ourselves, so too must we love *in ourselves* the qualities that we now love only in our partners. We must be proud of ourselves for what we admire in our partners, and praise ourselves as well.

🍂 *Recall a recent incident when you received a compliment, which you deflected. Recalling that compliment now, allow yourself to fully savor and acknowledge it. Say out loud, "This is true of me!" Share your pride with your partner.*

Breathing deeply, I visualize the disowned parts of my personality, seeing these nascent, undeveloped qualities as a fragile child dwelling within. I take this child onto my lap and hug it tightly, acknowledging this truth: "Joy will be mine when I embrace my full potential."

Sometimes our struggles with our partner seem so petty. But there is a larger purpose to these seemingly meaningless conflicts. In our struggle to heal our wounds, we are healing a wound in nature as well. The committed relationship is the conduit for nature's repair.

The wounds we bring to our partnerships are the culmination of thousands of years of untutored parenting and conflicted, loveless marriages. Failing to understand the source of their wounding, our parents and their parents pass their wounds on to their children, and the cycle continues.

Our wounds must be healed in the context in which they occurred—the committed dyadic partnership in which we reproduce our original environment. This has become possible only in recent history, now that marriages are no longer arranged. Couples can now consciously come together for the purpose of transforming their conflict into growth and healing, which breaks the cycle of the transmission of pain to the next generation of children. The healing of our relationships is the sacred, essential work of saving the planet.

❧ Do something today to heal your relationship. Grant your partner a behavior-change request; give them an extra caring behavior or two.

Today I visualize the wounds that I carry going back to our parents and our grandparents, spiraling endlessly into the dim past. This thought, my prayer: "With love and understanding, my partner and I can break the chain of wounding."

*I think the one lesson I have learned is that there is no
substitute for paying attention.*

—DIANE SAWYER

When we fall in love, we become enamored of our partner's every
deed and gesture. We hang on every word. But when we become
mired in the power struggle, we become equally fixated on our mate's
beastly behavior. We itemize every wart, every slight, every sideways
glance or harsh word. We collect evidence, specimens that prove
their perfidy. We're still paying attention, but our focus has shifted.

There is no substitute for paying attention to our partner, but we
often need to make a major shift in what we pay attention *to*. It may
require a change of heart, a compassionate awareness, to view our
partner from a more flattering angle. And it takes a bit of transcendence to allow them to exist as they are without turning them into a
copy of our projections. Our partner's good qualities would fill a book.
We need only change our focus to see them.

❧ *Be blind to your partner's faults today; have amnesia about
your gripes. Find that compassionate place in your heart. Focus
your attention on your partner without calling attention to what
you are doing. Write down every shred of evidence that your
partner is really terrific.*

**Today I move into quiet with increasing awareness that my attitude
affects what I notice about my partner. Restoring my spirit with
loving thoughts, I pledge this heart's vow: "I filter all impressions of
my partner through a compassionate heart."**

Physical pleasure is a sensual experience no different from pure seeing or the pure sensation with which a fine fruit fills the tongue.

—RAINER MARIA RILKE

Perhaps in no other area of our lives are we trained to measure our pleasure as in the area of sexuality. We compare ourselves to our friends, to movies, to former lovers, to articles we read in magazines. We want to know how long, how big, how often, am I like other people, did you come, was it good enough for you? Our enjoyment gets lost in the welter of taboos and statistics.

In a conscious relationship, the practice of pleasure is as important as the practice of communication or caretaking, and it requires the same atmosphere of safety and commitment. When couples fail to explore their potential for sexual pleasure, they are breaking their agreements to pursue the reclamation of their wholeness. Sexual union with our partners is a direct avenue to the aliveness and connectedness we seek, and should be measured only insofar as it moves us toward the reverberation of body and soul.

&. *Set aside time today for sexual pleasure, with no manuals, no orgasm counting, no preferred positions. The only goal is to feel safe and comfortable together.*

In time alone I envision sexual taboos and expectations as prison bars encasing my spirit, and picture myself breaking out of this prison and soaring to sexual and spiritual liberation.

How convenient to blame our partner for our problems. Acting as both judge and jury, we scan the evidence and declare our mate guilty of everything that is wrong between us. If only our partner would straighten out their problems—if only they would learn to communicate better, or make more money, or stop complaining—everything would be fine.

Take it on faith, you're half the problem. But because many of us grew up believing that no one could love us with our flaws and shortcomings, we desperately try and pin them on someone else. And who better than our partner? But admitting to our own culpability and finding that our partner still loves us—and respects us for our honesty to boot—take a big weight off our shoulders. There's even a chance for resolving the issue, instead of just meting out blame.

* *Think of a current conflict in your relationship that you've been blaming on your partner—the growing distance between you, a problem with your children, financial stresses. Identify your responsibility in this matter. Later today, talk with your partner about what you learned, and communicate your acceptance of the responsibility you disavowed earlier.*

Today as I enter the deep place within where God dwells, I allow myself to access the courage residing there. I accept my responsibility and free my partner of guilt. I acknowledge: "There is a healing value in confession."

*To be lucky in love requires falling in love many
times — and always with the same person.*

—MIGNON MCLAUGHLIN

The idea that we'll fall in love with just the right person and live happily ever after persists in spite of all evidence to the contrary. Fairy tales and Hollywood movies have conditioned us to expect everything to be smooth sailing after we say "I do." So why doesn't that happen in real life? It's a bummer. The minute we begin to feel safe and secure in our partner's love, to really believe that everything's going to turn out all right, our partner starts making demands and we see a side of them that they'd kept hidden.

We *can* live happily ever after, but first we have to slay the dragon. We do that by following love's path through storm and conflict, taking each scary step, changing and growing, along with our partner. As battles are won and wounds healed, as we see our partner's commitment deepen, we fall in love again and again with this stalwart person who is stretching to help us heal and grow. In a conscious relationship, we make our luck.

🌿 *In your notebook, itemize the lucky breaks in your relationship — the things you do for each other, the problems you've solved. Tell your partner how lucky in love you feel.*

Taking time for moments of ecstasy, I celebrate in prayer the riches of our journey together. I rejoice in the luck abounding in our relationship.

Wounded as children, trained to be responsible, exhorted to be good, we lose our innate aliveness. It's hard to remember how to have fun—how to walk in the rain, make funny faces, fly a kite, wear silly hats and blow party horns. Frivolity makes us nervous. It awakens old prohibitions.

Restoring our sense of aliveness goes with the territory of a conscious relationship. It's what happens as joy creeps back through the cracks in our armor. As we learn to trust our partner's love for us, somewhere inside of us, something wakes up, and we *want* to go out and play with our partner. We *want* to laugh and feel joyful. We recover our innate joy in just being alive, which is our deepest spiritual fulfillment.

ᨑ *Liven up your life. Take out your fun list and think of five new activities to add to it. Bubble bath? Foot tickling? Somersaults? Do something goofy today.*

In my time of quiet today I enter a place of joyful memory. I hold it in my mind, feeling the vitality of childhood aliveness, then merge the joyful feeling with an image of my current self until the two are one.

The art of love . . . is largely the art of persistence.
— DR. ALBERT ELLIS

So your partner forget your anniversary, and when reminded went out at the last minute and bought you a sweater two sizes too small in a color you don't like. They're still not helping with the laundry. And they haven't given you a single one of the caring behaviors from the list you made weeks ago. Well, if that isn't grounds for divorce!

At times we get so discouraged that it's hard to convince ourselves that things will get better, especially if we've been making an effort and our partner hasn't. It is at just such times that we need to step back from the fray, divorcing ourselves, not from our partner but from our anger and blame and sense of futility. This is the time for self-care and self-restoration, a time to renew our intention and our faith in the journey to real love. Things *will* change; they always do. Pulling back from despair and recrimination to renew your spiritual energy will assure that change will be for the better.

❧ *Take care of yourself today. Do something that is fun and relaxing and takes your mind off your problems. A long soak in the tub? A drive in the country? Lobster for lunch? Twenty minutes of staring into space?*

As I sit in quiet solitude today, I recognize the hard work of becoming an artist of love. For a moment I pause, breaking in and savoring my progress, renewing my spirit and my resolve to perfect this art.

The essence of pleasure is spontaneity.

—GERMAINE GREER

We humans are complex creatures. Though we crave reliable comfort and pleasure, eventually it loses its allure. Our neural system is designed to plateau after a period of regular input. Thus, after a few months of exchanging caring behaviors, you may be surprised to find that some of the original deep pleasure you experienced has diminished, and the loving attention that at first thrilled you has become predictable.

This is human nature. Though we enjoy presents on special occasions like birthdays, Christmas, and anniversaries, we come to take these gifts for granted. We want to be surprised; it's what's needed to spike our neural system again. That is how we are designed. Finding baseball tickets under your pillow, or unexpectedly having your favorite music played during dinner, or a surprise love note tucked into your lunch box—things like this have a powerful impact, creating a pleasant atmosphere of expectancy. It's the random, unanticipated gifts given purely out of love and affection that are the sweetest.

➚ *Begin a "Surprise List" for your partner, writing down at least three gifts or behaviors that would happily surprise them. Don't guess—instead draw on your memories of things that have pleased your partner in the past. Jot down hints or comments your partner has made about their specific likes and wants. Keep your list hidden.*

Moving into a place of inner strength, I experience a psychic shift as I let go of blame. I instead visualize myself being an agent of loving surprises. I let this phrase rest in my heart: "Joy is the greatest gift I could give to my partner."

Surprises, by Imago theory definition, are *random* caring behaviors above and beyond those requested by your partner. How do you know what surprises will touch your partner's heart? Your partner will tell you. If you listen carefully, you'll find that your partner frequently expresses interests, preferences, secret wishes, and dreams in day-to-day conversation.

So pay attention. Become a detective on the trail of your partner's hidden wishes and desires. Keep your ears open for clues. When your partner reminisces about how much fun they had going on an Easter egg hunt when they were a child, their secret thing for Silly Putty, or how they always wanted to spend just one first-class night on the town, you have uncovered a clue.

A surprise can be something you buy or make or do; whatever it is, your detective work tells you it will give your mate an unexpected thrill.

🍃 *Be a clue collector today! Listen carefully for the indirect hints your partner drops. Be especially attentive. As you unearth clues, you can begin to engineer future surprises. Add these to your list.*

I breathe deeply in this time of solitude, picturing my partner as a target, myself as an archer. Taking aim at their heart, I release arrows tipped with joy, and hear my partner laugh. Today I vow: "I can usher in the spontaneity that will heal my partner's childhood wounds."

Part of the pleasure of surprises is the enjoyment the giver has in planning them. Your partner experiences the thrill of receiving the surprise, but you get to know the rush of loving feelings as you give it. In addition, you actually get the surprise you give, because your old brain does not distinguish between what you give and what you get. It assumes that all action is directed to itself.

After pulling off a few successful surprises, it will feel more natural, a delightfully unpredictable element of your relationship. Continuing to give your partner random, unexpected surprises will sustain an air of expectancy; the biggest surprise of all will be your increasingly warm feelings toward your partner. More and more you'll see them as an opportunity to experience pleasure and joy.

🍂 *Choose one item from your list to surprise your partner with this week, and give it to them. It's okay to start with something simple like a single stem of a favorite flower, a limerick like the ones you used to write, or a pint of the year's first strawberries— your first surprise doesn't have to be the trip to Europe that has been a lifelong dream. When your partner surprises you, remember to acknowledge them appreciatively. Note the date of the surprises you give your partner on your surprise list or calendar; but no keeping track of the surprises your partner gives to you. Do a surprise no more than once a month.*

I'm aware in my time of meditation that these surprises, given without expecting anything in return, stretch me into new parts of myself increase my wholeness and joy. I celebrate these words: "Joy is in the giving."

Bickering over nothing is a sure sign of power struggle issues. Partners can fall into a rut of disagreeing for disagreement's sake— "You liked that movie? I thought it was the worst film I've ever seen." It's an indirect way of complaining that we're not getting what we need, or we're not being heard, without directly saying what our true feelings are or what we really want. Beneath the surface, the dialogue between the couple above is: "You don't love me!" "Yes, I do!" "No, you don't." "I do so!"

Who cares whether it's a bird or a plane anyway? Disagreeing with our partner can become an automatic response—it's how we tell each other (and convince ourselves) that our unhappiness is our partner's fault. But it doesn't solve any problems, nor do we learn anything about each other.

🍛 *All day today, be alert to signs of arguing over nothin'—what to have for dinner, the name of the little village where you ran out of gas last year. Check within yourself to see whether your disagreement with your partner reflects an issue you need to address directly or is just a habitual reaction. Ask your partner to engage in dialogue with you until you get your frustration clear.*

I open myself to renewal today and visualize our many petty arguments as a cover for deeper hurts. I utter in prayer: "Empathy heals."

*What I cannot love, I overlook. Is that real
friendship?*

—ANAÏS NIN

So often, when it comes to our partner's shortcomings, we overlook *nothing*. We notice the button left undone (the slob!). We grumble because they didn't say *please* pass the mayonnaise (how rude!). And they left the cap off the toothpaste again.

The cap off the toothpaste? Such a hard life we have living with such a terrible person. When we're unhappy enough, we can find something wrong with every little thing our partner says or does. With friends like us, as they say, who needs enemies?

Finding fault with our partner, blaming someone else for our misery, is such a safe, indirect way of expressing our unhappiness, a way of proving to ourselves the legitimacy of our misery. How much more friendly to divert the attention we give to identifying and enumerating our partner's faults to itemizing their good qualities in comparable detail. We probably wouldn't have much time left over for gratuitous faultfinding. Once we got into the habit of overlooking our partner's faults, we'd probably forget about most of them—the small, inconsequential ones, anyway. Out of mind, out of sight.

🍂 *List three traits you like most about your partner: their persistence, their snuggling style, their cornball jokes. Think about each one for a minute; fully experience how your partner expresses that trait. Tonight, before you go to bed, take your partner's hand, look deeply into their eyes, and say, "Three things about you that I think are really terrific are . . ."*

I visualize my partner's body covered with words describing all their good and bad traits. As I look on, all the words describing their good traits get bigger and bolder and brighter, and all the words describing their negative traits get smaller and more and more difficult to read. Though I know my partner has negative traits, I can barely see them now. I offer this truth in prayer: "In real love, there is no criticism."

Too much of a good thing is wonderful.

—MAE WEST

Sometimes we get parsimonious about love—too few hugs, too few compliments, too little time for each other. Sometimes this stinginess is our reaction to anger or hurt with our partner, so we parcel out our affection in proportion to what's coming in. More often our frugality reflects the scarcity or impermissibility of pleasure in childhood, our indoctrination that fun or pleasure is "evil." We take no pleasure in pleasure. And we find ourselves spiritually bankrupt.

There is no upper limit to the joys and pleasures of love. The supply is unlimited, so rationing is unnecessary. Time to begin retraining your old brain to revel in intense and abundant pleasure.

❧ *Come up with something that you and your partner can do today to stretch the limits of your potential for joy. A kiss-a-thon? Ten minutes of belly laughing? Staying in bed till noon? The world's largest banana split? Go for it!*

I spend my quiet time today visualizing too much love, too many kisses, excessive fun. I allow myself to be carried away by the pleasures of unlimited love and affection. I celebrate the power of the spirit within, saying: "There is no upper limit to joy."

Creative minds have always been known to survive any kind of bad training.

—ANNA FREUD

To some extent, we were all badly trained for relationships, raised by parents wounded themselves, in a society unschooled in the care of children. Many of us were pretty severely damaged, and it shows in the tempestuous tenor of our relationships. When we see the ways in which we continue to sabotage our happiness, the hurtful and unproductive ways in which we continue to behave, the picture looks bleak. Lacking in personal resources and in an awareness of how to turn our situation around, we blame our parents, or society, for our plight. Twenty years after we left home, we're still complaining—to our friends, our partners, and our therapists—about our alcoholic mother, our critical father, the year we moved four times, the time our brother locked us in the closet.

It is important to grieve for the pain and inadequate nurturing we received as children. But at some point we must put aside blame, quit looking outside ourselves for solutions, and take responsibility for getting the love we want. The only way to do this is to unlearn our old habits and learn to love.

No matter how stuck we feel, no matter how awful our childhood, it can be overcome. This is the blessing of a conscious relationship. The way things work, our Imago partner has usually sustained wounds of comparable severity. Pooling our creativity and our determination, we commit to overcoming our bad training, learning new behaviors to replace the bad habits we learned so long ago.

❧ *In dialogue with your partner today, come up with a creative solution for overcoming a difficult, seemingly intractable problem. See if you can devise a new approach to replace one that hasn't been working.*

Moving to a place of inner calm, I see the robotic habits and patterns that control me. I open myself to prayer and drink from the wellspring of compassion for my parents, my partner, and myself. Letting go of all blame for my past, I see myself coming alive with creativity.

*Pray inwardly, even if you do not enjoy it. It does
good, though you feel nothing. Yes, even though you
think you are doing nothing.*

—JULIAN OF NORWICH

If taking daily time for quiet and solitude is new for you, you may at
times feel discouraged as you move through the meditations in this
book. When at last we make the time to sit in stillness and cultivate
our inner life, we are often discouraged at the incessant inner chatter,
the fear and resistance and obstacles that arise. We are disappointed
not to be immediately rewarded wth inner peace, enlightenment, and
transformed relationships. Either we've failed, we think, or meditation doesn't work.

Simply sitting quietly, emptying one's mind and opening one's
heart, is an extremely difficult discipline, for which most of us have
little training. We know a great deal about how to be busy, we are
skilled at analysis, a whiz when it comes to getting things done; but
this meditation stuff is not exactly up our alley. What we need more
than anything is patience, and faith in the process. We must trust that
our bodies and souls crave a time for stillness, that this valuable form
of inner nourishment is worth our discomfort and frustration. Just the
act of sitting, the opening of ourselves to the God within, the mere
intention to give ourselves this gift of inner spaciousness, is sending
a message to our soul.

❧ *Validate your intention to find quiet time for yourself each day
by enhancing your place of solitude. Find images that are meaningful to you—a postcard of natural beauty, a picture of a
religious or spiritual figure with whom you connect. Bring in
candles or incense, or your favorite music.*

**During my time of quiet, I become aware of my restlessness and
recognize it as resistance to stillness. I breathe prayerfully and relax
into my discontent, releasing it slowly with each exhalation, holding
only this thought: "Meditation is doing one thing at a time with my
whole being."**

Sometimes, after years of fruitless conflict, the intensity of the power struggle burns itself out. The name calling stops, the anger turns to resignation, hopes fade, and partners settle into a kind of peaceful accommodation. They're used to each other, they've worked out the logistics of house and kids and chores. Though they've found a way to live in the same house, and perhaps even sleep in the same bed, they essentially live separate lives. She lunches with her friends, he goes fishing with his buddies, she knits while he watches the ball game, they rally together for the holidays. They're not unhappy, and they may even love each other, but there are no signs of passion.

When our relationship gets into a rut, a kind of inertia takes over, and what we end up with is an "invisible" divorce. It becomes hard to summon the energy and interest to exert the necessary effort to effect change. But when we give up trying to make things better, and let things slide rather than facing our conflict and speaking our truth, we are settling for second best. We may find peace and quiet of sorts, but we will never heal our deepest wounds, never recover our joyful aliveness.

❧ Have a couples dialogue with your partner about your adherence to the Imago process; focus especially on the ways in which you have slacked off in your commitment to fulfilling your dream of real love. Pick out something that you will work to improve together—more time to talk or just hang out together, more fun, better sex, updating your behavior-change request lists, closing another exit.

Making time for renewal, I acknowledge the ways I've simply given up. Gratified over the miracles of faith, I look afresh at my relationship. My hopeful prayer: "It's never too late for the birth of new love."

How love the limb-loosener sweeps me away . . .

— SAPPHO

Fantasies notwithstanding, most of us are afraid of being swept away by love. Wounded as children, hurt in past relationships, we aren't about to let ourselves get too carried away. Wary, withholding, skeptical, we're careful to keep one foot on the ground, afraid to trust our feelings until we're absolutely sure we won't be hurt again. We adopt a wait-and-see attitude.

Our very protectiveness keeps us from giving ourselves over to the power of love. But the safety we seek cannot be found in the restrictive security of a life jacket, something outside ourselves that gives us the illusion of keeping a toehold on safe ground. We can only be swept away when we know without doubt we are safe in the sea itself, sure that we will be buoyed up as we careen through the wildest waves. Our relationship itself must feel safe, and that feeling must be created with endless deeds of caring. How delicious, how liberating it is to give ourselves over fully to love, to put aside questions of who's right, to jettison fear, to cast practicality to the winds, leaving the world, and our fears, behind. Sweet surrender!

🐚 *In dialogue today, share with your partner your fears of letting go and expressing your love without restraint. Ask your partner to share their concerns with you.*

In my time of quiet today, I picture myself standing on the shore of an ocean of love on a balmy day. I am fully dressed in my worries and fears, wearing a life jacket to protect myself from danger. Piece by piece, I remove the life jacket and my clothes, pretending that each is part of my fear. I cast myself into the waves and am carried out to sea, free and buoyant. I surrender to the power of love.

"You want me to do *what?!*" Sometimes when our partner makes a behavior-change request we want to throw up our hands! How could we have connected with someone with such strange needs, someone whose demands require that we so drastically change the way we are? We rant and fume and resist—our partner is asking the impossible.

Too much for today, anyway. We don't have to change all at once; but perhaps we can change little by little, day by day. Keep in mind that when we balk at our partner's demands, it is often because our partner's request stirs up a part of ourselves that has been buried or denied. In stretching to fulfill our partner's need, overcoming discomfort and anxiety, we restore that lost part of ourselves. We rediscover our God-essence. We become whole.

   🐾 *Think of a behavior-change request your partner has made but you haven't yet granted because you think it is too difficult or even impossible. You know, the one behavior you think you're never going to change (it's probably also the one your partner most needs from you). Look again at your resistance, and see what personal gain there might be in granting this request. What small step could you take today to stretch a bit in this direction? Decide what it is, take a deep breath, and do it!*

Renewing my spiritual courage, I face the one thing my partner has asked me to change that seems impossible. I visualize myself making this shift, giving my partner the desired behavior, and see us both being transformed into a state of greater wholeness. I hold this image for twenty minutes: "We are the energy of love."

I have often wished I had time to cultivate modesty. . . . But I am too busy thinking about myself.

—EDITH SITWELL

Most of us operate on the unconscious assumption that others' experience—what they think, feel, want, and do—is identical or similar to our own. When we find out it is not, we devalue, reject, or deny the alien experience: "I can't imagine anyone eating well-done steak." "Why that should upset you I'll never understand." "I don't believe you really feel that way." Because our partner's experience doesn't conform to the way things are in our world (the only world we know), we are literally unable to comprehend them.

This is symbiosis, the inability to see the world as others see it, to value it, or even to acknowledge that such a world exists. A sign of symbiosis is the feeling that "We are one, and *I* am the one." This self-referential stance is a common response to childhood pain, the me-first attitude we felt we had to adopt in order to get enough love and care to survive.

In a conscious relationship, the cure for symbiosis is the diligent practice of the couples dialogue. When we actively listen to what our partner says in order to mirror them, when we verbalize our acceptance of their point of view in the act of validation, and open our hearts to feel their experience in the act of empathizing, we reawaken the innate compassion that we lost in the course of our wounding. It is a soul-expanding practice.

Make today a validation day. Make a conscious effort to validate your partner whenever they express themselves today: "I can see why you thought I was being petty." "I understand why you found that movie so hilarious."

I use my time of quiet to connect to the life force at my core, replenishing my resources so that I can see my partner's inner world. I treasure this wisdom: "Renewing my inner spirit prepares me to accept my partner's reality as being equally valid as my own."

Though we do a pretty convincing job of presenting ourselves as adults, inside each one of us there is still a child who remembers all the hurts we ever suffered and all the times we felt unsafe. We try so hard to armor ourselves against the slings and arrows of the world with our trappings and titles. But beneath it all, we are still bearing the wounds of childhood and longing for their healing.

In a conscious relationship, we slowly build trust that we won't be injured again, that those things that made us insecure in the past have no part in our present life. We do this by learning the details of our partner's wound, the unfinished business they have brought to us for healing, and we act as balm for those wounds. As our partner gains confidence in our healing ministrations, we create a cocoon of safety for that hurt child to come out and play.

❧ *Tonight, when you go to bed, put your arms around your partner and remember the wounded child inside. Hold and comfort that child as you fall asleep.*

Today in a holy stillness, I find a loving place where I recognize when my partner is reacting from a place of old injury. In this place I imagine the skills I can cultivate to make the five-year-old in my spouse feel safe and comforted. I acknowledge this potential: "I am my partner's healer."

All married couples should learn the art of battle as they should learn the art of making love. . . . Good battle . . . brings to a marriage the principles of equal partnership.

—ANN LANDERS

A container day is an expanded version of the containment process stretched over a twenty-four-hour period. During this time one partner is given carte blanche to express frustrations as they arise for a full day, while the other partner stays in containment mode. On a container day, no specific appointments are required.

Remember, a safe and healthy environment, or container, for our feelings involves *appropriate expression* and *appropriate reception* within agreed-upon parameters. Only one partner expresses at a time; healing and resolution can occur only if expressed feelings are fully and nonreactively received. "I" language is used to describe the frustrating behavior: "I feel so ignored when you pay more attention to the cats than you do to me." On a container day, the receiver listens, mirrors, validates, and empathizes all day without responding with communications of their own about their partner's frustrations. The sender simply expresses feelings as they arise, honoring the safety guidelines. The next day the receiving partner sends, but they must express only what comes up that day. No expressing frustrations about their partner's complaints the day before.

❧ *Review the guidelines and instructions for the containment process on Days 122 through 128. With your partner, decide who will be the sender and who the receiver. Begin your first container day right now.*

I go within and acknowledge how difficult it may be to contain my partner for a full twenty-four hours. So I move to that inner space that allows for growth and largesse, holding this prayer in faith: "Containing my partner for a whole day is teaching me the art of self-transcendence."

Fidelity means that when a woman wakes in the middle of the night from a frightening dream and feels lonely and worthless and afraid, she does not hesitate to reach for her husband, knowing that he has the strength, confidence, and tenderness to exorcise her primordial fears. It means she knows that not to seek his consolation under such circumstances would be infidelity, because it would mean that she is not willing to share with him her most intimate feelings of weakness.

—ANDREW GREELEY

To have a healing, loving relationship is to feel enough trust and safety to allow our partners to know every part of ourselves. Extending the healing effect of a containment process over the longer period of a day allows our deepest feelings to emerge and further reduces our fear of anger. As our fear of anger decreases, our relationship becomes safer and intimacy is deepened.

Container days provide a safe environment in which you and your partner can express frustrations and negative feelings of all kinds. Few of us have ever been in surroundings in which this was possible without fear of unpleasant consequences. As you allow each other frequent container days, you will both become more and more comfortable with the process. The expression of anger will become a normal and cleansing part of your life that brings you closer together, instead of something to fear and dread that pulls you apart. And your relationship will become a place where all your feelings can be expressed and accepted.

🍃 *Switch roles with your partner and do another container day today. Practicing this process for ninety days tends to replace defensive reactivity to frustrations with mirroring. Give it a try.*

Container days can be done mechanically. Then again, they can be done in the spirit of love. In prayer today, I draw upon my deepest resources so that I can meet my partner with the desired attitude and spirit. My partner feels that they are the beneficiary. But in this process, it is my own heart that is being enlarged.

*We challenge one another to be funnier and
smarter. . . . It's the way friends make love to one
another.*

—ANNIE GOTTLIEB

There are many ways to make love that have nothing to do with the numerous and elaborate positions of the Kama Sutra. Some of these ways are pretty obvious—the kiss and caress, the appreciation we express, the thoughtful gift.

But conversation is also a form of intercourse, with an endless variety of moods and positions. When we laugh together, when we goad each other into the next excruciatingly clever pun, when we truly engage each other in heated and passionate discussion, we are making love in a way that only intimate partners can share.

Unattended, devoid of challenge, our relationships fall into the doldrums. Without a mirror to reflect back to us our wit and intelligence, we look elsewhere to show off our stuff. We save our sparkling repartee for cocktail parties, apply our brainpower to looking good on the job. Partners in a conscious relationship are too clever by far to let that happen. They take up the challenge of keeping things lively. They call it making love.

❧ *Make it a point to tell your partner a joke or a story; brag about a problem you've solved; play a word game; quiz each other on state capitals or foods that start with Q.*

Today I tap into my spiritual resilience to visualize making love to my partner in all sorts of cerebral, riotous, spontaneous, nonsexual ways! I visualize each tease, each dare, each boast adding lively sparkle to our life together.

A human becomes an I through a You.

—MARTIN BUBER

Accustomed to seeing others as objects for our own gratification, it is hard for us to learn to see our partner as having value independent of their utility. We measure their worth in terms of what they are doing for *us,* how they are making *us* feel, which of their qualities are valuable to *us.* Our love is contingent on their usefulness. When we rate our partner according to the number of compliments they gave us this week, or the birthday gift they chose for us, or the amount of money they bring in, we are *in need* with our partners, not *in love.*

Love cannot exist until you see your partner as someone other than yourself, separate and unconnected to your needs. It is in loving your partner just because they are another being, equal in value to yourself, with their own thoughts and needs, that they can be transformed in your mind from an object to a subject.

Writing about the I/Thou relationship, theologian Martin Buber suggests that when two people love one another without conditions, then God is present. We can treat our partners as objects only as long as we remain closed to their inner world, so long as we insist that they are merely extensions of ourselves, and therefore the same. In practicing the couples dialogue, we are forced to give up the notion that there is only one world—the one that revolves around us—and we discover our partner as a subject. We become aware of our partner's own unique world and validate their independent existence. "I and you" becomes "I and Thou."

❧ *Identify five ways in which you expect your partner to be just like you. Pick one area, and in dialogue today, ask your partner to share their feelings with you about this topic. Instead of defending your opinion, try to really listen to what they have to say, and learn something about this new world.*

Today, I recognize that my need to merge my partner into my world indicates my failure to merge with my deepest self. I seek the foundation within that allows me to see my partner as separate and equal in value to me. In prayer, I contemplate this insight: "In honoring the deepest needs in my partner, I honor the deepest needs in myself."

Most people don't want your advice. They want your support.

—ANONYMOUS

We all act at times as if we're Ann Landers, giving our partner advice whether they want it or not. We think we know just what our partner needs, what our partner should do, even when they should think and feel and say. Our reasoning is that they should do what *we* would do. "If I were you. . . ," we venture, as if such a thing were possible.

Offering our wisdom to our partner has its place, and our concern is often welcome. But we need to be careful of the manner, the quality, and the intention with which we parcel out advice. A good indication of when to give advice is an invitation from our partner for our opinion. After all, they have their own ideas about what is good for them. They don't need a daily barrage of criticism or homework assignments or wisdom from us. We cannot fix them. Our constant second-guessing of what is good for our partners can eclipse their inner core of faith in themselves.

❧ *Don't offer any advice to your partner today unless they ask for it. Try it for one day and see if you can notice the difference it makes.*

When I talk to an animal, it simply sits there and stares. It seems to accept everything that I say, and doesn't have an overwhelming need to fix anything. Today in my time of quiet I draw on a deeper spiritual energy and cultivate the patience necessary to recognize that my partner is capable of taking care of themselves. I learn to listen to my partner as my pet might listen to me.

To love deeply in one direction makes us more loving in all others.

—MADAME SWETCHINE

A funny thing happens when we truly love our partner: we are more loving to everyone else as well. Once we discover that part of ourselves that loves, it spills over into all our relationships, to humankind, and to all of creation. As we become more whole through loving our partners, as our sense of safety increases, we free up the rich spiritual energy that we have been spending to protect and defend ourselves. We no longer spend our time in argument or despair or criticism or fear. The tensions in our bodies relax, our heart beats more calmly, our breathing slows. Less self-centered and consumed with our own survival, we have the wherewithal and the self-assurance to reach out and spread our love in the world.

Our troubled world, and our communities, desperately need each of our contributions. Our ability to make a difference in the world begins at home, with learning to love our partners, so that there will be plenty of love to go around.

ɞ *Discuss with your partner today a specific way that you can spread your love out into your world—to a needy friend or family member, to your community, or a local charity. Volunteer to clean up the park, visit rest homes, take care of a sick friend's kids, plant trees.*

Drawing strength from a period of stillness, I relax into the love between my partner and myself. I hold this thought in quiet prayer: "As our love grows, it expands into the world around us."

*One of the oldest human needs is having someone to
wonder when you are coming home at night.*

— MARGARET MEAD

Sometimes we feel limited by the imagined restrictions of our
relationships—"If I were single again, I could just stay out and watch
the game at the bar." "If it weren't for my partner, I could take that
vacation to Peru." But, really, would we trade places with our single
friends?

Very few things about our childhoods were more influential than
whether our parents were there when we needed them. To this day
that very human need persists, no matter how reliable our caretakers
were, no matter how well we've compensated for any past unreliabil-
ity, no matter how independent we've become. This is true for the
captain of industry, the factory foreman, and the daredevil stunt-
woman.

We all want someone to come home to. No matter how busy and
self-sufficient we are, there is something reassuring about being
welcomed home by our partner after a long day of slaying the dragons
of commerce or child care. Being reliable for our partner is a basic
ground rule of a conscious relationship. Just being there satisfies a
basic human need for security.

*Greet your partner with a warm embrace this evening and tell
them simply how good it is to have them in your life, and how
much you look forward to seeing them at the end of a long day.*

**Today I offer thanksgiving for the constancy of my partner's presence
in my life. I hold this thought: "As we are more rooted in each other,
we are more rooted in the power of the ultimate."**

Have you even wondered how it all happened? How one day you thought your partner was the answer to your dreams, and now that you are awake, you are living in a nightmare? It's that way for a reason. Nature knows that if you had known the unvarnished truth about your partner from the beginning, you would have run screaming in the opposite direction. So nature created romantic love to numb you to the harsh reality of the problems you will face with your partner. By the time the romance fades—when the scales fall from your eyes and you see the awful truth of your Imago partner—it's already too late. You're hooked.

Romantic love is nature's anesthesia, a dirty trick to bond us to our partner so that we are willing to go through the struggle to real love. The intensity with which we fall in love is an indication of the degree of our need. Nonetheless, romantic love *is* wonderful: it is nature's siren call to healing and self-completion.

• *Describe in your notebook your partner when you met, and your partner today; note the differences. Considering that your disappointment is natural and universal, focus on the positive that is still there, ignore the negative, and, throwing caution to the wind, do something incurably romantic today.*

I strengthen my inner spirit with this thought: "Romantic love is only a window to the paradise of real love."

The loving are the daring.

—BAYARD TAYLOR

How many times do we wish we could just go away and not have to deal with the anger and disappointments, not even have to look at our partner?

Most of us, of course, don't run away. We stay with our partners but avoid conflict. We busy ourselves with work and outside interests and the children. We keep our secrets, nurse our wounds in private, and hope for the best. It's only a partial solution, and it's not real love.

Love never comes easily, except maybe to infants and kittens. To love fully and be loved is a high-risk proposition, involving daring feats of self-disclosure, death-defying exertions in our partner's name. To love someone, to go through the valley of anger and conflict without flinching or pulling back, requires courage and tenacity. It's not for the fainthearted. To stay with the Imago process day after day, learning and practicing difficult or tedious new skills, is a daily act of daring for which you deserve credit. Congratulate yourself for facing the challenge of this great adventure!

❧ *Do something daring today. Face a problem you've been avoiding; use the containment process to say what's on your mind; fulfill a difficult behavior-change request; ask your partner for something outrageous.*

In quiet contemplation today, I descend into the depth of my courage and bravery and imagine myself going beyond the boundaries to create an outrageous new aspect of our relationship that deepens our love.

You grow up the day you have your first real laugh at yourself.

—ETHEL BARRYMORE

It's hard to do—to laugh at yourself. Almost as hard as growing up. Our society rewards us for being businesslike, solemn, respectable. We carefully groom our image in the world to convey confidence, competence, or stylish charm. Not a hair or an adjective is out of place. We take ourselves *so* seriously.

In our intimate relationships, though, it's impossible to hold it together every minute. Our partner sees the unedited version—the clumsiness, the mistakes, the valiant attempts to hold in our stomach. Our partner knows about the time our fly was open when we made the big speech, the time we introduced the boss's wife by the wrong name, the time our bridge work fell out at the dance. Isn't it a relief that someone knows the truth and still thinks we're grand?

So lighten up! Teasing, joking, mimicry make our all-too-human foibles okay. Laughter comes from the spirit and allows for the magic, the transcendency that can transform the negativity between you and your partner. If we can laugh at ourselves—if we can be the first to laugh—we are on the way to accepting ourselves, all of ourselves, just as we are.

&❧ *Go look in a mirror and make faces at yourself until you laugh. Tonight, tell a funny story about yourself. Then ask your partner to tell you about a time when you did something goofy, or absentminded, or embarrassing. Be the first to laugh.*

In my time of sacred solitude today, I relax into a hall of mirrors in which I see many distorted images of myself. As I relax even deeper, I release my seriousness and allow a laugh to come up from deep inside me. This release is a step toward spiritual freedom.

Love doesn't make the world go 'round. Love is what makes the ride worthwhile.

—ELLA FITZGERALD

We are all on life's roller coaster, with its ups and downs, twists and turns. At times life is smooth and easy; at others we are beset by problems and crisis. But what makes life tolerable and worthwhile is the love that accompanies us on the ride. This love is not something we find by the side of the road. We must create it through our actions and intentions. Whatever our outer circumstances, a life where love is scarce is a bumpy journey. But when we have love in reserve, it can be a powerful buffer against hard times.

❧ *Do something today to make the ride worthwhile. Tell your partner that you would like to do something to make them feel loved. Let them choose it—a special meal, or special words they want to hear, a behavior change they would like from you. Whatever it is, grant their wish.*

Today I visualize the journey of our relationship as a road in which there have been stretches of smooth pavement, interspersed with patches of slippery rocks and high mountains, even walls that seemed impossible to scale. I reaffirm my intention to make the ride worthwhile, with acts of love to smooth the way.

What we must decide is how we are valuable, rather than how valuable we are.

— CHRISTOPHER ISHERWOOD

We all have attributes that are of value—to ourselves and to others. We award points for looks, income potential, entertainment value, parenting skills, kindness. We tally up our assets, determine our personal worth, and put a price tag on ourselves. Then we expect our partner to make it worth our while to expend our assets in their service. And once we've determined what it is that we deserve in return, we spend more of our time making sure that we're getting a fair trade than spending our valuable assets to give our partners what they need.

Like cash kept in a safe-deposit box, hoarded personal assets actually decrease in value. When we spend freely of our ample gifts, we generate an abundance of love, energy, expertise, knowledge, attention, and much more wealth that both we and our partner can draw upon.

Marketplace economics have no relevance to relationships. Instead of dwelling on whether we are being repaid in kind, whether we're showing a profit or loss, we should be trying to see how our assets can add value to our partnership. How can you contribute to your mutual growth? What do you have to give to your partner? Where is that generosity of spirit?

&❧ *Give your partner something of yourself that is of value to them today. Does your partner need some help refinishing a piece of furniture, choosing some new clothes, moving some boxes? Would a little extra affection or concern be of value?*

In wordless prayer today, I contemplate the qualities and skills that I can make available for use in my relationship. I picture myself filling a large box with these attributes and presenting them to my partner.

To thine own self be true. . . . Thou canst not then be false to any man.

— WILLIAM SHAKESPEARE

We begin keeping secrets as children, hiding certain thoughts and behaviors from adults. If Dad thinks our imaginary playmate is babyish, we talk to her only when we're sure no one can hear us. We sneak sugar from the sugar bowl because we've been scolded for doing it in the past. We play doctor when we know we won't get caught. We figure out that if we want to suck our thumb or play with our genitals, we'd better keep it to ourselves. We develop a hidden self, known to us but unknown to others.

As we grow older, we learn, if we're lucky, that society's rules aren't all they're cracked up to be, and that we can set our own standards. We are able to let go of some of the guilt and shame that normally attend going against society's demands, and find ways of being ourselves and preserving our idiosyncrasies and our own way of doing things—as long as we don't tell anyone. For the next three days, you'll be guided in looking at your hidden self and see if that secrecy is helping or hindering your desire to be whole.

&❧ *At the top of a new page in your notebook, write "My Hidden Self." Ponder for a few minutes the traits and habits that you keep hidden from others, traits that don't fit your public persona or that would embarrass you if others knew about them. Write each one down as if you were completing the following sentence: "What would people think if they knew . . ."*

In my safe place today, I meditate on the hidden places within me and the shame I sometimes feel about them, and tenderly embrace them as my "inner children." I hold this thought: "Embracing the hidden parts of me is an act of self-love."

Our hidden self is made of the things we believe or do that we keep to ourselves in order to avoid criticism or judgment. What are examples of hidden-self traits? "I write love songs that publishers keep turning down." "I cheated on my husband." "I sometimes wear the same underwear for three days straight." "I eat dinner straight out of a can."

Keeping your hidden self under wraps requires energy and vigilance. But many hidden-self traits are parts of your authentic core self that deserve to go out in public with you—your teary response to movies, your love songs, or playing the flute. For one thing, once our secrets come out into the open, they often lose their dark, shameful quality, and we are able to enjoy them as a gift of ourselves to ourselves.

❦ *Look again over your list of hidden-self traits. Decide which should remain private and which should go public. Select one that stands a good chance of being accepted in a hospitable environment.*

Reflecting on the way I present myself to others, I take a new perspective. As I enter my safe sanctuary, I envision myself going public with parts of myself that can be shared with others without shame. I relax into this thought: "It is okay to let others know who I am."

I think Dostoevsky was right, that every human being must have a point at which he stands against culture, where he says, this is me and the damned world can go to hell.

—ROLLO MAY

The problem with many of our hidden-self traits is not the traits themselves; we all have secrets, we all have our little ways. The issue is: what motivates our secrecy? Do we keep parts of ourselves hidden because we are ashamed of who we are, afraid that our behavior would draw ridicule or rejection? Are our secrets a barrier to intimacy with our partner?

Some of our hidden-self traits are inherently private: masturbation is not appropriate public behavior, and no one is interested in seeing us wolf down a quart of ice cream standing in front of the refrigerator.

But in many cases, the problem is not you but society's stifling rules. What you really need is a more tolerant environment than the one you grew up in, one that enables you to reclaim your authentic self, to regain confidence that you're okay as you are. That environment begins in your home, with your partner.

🍂 *Share one of your secrets with your partner—perhaps the trait you identified yesterday—and ask your partner to do the same. Welcome the confidence your partner reveals to you.*

In time of prayer, I celebrate eccentricity! I envision daylight surrounding my secrets, and honor this thought: "I cherish my partner's secrets, as well as my own."

To behave with dignity is nothing less than to allow people to be themselves.

　　　　　　　　　　　　　　　—SOL CHANELESS

One of the benefits of having a partner who loves and accepts us unconditionally is that we have an ally who can encourage us to be ourselves, a friend with whom we can practice being eccentric in the best sense of the word.

Our home should be a safe haven where, protected from the stares and comments of society, we can explore expressing those parts of ourselves we used to think we must hide. Here it is safe to practice our yodeling or clog dancing, safe to lick the icing off the Oreos, to watch "The Newlywed Game" without embarrassment, to spend the day in our bathrobe without guilt.

Sharing secrets with your partner builds intimacy. As you and your partner reveal your secrets, you can be for each other a bulwark against the judgments of the world.

🍃 *Today, select another trait from your list of hidden-self traits and pick a close friend or coworker and share it with them.*

In quiet, I rejoice over the conscious reclaiming of the parts of my life I keep hidden and begin repairing the self-damage caused by my secretiveness. I celebrate this holy work, the work of becoming whole, and allow myself to find constructive ways to reclaim all of me. I commit today to these words: "Wholeness is holy."

Our whole energy remains blocked either in the past or in the future. When you withdraw all your energy from the past and future a tremendous explosion happens.

— BHAGWAN SHREE RAJNEESH

Sometimes we feel so ensnarled in past hurt and anger, so consumed by blame and recrimination and regret, that we can't relax our grip and let go. At the same time, in another part of our mind, we are just as enmeshed in an image of the way we want our partner to be, of the relationship that we hope we'll have someday. When we're not blaming our partner for the pain of the past, we're counting on them to provide the pleasure of the future.

What about today? It is only in the "now" that the holy can explode into consciousness. The past is gone, and tomorrow may never come. It is only in the here and now that you have the opportunity to fully enjoy your partner. Today, try simply to see your partner in the present. Let go of the past, and hold the future at bay. What could you do, right now, to experience a special feeling of closeness with your partner? What innovation to the relationship could you suggest that would make this day a truly wonderful memory?

❧ *Look over your partner's behavior-change request list and choose something that you feel comfortable dealing with at this moment. Surprise your partner with this gift today.*

I let go of past and future thoughts, focusing only on this moment of nurturing solitude. Feeling an inner renewal and awakening, I make this decision: "I choose joy today!"

How much happier we would be if we were to focus on the little things about our partner that we love, instead of finding fault with every little thing that we don't. How loved and validated they would feel if we were to share all the small and loving observations we make of them that we usually keep to ourselves: "I love the way that little lock of hair keeps falling in your eyes," "You look great in that shade of green," "Your touch is so gentle," "I still get a thrill when you say my name."

Our thoughts have power to create our reality. When we focus on accentuating the positive, we drive out the negativity that usually inspires our image of our partner. Over time, basking in the goodwill and positive regard reflected back to them, our mate comes to embody the picture we paint of them.

❧ Be especially aware today of the little things you love about your partner; write each one down. Whenever a negative thought arises, see how you can substitute or balance it with a positive one: "He always leaves the lights on!" could be balanced by "He never forgets to kiss me good-bye in the morning." At the end of the day, have your partner sit in a chair as you walk around them and reel off your list in a deluge of positive flooding.

Today I commit to embracing the positive, and I focus on this truth in prayer: "Our thoughts have the power to shape our reality."

A good marriage is one which allows for change and growth in the individuals and in the way they express their love.

—PEARL S. BUCK

Think back to when you and your partner first met. How different you are now! Planned or unplanned, welcome or not, things change. Even without conscious effort, nothing stays exactly the same for very long.

But change is often threatening, and makes us feel as if we're on shaky ground. Our relationships often operate according to specific tacit arrangements that depend on an unspoken balance of power. If one of us gets a promotion or loses a job, if one learns to play tennis or wins an award, if one gains twenty pounds while the other trims and tones at the gym, the status quo is disturbed. We worry about how the change will affect our relationship. Will there be a shift in the power balance, will they meet someone new, will we stay together?

As always, the discussion returns to the issue of safety. When partners trust each other, when they feel valued and loved as they are—and were and will be—they welcome the fresh air and new ideas that change brings. Though they may feel anxious or uncomfortable at first, and unsure about how it will affect the partnership, they trust that it will lead to growth and evolution of their feelings for each other. They talk openly about their fears, they anticipate adjustments. They use change to work for rather than against their partnership.

❧ *This is a good time to update your relationship vision. Has your vision changed to reflect the changes in your lives? Make any alterations and additions that are needed.*

I turn in meditation toward my relationship today and see it as a flowing river, always changing but always remaining the same. I view this scene with peace and celebrate the constant birthing of the new.

Then let thy love be younger than thyself,
Or thy affection cannot hold the bent.

—WILLIAM SHAKESPEARE

There is much talk about the wounded inner child but little talk about its counterpart—the resilient, joyful inner child. This joyful child was there first—the wholly alive being whose vitality was slowly squelched by inadequate caretaking by parents and a society not yet evolved enough to know how to rear children without wounding them.

What we all unconsciously seek in our lives is to recapture the aliveness of that child. One way of doing that is to remember what that child was like, and to do again what that child did, re-creating some of the pleasure that once made that child laugh.

Think back to the things that once made your eyes shine: the jingle of the ice cream truck a block away, jumping through piles of fall leaves, making angels in the snow, running willy-nilly around the schoolyard until you could barely catch your breath. Inside you is a kid who would still enjoy riding the swings at the park. There's no better medicine for that wounded inner child than to begin to incubate the resiliency and vitality of a "love younger than thyself."

❧ Spend a little time playing with your partner today. Buy finger-paint soap and take a shower together. Get a kite or Frisbee and suggest a picnic in the park, or go to a slapstick movie tonight. Be a kid again!

In my time alone, I call up those memories of myself as a strong, fun-loving child. Recognizing that the vibrant spirit of that child still resides within, I open my arms in welcome, allowing the sense of full aliveness to permeate my soul.

All our lives we're taught to play the part of a "man" or "woman." We cultivate certain gender-specific traits at the expense of others. Then we hook up with someone who has the opposite gender qualities, which we've buried or let atrophy, and expect them to take up the slack.

At first it works out all right. But under pressure, we end up deriding the masculine or feminine qualities we once found so appealing in our mates. What we once praised as confidence we now criticize as control. What was once appealing affectionateness now strikes us as intrusive or smothering. No wonder our gender roles sometimes seem like just another huge hurdle to intimacy.

The macho man and the femme fatale have much to learn from each other. To break out of their gender straitjackets, each needs to take the pressure off the other to measure up to artificial standards of masculinity or femininity roles that deprive them of their own potential to express their full nature.

Figure out one specific thing that each of you could teach the other to begin to break out of your role-bound patterns, and dialogue about it. Learn to bake a cake or throw a football, to change the oil in the car or supervise the kindergarten birthday party.

I imagine that I am someone of the opposite sex, and notice that the new qualities and skills I now possess make me feel more whole. This truth is mine today: "I am both male and female."

Keep your eyes wide open before marriage, and half shut afterwards.

— BENJAMIN FRANKLIN

This is great advice, but who can say they follow it? It usually works the other way around. We're blind to the flaws in our partner until we are deeply entangled; then we open our eyes and see every blemish. If we could just learn to look through half-closed eyes at our partner's imperfections and let small things pass, while opening our eyes wide to the love and goodness, life would be easier and more pleasant.

Everyone likes to be seen in a flattering light. In the movies they achieve this effect with a little Vaseline on the lens; all sorts of minor flaws and wrinkles vanish. Why shouldn't we do the same for our partner? What a great ego builder it is to comment on what is good and loving about our partner rather than honing in on what is petty or mean. To notice the blue shirt that flatters rather than the yellow one that makes them look washed out. To praise the perfect roast rather than criticize the burnt toast. Such selective vision can have a powerful effect not only on our partner's feelings of safety and acceptance but on our whole outlook on the relationship. Sometimes all it takes is to shift focus slightly so that we see things from a different angle.

&. *Half shut your eyes today to your partner's faults that you usually see in gory detail. No nagging, complaining, criticizing, or suggestions.*

I imagine myself looking through binoculars at my partner, enlarging every flaw. I reverse the binoculars and the flaws disappear. I recognize that I have the power to decide which end of the binoculars to look through.

Anyone who's a great kisser I'm always interested in.

—CHER

Affection between partners can be the glue in the relationship, smoothing over rough spots, signaling caring, quieting fears. Whoever invented kissing was a genius. It's fun, it's loving, it comes in infinite varieties, and it doesn't cost a penny. You can never have enough kisses around the house.

❧ *Strive for greatness in kissing today. Practice on your partner.*

Drawing strength from my time in stillness, I hold this reality in my consciousness: "My kisses are balm to my partner's wounds and worries."

We're all guilty at times of weighing our partner's performance against some ideal we hold in our mind. We measure our partner's meatloaf against Mom's, their sexual style against a former lover's, their income against our best friend's partner's, our entire relationship against one we fancied in a romance novel. We run endless comparison tests.

But what does all this comparison have to do with *our* partner in *our* relationship, here and now? Nothing. Will our judgment improve our partner's performance, enhance their security, reassure them of our love? Doubtful. Better to see, accept, and praise our real, unique, in-the-flesh partner.

🍂 *Take a close look today at the scale by which you judge your partner. Make a list of categories that you judge and the source of the standard you use to judge them: "Cooking—Mom's," "Sex—first lover," "Clothing—GQ magazine." When you've completed your list, go through it again and reevaluate your partner in each of these areas, without the comparison. Maybe your partner doesn't kiss like your first lover; what about those soulful caresses? Jot down these discoveries, and compliment your partner on them throughout this week.*

I confess to making comparisons with others and, during this quiet time today, slowly surrender them. I think of my partner as I focus on this important reality: "We all carry a divinity within."

Sympathy is a supporting atmosphere, and in it we
unfold easily and well.

—RALPH WALDO EMERSON

How many times have you gotten angry at your partner for being
irritated or angry—even if the irritation wasn't directed at you? It's
like a chain reaction; when faced with frustration, we respond with
defensive upset rather than compassion. Soon we're snarling at each
other, and what originated as a frustration with work or traffic or the
kids ends up as a shouting match about what's wrong with the
relationship. And all our partner wanted was a chance to vent
frustration to a sympathetic ear!

The inability to hear our partner's frustration without personalizing
it is the result of our defensive self-centered symbiosis: they must be
angry at *us* (after all, we are the center of the world), we must have
done something wrong, we'd better quickly defend ourselves against
further attack. The ability to refrain from self-referential reactions
and listen to our partner's frustrations compassionately but dispassionately, without assuming our own involvement, is the beginning of
real love. Setting aside our reactivity and emotions so that we may
empathize with our partner, we create a container in which the
seedlings of *agape* love can grow.

❧ *Make today an empathy day. Listen openly and attentively*
today to your partner's frustrations. Just allow your partner to
talk about the pressures of work or their worries about the
children or money or the nasty phone call. Empathize with what
they are feeling while keeping in mind that these are not your
frustrations; you are not responsible for their resolution, nor are
you their source.

Today I recognize my ability to help my partner move pain and
suffering through them so that they may release it and begin to heal.
I draw upon the sustenance of an inner power that I feel during this
time of prayer, so that I may handle my partner's frustration with
compassion instead of anger.

As we bury parts of ourselves and hide or disown others in order to be loved and accepted, there isn't much left of our original core self. Of necessity we fashion a new substitute self to fill in the gaps and give the appearance of wholeness. This new public persona has what it takes to win love and approval.

This persona is the presentational self. We replace our hearty laugh with a ladylike giggle, give up poetry in favor of public speaking. Sometimes the performance is so good, the mask so seamless, that we don't even remember that it's all a facade.

But every facade cracks under pressure, and the pressure inevitably comes in the form of the level of intimacy in a committed relationship. We cannot be onstage with our partner every minute; the theater's too small and the close-ups too intimate. Don't forget that the self you present to others is only a poor substitute for the real you underneath. In peeling away the presentational-self traits, your true self reemerges.

ঞ *Title a new page in your notebook "My Presentational Self." Make a list of your presentational-self qualities by describing the traits you use to cover up or replace the lost-self aspects you itemized on Day 225, your denied-self traits (Day 240), and your disowned-self traits (Day 249).*

In a time of wordless prayer, I allow myself to feel the energy expended in keeping my cover intact. It's exhausting. I visualize letting the mask slip a bit to reveal the flesh-and-blood face underneath, longing to see the light of day.

All the world's a stage,
And all the men and women merely players.

—WILLIAM SHAKESPEARE

We cultivate the face we present to others in order to generate applause on the world's stage. If we look beneath the surface, however, we see that it is just a mask that we wear to play our role.

Society encourages us to cultivate a presentable self, an image of what is considered acceptable. Polite society doesn't applaud anything out of the ordinary—too much confidence or timidity, or too much or little of anything for that matter. We're all supposed to play stock characters: the clever businessman, the dizzy dame, the smart cookie, the wise old man.

But our partners need our truth; they demand the real thing. This demand makes us squirm—we're more comfortable with our stage role. But their demand is an indirect gift. In revealing our authentic self to our partners, and seeing that they love us as we truly are, we can step out of our stifling roles. We are able to give up measuring ourselves by society's standards and instead live according to our own. Shedding the presentational self is a liberating process that reveals the truth of who we are. That's something we can live with.

❧ *In a couples dialogue with your partner, choose one presentational-self trait to let go of. Identify a situation in which that trait typically emerges, and talk about how you could behave differently as your true self. Ask for your partner's acceptance and support as you stretch to behave in this new way.*

Looking into a mirror, I see the mask I wear to hide my true self. I hold this thought in prayer today: "Give me the courage to go naked into the world."

*Some emotions don't make a lot of noise. It's hard to
hear pride. Caring is real faint—like a heartbeat.
And pure love—why some days it's so quiet, you don't
even know it's there.*

—ERMA BOMBECK

We're trained to associate true love with certain obvious, larger-than-life signs: the passionate kiss, the floral extravaganza, the sweeping gesture, the roller-coaster emotions. No wonder we tend to measure the depth of our love according to its decibel level.

But real love is not normally loud and obvious. It whispers through the little things that lovers do for each other every day—the fresh sheets on the bed, a kind word, the loving glance, the help with typing a letter, the silent hand holding. But even though it may not be visible to the naked eye or audible to the untrained ear, it is unmistakably and unfailingly present, an invisible vibrational catalyst that keeps everything humming along smoothly.

❧ *Tune in today to the almost imperceptible vibrations of love
and caring in your relationship. Can you pick them up, or are
they too faint to tune in to? Come up with something you can do
right now to strengthen the heartbeat of your partnership, something so pure and quiet that your partner may not even notice.*

**In silence today, I attune my spirit to register the countless small
gestures between us that indicate the undercurrent of love present in
our relationship. I hold this image in my heart: "Acts done in quiet
speak the loudest."**

We learn nothing from the things we know.

—JOHN CAGE

We get stuck in knowing—knowing what is right, who we are, what our partner needs and wants, how to do things, how to fix things. So why isn't everything working out as we expected? Sometimes our powerful new brain tyrannizes us with false knowledge, leading us to think that merely believing something makes it true. Rigid beliefs can be a barrier to seeing what's really going on. Sometimes not knowing is the door to clarity.

Allow the unknown to become your teacher and your guide. Where are the areas of intensity in your life? Unresolved problems with your mother-in-law, your boss, that long-standing impasse with your partner? The intensity that you feel means there are new truths embedded in the struggle, waiting for clarification and integration. Release yourself from the tyranny of the known and relax into the lessons the future holds in store.

Identify one problematic issue in your relationship, and then try looking at it without the blinders of your beliefs; try not knowing what to do. See if you can stretch into new knowledge. For example, allow your partner to give you feedback about parts of yourself you're not aware of. Mirror back and consider each statement as a potential new truth. Allow yourself to stretch into fuller knowledge.

Today I suspend my certainty and allow myself to enter the place of not knowing. Breathing slowly and deeply, I allow my rigid defenses to relax. I feel aroused by the excitement of learning. This ancient truth becomes my prayer: "Acknowledged ignorance is the beginning of wisdom."

What you are becoming is much more important than what you are accomplishing.

—ANONYMOUS

We tend to measure our success by our accomplishments—the promotion, the new patio, the winning soccer game. We often get so caught up in our plans or in measuring ourselves against the accomplishments of others, that we come to think of our accomplishments as evidence of our net worth.

But we are not what we do. It is much more important to be aware of the particular ways in which what we are doing and how are going about it affect the person we are becoming. What counts is the way we handled the interpersonal relationships that led to the promotion, the patience with which we responded to our partner's forgetfulness. Long after the thrill of the accomplishments is forgotten, our character will have been shaped by our attitude in the process of achieving them. When we have a clear idea of the person we hope to become, we can take stock of what we need to do to get there.

❧ *Read over the relationship vision that you and your partner wrote on Day 46. What do you need to accomplish to become the person in your dream relationship? Do something specific today that will lead to becoming that person: expressing empathy for a concern of your partner's, offering tenderness, or, harder yet, true forgiveness.*

Today I acknowledge that the way I handle routine, mundane activities reflects and shapes the person I truly am. In contemplation I acknowledge this truth: "I am what I do."

Here's a two step formula for handling stress. Step number one: Don't sweat the small stuff. Step number two: Remember it's all small stuff.

—ANTHONY ROBBINS

Many of us are far better at making mountains out of molehills than vice versa. Maximizers, in particular, are exceptionally skillful at this. One can readily identify a maximizer by their elaborate emotional agenda, their schemes and lists and backup plans for every eventuality.

To a maximizer, it's all big stuff; they learned in childhood that if you didn't pay attention every minute, and make a fuss to get attention, you might be overlooked or abandoned. If you don't pay attention to every detail, something could go wrong, and then what?

To achieve a loving relationship, that traumatized maximizer child needs to feel safe enough to relax, to have enough trust in their partner, and in life itself, to know that their worries are unfounded. The minimizer partner, who copes with fear by pretending that *nothing* is important enough to work up a sweat about, needs to find the compassion to be able to hold their scared and worried partner. In the process, their own buried fears will be comforted as well.

&❧ *Invite your partner to talk about their childhood wound and explore the present-day circumstances that still trigger the feelings of the past. Talk with your partner today about a specific way to keep those feelings from being reactivated.*

In peace today, I confess to overworrying, exaggerating, and thus creating mountains that weigh both me and my partner down. I laugh with this universal insight: "Nothing is worth such stress. It's all small stuff."

You must do the thing you think you cannot do.

—ELEANOR ROOSEVELT

Sometimes in our relationships we feel as if we've hit the wall. We can't change another thing; we can't go any further, and we're not sure we want to. Changing is no fun! But it's not such a bad thing to stretch beyond our limits, for that's when we encounter our potential for spiritual growth and the gift of a greater consciousness.

If we're quiet and accustomed to keeping our own counsel, our partner will badger us to share our feelings, to open up, to tell us what's on our mind—all of which feels intrusive and threatening. If we're outgoing and like parties, our partner wants us to spend a quiet weekend away at a lakeside cabin where they can have our undivided attention, but where we pace the floor and putter around and rearrange the furniture to avoid just sitting still.

Giving our partners what they need often requires major change on our part, for it calls on our most deeply buried qualities. We are forced to give up what feels natural to us, and substitute behavior that makes us uncomfortable. Sometimes it even feels as if our partner is asking us to give up core aspects of our personalities. In fact, that is just what we are doing—we are putting aside our accustomed behavior in favor of calling forth the buried or atrophied parts of ourselves that our partner needs from us.

But in doing the impossible to meet our partner's needs, we force the lost, buried parts of ourselves to emerge that must be healed and reintegrated for us to regain our spiritual wholeness. The thing we think we cannot do is exactly what we *must* do to reclaim our true potential.

&. *Think about a difficult behavior change your partner has asked of you. Can you see what part of yourself you might recover if you were to honor that request? Take a small step today to begin to make that change.*

I see my partner's needs as a mountain I cannot climb. But as I move closer, mustering all my effort and courage, I see that there is a path that leads up the mountain. With rope and tools for the ascent, I fortify myself with this assurance: "With love, all things are possible."

It's only in winter that the pine and cypress are known to be evergreens.

—CONFUCIUS

It's not difficult to be pleasant and easygoing when things are going well, as we all know from the early days of courtship. But crisis tests our mettle—as we also know from the conflicts that have come up since.

All relationships have their seasonal cycles—the bloom of spring, the passion of summer, the fall from grace—and the winter of our discontent, where most of us get into trouble. When couples fail to understand the pain and unfinished business that will surface in their partnerships, the winter can be very long indeed. It behooves us to learn and practice the process that most helps us to weather the wintry storms—containment. Being able to hear our partner's hurt and frustration without feeling overwhelmed or denying their feelings is one of the hardest tests of our character and commitment. Today you will begin an exchange of container days with your partner, in which you will practice the safe management of your frustrations. If you and your partner can master this skill, you'll be able to hang on to your needles through the harshest winter.

❧ Declare today a Container Day (Day 271). If you are to be the receiver, take a minute to visualize your partner as wounded to prepare yourself to simply listen to your partner's frustrations without reacting. If you are to be the sender, articulate your frustrations to yourself beforehand, so that you are describing behavior, not labeling your partner. Tomorrow, switch roles.

Today I imagine a vast expanse of trees, fully green, in the spring of the year. As I watch, the season changes to summer bloom, then to riotous fall color, then to winter, when the leaves fall, leaving the branches bare and gray. Only the stately, patient evergreens are still lush and lively, like our love. This thought focuses my attention: "Love survives the winter of discontent."

How sweet it is to realize that love becomes richer with each passing season. How precious is the love that arises out of mutual concern, respect, and support. We've seen all the movies about insatiable passion, read the books about the thrill of romance, but nobody told us about this—the extraordinary richness and intensity that are the reward of years of togetherness. When we are caught in anger or unhappiness, when we feel that great love will never be ours, we need to remember that it is in the process of working through our troubles that we enrich our future.

🍃 *Tonight, surprise your partner by taking them on a trip down memory lane. Unpack your wedding album and savor the memories, dig out the pictures of your first vacation together, or simply reminisce about that first date. Remember how happy you were then, and talk about how your relationship is happy in a different way now. Celebrate the nuggets of richness that are beginning to accumulate.*

In contemplation today, I see our lives as a mighty river flowing on forever. This thought—a constant undercurrent—strengthens my soul: "I can be the source of endless love."

You can live a lifetime and, at the end of it, know
more about other people than you know about
yourself.

— BERYL MARKHAM

"**I**f I were she, I'd never put up with it." "If I were in his place, I wouldn't wear that style of jacket; it's so unflattering." "If I were president, I wouldn't pay any attention to opinion polls." "Can't she see that they're never going to move to a bigger house until she puts her foot down?"

We're so insightful and observant when it comes to others. Our friends seek out our counsel, we freely offer our opinions on solving the world's problems, we stand up at the PTA meeting and tell them how to solve the high incidence of truancy.

It's so clear to us how others' behavior sabotages their friendships and happiness. We know just what we would do if we were in their place, and often we tell them. We can certainly see what's wrong with our partner, and pinpoint with remarkable clarity their responsibility for the problems we're having. Focusing all our attention on causes and effects outside us, we remain ignorant about our own complicity in events, and therefore blameless.

When we project our negative behavior onto our partners, it may protect us from having to see our own problems, but it protects us as well from knowing ourselves and growing. This is one of those situations in which ignorance is not bliss.

🙐 *Write down five criticisms you make of your partner. Look at each one and ponder how that criticism might be true of you.*

In contemplation today, I listen to my criticisms of others and hear them as attributes I might apply to myself. I am instructed by this ancient wisdom: "I'll focus on that beam in my own eye and forget about the mote in my partner's."

Let us not look back in anger or forward in fear, but around in awareness.

—JAMES THURBER

Stop for a moment and think back over what's been going on in your mind just in the last few minutes. Chances are, your stray thoughts and reactions were concerned about something that happened in the past or might happen in the future. Were you thinking about what your partner said about paying the bills last night, or worrying about having good weather for the barbecue this weekend? Many of us spend so much of our mental time living in yesterday's anger or projecting tomorrow's fear that we obliterate the present. We don't experience our lives as they happen—they exist only as memories or future possibilities.

This is useless, time-wasting activity. Nothing is amenable to change and improvement except what is going on *right now*. In a conscious relationship, partners bring their pasts, and their hopes for the future, into the open so that they know the territory they are exploring together. Having done so, they concentrate their attention on the love that is available between them *now*, what's needed in the relationship *now*. They work to let go of entanglements of both past and future, so that they can live in a present time that carries them, moment by moment, in the direction they want to go.

❧ *Today, focus only on the present. Be aware of your partner as they are today, as if you are seeing them for the very first time. Forget about what you thought or felt about your partner earlier this morning or yesterday or last year. Mirror your partner as they are today. Tell your partner something that you appreciate about them today — not "I always like it when you wear that shirt," but rather "I love the way you look in that shirt today."*

In my time of prayer, I close my eyes and focus my attention on the present. I notice feelings, sounds, smells. As stray thoughts come to mind, I notice which are about the past, and which are about the future, and release all those that are not about right now. I awake to the power of this thought: "My life is in the present."

*A spirit filled with truth must needs direct its actions
to the final goals.*

— MAHATMA GHANDI

Most of us grew up believing that a good relationship comes easy.
Meeting the right person and falling in love might be difficult, but
once we've found the partner, it's happily ever after from that point
on.

One of the main reasons couples are so shocked and unprepared
for the difficulties they come up against in their partnerships is that
falling in love with their partner *was* the goal, and in fact their actions
were directed toward that goal. They made a point to get out and
meet people, they presented themselves in a way that made them
desirable as mates, they gave their beloved lots of care and attention.

But now what? How do they travel the long road ahead? What do
they need to do to live happily ever after? The Imago process fully
delineates how an individual can direct their actions to the final goal
of a conscious marriage. But learning the truth about how relationships work is only a partial step toward that goal. It is the action we
take, every day, learning and practicing the Imago skills, caring for
our partner, that actually propels us ahead toward our destination.

~ *Identify one aspect of Imago relationship therapy that you will
practice — perhaps it's using the couples dialogue in all conversation today, or springing a surprise behavior on your partner.
Whatever you choose, be proud that you're taking action toward
your goal.*

Today I recognize all the more deeply how important it is to be an
active agent in my relationship. In my time of renewal, this thought
takes life: "I have the ability to actively create the relationship I've
yearned for."

The golden rule of relationships: Do unto your partner what your partner would have you do unto them.

—HARVILLE HENDRIX

The time-honored golden rule, "Do unto others as you would have them do unto you," is a profound instruction for relationships in general. But in intimate partnerships, we need to take this admonishment a step further. Instead of treating our partner as *we* would like to be treated, we need to treat them as *they* want to be treated.

This is harder than it seems, for at least three reasons. One, we're all pretty self-centered, far more in touch with our own desires than with those of our partner. Two, most of us think other people's desires are similar, if not identical, to ours. Three, we are so protective of our own ways and means of doing things that we find it hard to accept and honor our partner's desires (even if we do know them) when they seem odd or difficult to us.

Yet we all know how wonderful it feels to be cared for in just the way that makes us feel loved. So why not do it right—*exactly* right? In these next three days, you and your partner will be encouraged to focus on turning the caring behaviors you already give to each other into the fine-tuned target behaviors that will enhance both your pleasure and your understanding of each other.

&c. *Remember "The Newlywed Game" on television? The object was to find out how well each partner knew the other. Here's a home version of "The Newlywed Game" to play with your partner. In a spirit of fun and mutual fact gathering, quiz each other about your tastes and preferences. Ask each other questions to see how well you know each other: "What is my favorite color?" "How do I like my coffee?" "Where would I go on a dream vacation?" "What is my favorite meal?" "What is my favorite song?" "What is my lifelong dream?" When you don't know the answers, fill each other in. Be specific in your responses, and don't hesitate to voice any additional specific likes or dislikes. Then, because you're newlyweds for the evening, have a honeymoon.*

Letting go of preconceptions during the stillness of meditation, I listen instead with my heart to the nuances of my partner's desires. Today I honor this hope: "Love specifically targeted is life-transforming."

Our partner's preferences are usually very different from our own, no matter how much we might have in common. Unfortunately, partners often feel miffed and upset when they don't get their heart's desire. But we cannot read each other's mind. The only way to get exactly what we want is to tell our partner just what that is, in every detail. Sometimes our desires are quite simple: "When you bring me a cup of coffee, I'd like it in that cracked blue mug, with just a half-teaspoon of sugar." Some are rooted in pleasant childhood memories: "I love it when you set out the lap robe for me, but it would feel so good if you would cover me and tuck me in sometimes like my mother used to do." Some are fantasies: "You know what I would love the next time you fix a special meal? A fancy soufflé and a bottle of white wine." To get to our partner's heart, it helps to know the way.

❧ *Identify three caring behaviors that you already get from your partner, which you would love even more if they were fine-tuned to your exact specifications. In conversation tonight, thank your partner for their caring behaviors toward you, and tell them very clearly exactly how they could make those acts of caring even more pleasurable in the future.*

Retreating into stillness today, I imagine myself holding a bow and a quiver of arrows, each signifying a special way my partner wants to be loved. I aim my arrows at a target pinned to my partner and hit the bull's-eye every time.

Chains do not hold a marriage together. It is threads, hundreds of tiny threads, which sew people together through the years.

—SIMONE SIGNORET

Like subtle threads in the fabric of our relationship, target behaviors sew us together. It's the little, seemingly insignificant things we do for each other that create invisible stitches: a kiss (on the ear with your hand in my hair) when you leave the house; a piece of (bitter-sweet) chocolate (that's been kept in the freezer) brought from the kitchen during a commercial while we watch our favorite show to-gether; coming home to a warm house because your partner lit the fire (with some pine boughs in it for the scent) and pulled your chair (with your needlepoint) up close.

Caring behaviors that are right on target weave especially strong threads. One cup of coffee with just the right amount of sugar tastes better than ten too-sweet cups. One perfect peach-colored French tulip beats out a dozen long-stemmed roses in the you-know-just-who-I-am-and-just-what-I-want department any day.

❧ *Give your partner one of the target behaviors they asked for yesterday, exactly the way they want it in every detail.*

I contemplate in prayer today the richness of the tapestry my partner and I can weave with thoughtful loving.

Do you love your partner for what goods and services they have to offer? Because he is good in bed, or because she is a corporate executive? Because she is beautiful, or he is strong? Love attached to a reason is conditional love. Will you still love her when she changes careers and makes less money, or when she gains weight during pregnancy? Will you still love him if he becomes impotent or injured?

The fact is, real love is unconditional—it appears when you value your partner even when they are of no value to you. It flourishes as you value your partner simply because they exist in your world, not because they have value as a resource. Partners in a conscious relationship do not base their love on a balance sheet of their partner's assets, or a tally of their partner's deeds. They love each other as they are, without measuring its reasons. Unconditional love is the only love that heals.

Take a look today to see if there is a hidden contract in your relationship, a list of requisites that are the conditions on which you base your love. What if these conditions were no longer met? Would you still love your partner? In your mind's eye, tear up that contract today; reaffirm your commitment to loving your partner unconditionally.

Drawing peace from a time of stillness today, I focus on my deep breathing, and let go of the conditions I place on love. I bathe my soul in this moment of serenity, and hold this thought in mind: "Real love knows no bounds, keeps no records, and asks nothing in return."

Between whom there is hearty truth, there is love.

— HENRY DAVID THOREAU

Most couples would say they put a high premium on honesty in their relationships. But if you were to examine their actual behavior, you'd see many ways—some of them well-meaning—in which truth is sabotaged. Rather than saying what they mean directly, they resort to all sorts of indirect tactics to get their message across. They rely on whining or psychological jargon or half-truths to make their point. They use anger, they clam up, they retreat, or act insulted, in order to avoid hearing what their mate has to say. They remain silent in order not to rock the boat, or to avoid hurting their partners. All these strategies are adult carryovers of patterns learned as powerless children, when we had no way of getting what we needed without resorting to various forms of subterfuge.

It's not always easy to tell the truth in a relationship, especially when there is conflict or complaint or fear of reprisal. But each time we withhold or bend the truth, we take a step backward on the journey to real love. Truth in a conscious relationship is maintained through using the containment process to express our frustrations. In practicing the mini-container exercise, we establish a whole new framework in which we can tell the truth in a loving, straightforward, and effective way. We learn that truth and love can—and must— coexist.

❧ *Today, use the containment process (Day 122 to 128) to tell your partner the truth about something that is frustrating you.*

With faith in the power of self-disclosure, I access a deeper inner courage. I imagine myself opening all of my being to my partner in calm dignity, claiming: "Truth is the path to intimacy."

Light tomorrow with today!
—ELIZABETH BARRETT BROWNING

There is plenty to worry about in this troubled world we live in: the fighting going on around the globe, our kids' troubles in school, the mortgage payments we can barely meet, the fighting going on in our home. The landscape of our lives seems fraught with darkness at times; no matter how hard we try, our efforts make little difference. The future looks bleak.

It's natural to worry about what the future will bring. But we have the power to shape the future, to create the potential for hope. The future does not just happen, on either a global or personal scale. It is what we do today, in this moment, that prepares the way and ultimately determines the brightness of the days ahead. In a conscious relationship, this is called intentionality—the power to determine a desired outcome. If we react out of fear, as we do when we are unconscious, we fill our todays with strife and recriminations and conflict, and we cannot expect a loving future. If we want tomorrow to be safe and sunny, our decisions and actions today must contribute toward that goal.

🍃 *Do something today that will light up tomorrow—give your partner a caring behavior, offer to use the mini-container exercise so your partner can heal a frustration, bring a creative idea to your relationship that will make your partner smile, or have a couples dialogue about your concerns for the future.*

During my time of quiet, I offer a prayer of thanksgiving for my freedom to create my future for greater light and enlightenment. I focus on this truth: "What I do today will create my tomorrow."

Compassionate toward yourself, you reconcile all beings in the world.

—LAO-TZU

However critical we may be of our partner, our friends and family, or our government, it probably doesn't hold a candle to the judgment and criticism we heap on ourselves. Most of us have such a low opinion of ourselves, we are our own worst enemy. Self-hatred, shame, and low self-esteem are epidemic in most cultures; we as a species seem desperate to be good enough to feel worthy of love.

Open and trusting as children, we accepted the advice and opinions of our caretakers as truth. Whatever our parents rejected or criticized in us, we assumed was in fact no good, so we disassociated ourselves from our unacceptable parts. As adults, we assign our partners responsibility for the penny-pinching or ill temper or evasiveness that we cannot abide in ourselves.

The restoration of self-love is possible only when we understand that the traits we so abhor in others exist in us. They have the self-protective function of shielding us from further wounding. To experience self-love, we must love the partner in whom we see the hated traits.

Our unconscious cannot distinguish between the self and the other; it receives the love and acceptance we give to our partners as if directed at itself. Without this process of loving in others what we unconsciously hate in ourselves, we are stuck with our unconscious self-hatred.

❤ *Pay particular attention to empathizing with your partner's experience today, especially in situations where your usual tendency would be to judge or criticize what you perceive as their oversensitivity, or irritability, or pettiness, or stinginess. Say "I can feel how irritated you must be," or "I feel ripped off, too." Know that there is a place inside where your own irritability or stinginess is being accepted and loved as well.*

Today in stillness, I acknowledge the tensions I carry as evidence of my own self-rejection. Focusing on my partner with a prayer of compassion, I allow myself to relax and absorb this truth: "Self-love is the outcome of other-love."

Whatever possesses us to think that accusing our partner of being a wimp will make them strong, or proclaiming them a cold fish will make them wild in bed? Even as kids we knew that the adage about "sticks and stones will break my bones, but names will never hurt me" was a big lie.

Criticism is a powerful form of emotional abuse, but its effectiveness in getting our partners to change or to love us is just about nil. Name-calling is a particularly childish way of showing our displeasure, an indirect expression of a need or frustration. A grown-up would identify directly the behavior that needed changing, rather than indulging in character assassination.

In a conscious relationship, *there is no criticism*. Instead, there are skills that enable us to express our frustrations directly, and to understand their source. Next time you are about to scream insults at your partner, stop. Take a few deep breaths, and ask your partner to do a mini-container exercise.

❧ *Think about a derogatory name or label that you use on your partner when you're angry or frustrated. Do you call your partner a slob because they left their dirty socks on the floor? What is the frustration behind your name-calling, and what do you want from your partner? Once you've figured it out, ask your partner to do a mini-container exercise and tell them specifically what would make you happy — to put the laundry in the hamper.*

In my time of quiet, I release all vindictive feelings and visualize the expression of frustrations in ways that promote healing. I celebrate this truth: "We both deserve respect."

Familiarity, truly cultivated, can breed love.

                          —DR. JOYCE BROTHERS

The old saying that familiarity breeds contempt arises out of a fear that if we let others truly see who we are and what is in our hearts, they will reject us. If our partner sees us shaving, or brushing our teeth, or putting two teaspoons of sugar in our coffee every single day, we'll become invisible to them or, at the very least, dull. If they really get to see our obsessive penny-pinching or our inability to think straight before noon, they'll want nothing to do with us. So we keep our masks in place as well as we can, exhibiting only the traits we've learned are desirable. The rest we bury. How sad this is. If we hide, then we haven't a chance to be known, or loved, for ourselves.

What matters is the way in which familarity is cultivated. There is a fine line between the kind of tenderness that grows from watching someone dear to us brush their teeth in their quirky way, or seeing them panic at the sight of a mosquito, and the aversion or contempt that result when we abuse the privilege of being ourselves, insisting that our partner see and accept the intolerable or the unnecessarily unpleasant. No one wants to feel obligated to become familiar with our temper tantrums, or our uncleanliness, or our bigotry.

In an atmosphere of discretion and respect, familiarity indeed breeds content. As we slowly but surely shed our masks, we learn something truly wonderful: if we will be ourselves, our partners will love us just as we are, *because* we are just as we are.

🍂 *Reveal an unfamiliar aspect of yourself to your partner—the tattered T-shirt that you've saved since college, your secret love for the* National Enquirer.

Today I visualize encouraging my partner to let me know all that is now hidden. I show love and acceptance, and cradle this thought securely in my heart: "Knowledge is a precondition of love."

It's surprising how many couples in long-term partnerships give up on their sex life, as though sex belonged exclusively to the young and the restless, and was improper and undignified for anyone over a certain age. For those couples who never worked through their sexual fears and taboos, or were never able to talk through their desires and differences, putting their sex life behind them can be a relief.

But sex is not just for teenagers and movie stars. A satisfying sex life has no age limit, and it can begin at any time. Making love takes many forms. And one of the ways sexual bonds deepen is through openly and unabashedly sharing our sexual fears, needs, and fantasies with our partners. It's the first step to creating the safe and intimate ambiance in which to make love.

🍃 *Start a dialogue about the current status of your sex life. Begin by telling your partner a sexual secret, something that has been difficult for you to talk about. "I am so self-conscious about my stomach when we make love." "I have fantasies of making love in a public place." "I've always wanted to explore Tantric sex." "I am embarrassed to make noise when I have an orgasm."*

In quiet contemplation, I decide to share my sexual self with my partner. I absorb this truth: "It is a part of my inner divinity to be a sexual person."

Does life always have to be so serious? Is this what it means to be an adult? It's so easy to get caught up in routines and problems, to become slaves to our carefully preserved self-images. We're afraid to reveal that part of us that loves to goof off. If we keep our spirit under wraps long enough, we forget how to be silly. But, like all red-blooded animals, we are innately playful. That buried part of ourselves that wants to let it all hang out is calling for attention.

So how about taking ourselves *lightly* for a change? It's such a relief to leave public propriety behind, to let our hair down and make a fool of ourselves in the safe and conspiratorial presence of our partner. The ability to laugh at ourselves should be encouraged; it is a priceless relationship asset.

🍃 *Do something silly today, something that shatters your self-image. If you're too shy or embarrassed to act up in front of your partner, try doing something foolish all by yourself: dance madly around the room, wear mismatched socks or your partner's clothes, do animal imitations. Work up to exposing yourself to your partner — by tomorrow!*

Today I let go of the version of myself that the world sees and locate that playful part of me that sees life's humor and loves to have fun. I recognize this as part of the sacred in life. This truth is mine: "The ridiculous and the sublime are one."

*There is no more lovely, friendly and charming
relationship, communion or company than a good
marriage.*

—MARTIN LUTHER

No one is forced to be married. Some people avoid it like the plague.
Some try and fail, and never return to it. But most of us hang in
there, and even if it doesn't work the first time around, we come back
for more. Even in its darkest hours, somehow we know deep down
inside that nothing can compare to the deep and nourishing intimacy
of partnership. However else we might get our kicks, however
disappointed or frustrated we may have been by past love, nothing
else offers the opportunity for reclaiming our innate joyfulness, the
aliveness we yearn for.

All life on earth is the result of the pulling together of opposites
into a whole—as a day is composed of light and dark, a year
encompasses summer and winter, so are two people pulled together
into their quest for completion. To seek union, to live in communion,
strengthens our continued spiritual and psychological development on
the most profound level. Marriage experienced as sacrament awakens
us to the wonder of life.

❧ *With your partner, recommit to applying the Imago processes
in a more intentional way on a daily basis. Read your relationship
vision to each other as an affirmation of the vibrant, healing
relationship you are creating day by day.*

**I celebrate the concept of deeper communion with my partner, seeing
them as a separate and equal person whose inner life I honor and
experience.**

Nature does not care that you are comfortable, only that you evolve.

—HARVILLE HENDRIX

Most of us resist change because it makes us uncomfortable. We prefer the predicatable misery of the familiar to the potential splendor of the unknown. We would like the outcome of an improved relationship—if only we could achieve it without the anxiety and pain of change. But nature is never static; it is always changing, always growing, always creating new life. Fear of change is the logical outcome of our childhood wounding; it is a fear of further injury, and a decision to cut our losses. But it blocks our spiritual development and is contrary to our true nature. If we are uncomfortable with growth, that fear itself is part of what needs to be changed.

Nature is much less interested in our comfort than in its own self-completion. We are a part of nature, and nature seeks to repair itself through us, as we heal our own wounds through the journey of the conscious relationship. In cooperating with that process, we are fulfilling nature's plan. Nature's only goal is to repair itself and complete itself, no matter how difficult or painful the process may be. However we have been going about it—or resisted going about it— our unconscious goal is the same as nature's. We might as well stop fighting it, and get with the program.

❧ *Go for a walk today in a place where you can observe nature at work—your backyard, a forest, a park, a beach. Find a comfortable spot and sit. Look around you attentively and become aware of how nature is in a constant process of healing: bumps where bark was healed over a tree, grass springing up through a crack in the sidewalk, new growth or flowers on a bush, earthworms turning dried leaves into soil. Sitting quietly, become aware of how you are a part of nature too, and nature is working to heal you, just as it heals everything else. Entertain the thought that your love is nature's healing balm for your partner's wound.*

Taking the time to awake to nature today, I draw strength and fresh perspective. I prayerfully hold this thought: "I join in nature's healing plan by committing to heal my partner's wounds."

I realized a long time ago that a belief which does not spring from conviction in the emotions is no belief at all.

          — EVELYN SCOTT

"**P**eople who assert themselves get respect." "Wealth is a measure of success." "When you loan money you never get it back." "Italians are talkative." "There's nothing I can do to change the world." "Children should be seen and not heard." "Men are violent."

Many of us take pride in "living by our beliefs," without ever having thought about where our beliefs come from. Are they the product of our own experience, the result of accrued wisdom? Probably not. It's more likely that our beliefs are the received wisdom of our culture, the unwritten code of conduct our society promotes. We absorbed them from our parents in childhood, and they were reinforced through the acceptance or rejection of others.

Belief systems differ markedly from one part of the country to another and from one community to the next. What is accepted and encouraged in a southern California beach town is vastly different from what is proper on Boston's Beacon Hill. Beliefs can be insidious; when we accept them at face value, as just the way the world is, they blind us to seeing things as they really are.

Over the next three days, you'll gain some insight into the beliefs that motivate your behavior and relationships. When we become aware of our beliefs about how women are or how relationships are, they begin to loosen their hold on us, and we can base our actions on our actual experience.

🍃 *Title a new page in your notebook "My Beliefs." Write down at least three beliefs you hold about how the world is and three about how people are.*

In quiet today, I enter the deep place of my own wisdom, the divine that is my own truth, and see myself shedding the prison of beliefs I have inherited. I acknowledge: "I carry within me the source of my truth."

Pleasures may come out of illusion, but happiness can only come out of reality.

—NICHOLAS CHAMFORT

Our beliefs perform a valuable service, for they temper our instinctual nature, providing a framework of order and stability in a chaotic world. By conceptualizing our repeated experiences into a codified canon that is fixed and stable and logical, we can say, "If I do this, then *that* will happen," "This is how my mother takes care of me when I am sick . . . ," "This is how my father reacts when I . . ." Our pattern-forming new brain enables us to input mountains of stimuli and to formulate a proper and effective response. With our belief systems firmly in place, we have guidelines for responding to our experiences. We short-circuit the mindless reactions of our old brain, so that we are not at the mercy of our primitive instincts to fight or flee, and don't have to start from square one to figure out how to react to every situation.

But we get tripped up in our belief systems as they become ingrained, fixed, and unyielding. Our belief about how our father reacts becomes a belief about how *all* fathers will respond to a situation. Our experience with our chum becomes a belief about *all* friends or *all* men. However useful belief systems are to us, and however comfortable we are in their certitude, we must break free of them if we want to function in the reality of relationships.

❧ *On the page titled "My Belief Systems," which you started yesterday, list at least three beliefs you hold about relationships, and three about the opposite sex. For example: "Passion never lasts beyond a few years." "All couples fight." "Husbands should provide for their families." "Women talk too much."*

I use my time in contemplation today to move to a deeper level of experiencing. Breathing deeply, I relax preconceived ideas about the opposite sex, allowing in an openness to the uniqueness of the other.

What we want, and what we do, in any society, is to a very great extent what we are made to want and what we are allowed to do.

— JAMAKE HIGHWATER

Because our beliefs are so often formed without questioning their source or value, and because they so powerfully influence our behavior, it is important to be aware of them and to insist that they reflect our reality. Is our belief that "men have a hard time expressing their feelings" or that "women and men can never get along together" really true in our own relationship and among the people we know? Have they determined how we behave and what we expect from our family and friends, our job, the world? Do you and your partner fight because you've learned from experience that all housework should be done by women or that men should be the sole breadwinners in a family—or is that just a belief you grew up with? Are you acting out a belief that sexual interest fades over time or that yelling, screaming fights are normal? It behooves us to be sure our beliefs are in alignment with our inmost convictions.

❧ *Have a couples dialogue with your partner about the beliefs you both hold about committed relationships, how partners should treat each other. Share how they influence your behavior in relationship. Identify one belief about relationships you each hold that is accepted in our society but that you realize is not true for you. Talk about how your partnership can be different when you let go of the behavior behind that false belief. For example: "I now see that I've just turned off on our sex life, believing that we 'shouldn't' or 'couldn't' keep up our attraction to each other. Now that I am aware that this is a belief, I am noticing that the reality is that you often touch me or flirt with me, and I feel myself beginning to respond again."*

In my time of quiet I recognize how enslaved I am to my own conditioning about relationships. With each deep breath, I release a belief and move toward spiritual liberation.

The crossing of the threshold is the first step into the sacred zone of the Universal Source.

— JOSEPH CAMPBELL

"**I** can't be what you need and still be me!" We sometimes feel that our partner's requests are overwhelming. What they need is more than we can give; to respond would take us beyond the breaking point.

But we must cross the threshold of our fear and discomfort to enter into paradise, to touch the deep source within. Touching that core makes stretching to meet our partner's needs worthwhile; it moves us into the zone of the divine source. The ability to move empathically beyond our limitations and heal our partner strengthens us psychologically and deepens us spiritually. It's difficult, even painful to move out of our own safe sphere, out of our own secure and familiar world, and enter into another's reality, but that is the only way to the destination we seek.

❧ *Identify the issue your partner raises that is the most difficult for you. Recognize that meeting this need will provide you with your greatest opportunity for growth. Ask yourself: Am I willing to work on my partner's request, a bit at a time?*

Today, in my time of quiet, I hold this one, most difficult behavior in mind and offer to do it from a place of love. This is a holy place. It has the potential of developing the sacred in my own being.

Our partner is a mirror in which all aspects of ourselves are reflected back to us. If we are loving, love is reflected back; our criticism, however subtle, will be seen for what it is; our shyness or coldness or dishonesty will be clearly illuminated. We cannot edit or distort the picture; mirrors don't lie.

The brutal honesty of the mirror our partner holds up to us can be shocking. It reveals what we think we have successfully hidden as well as what we willingly display. Its benefit is that it will always accurately tell us about ourselves and will register every small change that we make to create a better image. There is only one way to improve on the picture, and that is with acts of love and caring that create a more flattering reflection.

❧ *Today, be aware of the image reflected back to you by your partner. If you are not completely satisfied—if you have gotten feedback about being too angry, or whiny, or slovenly, or over-dependent—do something today to improve your image.*

In time of contemplation, I welcome the truth about myself that my partner mirrors back to me. I honor this perspective: "My partner mirrors what I am and what I can become."

The giving of love is an education in itself.

—ELEANOR ROOSEVELT

With all our schooling, with all we read about or see on television, many of us are hopelessly uneducated about matters of the heart. No matter how many books we've read or movies we've seen, we find out that what we have learned doesn't seem to apply to our situation.

We are shocked at how much we don't know, about ourselves and our partners, about life and love. Used to being competent at everything we do, we find that we are all thumbs when it comes even to simple things like listening, or helping out, or saying what we need. The harder things—giving unreservedly of our time, overcoming a lifelong temper, loving our partner when they are acting unlovable— seem nearly impossible. They didn't teach us this in school. We must learn the lessons of love by experience, by trial and error. A conscious relationship is a lifelong educational as well as spiritual process. Partners who embrace the Imago system are involved in a constant process of learning from the heart.

❧ *Love your partner today in a way that requires you to learn something or stretch yourself. Look over their list of behavior-change requests (Day 200) and grant one that you have been avoiding. Maybe you'll have to learn a new skill or open yourself to a new experience. Get an education today by loving and healing your partner.*

Today in meditation I open myself to the joy of new learning, and I dwell upon this truth: "Learning the lessons of love increases my own spiritual deepening."

*"If you don't mind by boldness, you look stunning.
Make-'em-run-around-the-block-howling-in-agony
stunning. I'm serious. You're big-time elegant,
Francesca. In the purest sense of the word."*

—ROBERT JAMES WALLER

When was the last time you told your partner how beautiful or handsome or elegant or sexy they are? We sure know how good it feels to receive such a compliment, so we can assume it feels just as good to our partner when we dish it out.

We are so vulnerable to others' evaluation of our looks, our sexuality, our prowess in bed, our allure and appeal and attractiveness. When we let our partners know that we're well satisfied with them in these ways, we build a nest of safety and confidence in which we can freely make love to each other

Spend a few minutes thinking of all the good things that come to mind about your partner in the area of their attractiveness, sexuality, and lovemaking skills, the ways in which they please you and allow you to express your sexuality. Tonight, tell your partner all about it in a wave of positive flooding. Have them sit in a chair while you circle around, showering them with praise for their many attractions. "You look so yummy when you just come out of the shower all wet; The skin on your tush is so soft; I often think about making love to you when I'm driving home; you have such a gentle touch . . . juicy lips . . . you smell so good . . . make my toes tingle. . . ." Don't stop now.

Rejoicing in the sacredness of our sexuality, I imagine blowing upon the coals of life in my partner, stirring up flames of pleasure. I hold this thought: "It is holy to celebrate the joys of sexual love."

Sometimes it seems as if we will always be locked in a struggle with our partners to see who is right, who is more loving, who gets to go first, who has to pick up the kids at school. But the power struggle is supposed to end. It's only a stage on your journey, the seemingly endless period during which you fight tooth and nail to get your needs met—using tactics that don't work. How long it lasts depends on your intentions and on how diligently you work to heal your partner's wounds. It helps to know that if you keep using the Imago tools, you will break through to real love. What can you do today to shorten the trip?

Practice one of the Imago skills that will move you through the power struggle—use the couples dialogue, grant your partner a behavior-change request, do an activity on your fun list, give your partner something from your surprise list, shower your partner with positive flooding, or read your relationship vision to each other.

In my time of quiet today, I see myself holding the rope in a never-ending tug-of-war. From a place of deeper wisdom, I let my partner win, liberating me from competition. This thought is mine: "Holding on to the struggle impedes my journey to real love."

We are what we pretend to be, so we must be careful
about what we pretend to be.

—KURT VONNEGUT, JR.

By the time we meet our partners, we are pretty good at pretending. We have cobbled together a self—some of it authentic. But much of it is pieced together of traits that make us look good in the world, that enable us to function, that cover over unhealed pain. But that self we present to others takes on a life of its own, and we are no longer in touch with the parts of us that got lost in the shuffle. We have been careless and lost our true selves.

It's so tempting to continue to put up a false front. The world rewards our pretense, after all. But if we're not comfortable with the person we pretend to be, we can find ourselves in a life we don't like, afraid to be ourselves, or amnesiac as to who we are underneath the disguise.

In a conscious relationship, we don't have to pretend to be anyone other than ourselves. We are called on all the time to remember our true selves and our true feelings. This is after all our innate divinity. Our partners need to have access to these covered-over parts of us; they demand and deserve our authenticity. Meanwhile, with awareness and intention, we can help the process along.

❧ *Take a step today to begin dismantling your presentational self.*
Pick a trait that isn't really you—the officious phone voice, the
false humility, the sexual prissiness, the flashy clothes, the shyness
when you're around your in-laws. What can you do today to stop
pretending you're someone other than yourself?

Today in my twenty minutes of quiet, I let the masks fall and the self
I really am, that whole/holy part, be all there is in my consciousness.
I ponder this revelation: "What I hide from others diminishes me."

I learned the real meaning of love. Love is absolute loyalty. People fade, looks fade, but loyalty never fades. You can depend so much on certain people, you can set your watch by them. And that's love, even if it doesn't seem very exciting.

—SYLVESTER STALLONE

Can your partner set their watch by you? It may not seem very exciting, but knowing—without a doubt—that you will be there when they wake up in the morning and when they go to sleep at night, greet them at the door with a kiss, work through any problem, take care of them when they are ill is the bedrock of a lasting relationship. It's this kind of unwavering dependability that allows us finally to relax and feel secure and safe. Believe it or not, when you offer your partner this kind of bottom-line security, it's a powerful aphrodisiac. The secure knowledge that they can be themselves, that all of who they are is accepted, even welcomed, that they have a rock-solid haven in which to grow and heal, to laugh and love—now, *that* is exciting.

❧ *Take an honest look at your loyalty to your partner today. Then do something specific today to prove your reliability, to demonstrate to your partner that they are in safe hands with you. Hold your temper. Call from out of town to reassure your mate that you miss them. Be on time.*

Moving into my inner sanctuary, I visualize in detail our home as a place where my partner and I can be ourselves in total safety. I hold this prayer; "The passions of love flourish in a reliable environment."

*If we could read the secret history of our enemies, we
should find in each man's life sorrow and suffering
enough to disarm all hostility.*

— HENRY WADSWORTH LONGFELLOW

When we live in hostile territory, battling for whatever love and
attention we can get, our defenses are up. We get to know our enemy
well, and seek to exploit their weaknesses. They're making life
difficult for us, so we feel entitled do the same to them. Hardened to
their plight, we find it hard to feel compassion for their pain.

Our lack of empathy did not begin in our relationship; it has its
roots in earliest infancy when, finding that our needs were being
ignored, we learned to hoard our meager ration of compassion for
ourselves. We are often so desperate to get first aid for our own pain
that we are incapable of empathy for the pain of another.

In a conscious relationship we become aware that our self-absorption and lack of compassion for our partner are the result of our own
wounding, and we consciously strive to overcome our instinctive
tendency to protect ourselves first. In hearing from our partners
their tales of neglect or abuse, we come to understand their hurtful
behavior toward us as rooted in their pain. When we are able to
empathize with their suffering, we cannot maintain our cold, uncaring
defense. The sharing of our wounds breaks down barriers and
reawakens compassion—for our partner and ourselves.

 *Visualize the childhood suffering and sorrow that your partner
has shared with you. Can you see how their behavior is influenced
by that experience? Tonight, offer to hold your partner and invite
them to tell you about a past incident that still causes pain.*

As I relax into a place of prayer today, I access the courage to
examine my heart for compassion. I choose to surrender my self-
absorption, and hold this thought: "Compassion for my partner opens
my heart."

*If we say that we have no sin, we deceive ourselves, and
the truth is not in us.*

—1 JOHN 1:8

We have such a tenacious need to be right. It's hard for us to own
up to our mistakes, to admit that we were petty or selfish or mean.
In part, our fear of being found wrong is rooted in a fear of punishment. But our greater fear is that if we are not perfect, if we display
the traits that were criticized in us as children, we will not be loved
by our partners, as we were not loved by our parents. This is indeed
frightening, so we go to outrageous lengths to maintain our innocence.

This need for innocence—the inability to confess our wrongs and
atone for them—can be a tremendous barrier both to trust between
partners and to self-love. The real sin is not our mistakes themselves
but our tenacious hold on our character defenses, our refusal—out of
fear or self-righteousness—to change our hurtful ways.

In the safety of a conscious relationship, we can confess our
mistakes without fear of retaliation or annihilation. We all make
mistakes; we are only human, after all. In order to cure our self-
hatred, to learn that we can be loved with our faults, we must admit
it when we have done something wrong. The atonement for our
mistakes invites forgiveness. When we break down barriers between
our defenses and our innate innocence, we open ourselves to our
innate spiritual wholeness.

ᐤ *Confess a recent mistake to your partner today. Tell them that
you were seduced by a $400 leather jacket during a shopping trip.
Confess that you were intentionally rude the last time your
partner's best friend visited, or that your sulking last night was
intended to make them feel bad. Tell your partner what you want
to do to atone for your mistake. Notice the closeness that can
develop in this process—and the self-love.*

**In a time of quiet, I acknowledge that making atonement to my
partner brings me to at-one-ment with myself. In the spirit of
celebration I acknowledge: "To unburden the darker human aspects
of my soul in confession is an important step on the journey toward
wholeness."**

Do you ever have days when you just want to pull the covers over your head and sleep all day? When you just don't have the energy or interest to work on the relationship? When the only thing that sustains you is the guilty fantasy of lazing under a palm tree sipping piña coladas—*alone*?

It sounds as if you need a day off! Sometimes body and spirit just need time to rest and recharge. Your partner, your family, the world, will not fall apart if you take a day off—but you might if you don't. Nor will their love for you diminish if you're not on duty twenty-four hours a day.

So drop out today; play hooky from responsibility. Do what it takes to give yourself the soul food you need.

𝒶 *Have a dialogue with your partner about taking an official mini-vacation day, a day when you can abdicate all but the most necessary responsibilities and just let things slide. This is a day to stare out the window, wander aimlessly, take naps—to recharge those batteries. Your partner may want their own mini-vacation day very soon!*

Today, I simply let myself feel my exhausted state and recognize that all of me is lovable, even the parts that are tired, worn, and grumpy. I honor this thought: "Caring for my soul, I can better care for my partner."

To love the conscious need in your partner is to discover a hidden need in yourself.

— HARVILLE HENDRIX

Do your partner's needs seem strange or irrational to you? Do you have trouble comprehending why it's so important to them that you be on time, that you call every single day during work, that you show interest in their friends, or go with them to the ball game, or refrain from kissing them on the ear? You would never want these things; why would they? Not only do their requests seem bizarre to you; you find it particularly difficult to grant them.

While this may seem like a mystery, the truth is that what our partner wants is also a hidden desire in ourselves. The difference is that our partner is conscious of the desire while we have repressed it. Our partner wants to touch, or to boogie, but we were told not to touch or to wiggle our bodies. Being asked by our partner stirs our own similar but unknown needs into awareness. This makes us uncomfortable, because we long ago buried our needs—these forbidden impulses—out of fear. To avoid the danger of having these needs, we belittle our partner or label them strange rather than trying to meet them. But overcoming our fear brings back on line a lost and undeveloped part of ourselves, and simultaneously meets that need in ourselves, thus bringing us closer to wholeness.

&❧ *Of all the things your partner has asked you to do, which one is the most difficult—to wear sexy lingerie, show more affection, spend Sunday morning in bed instead of jumping up to clean the house, say what you are feeling instead of going off and sulking? What lost aspect of yourself would you recover in meeting that need? Take a risk and discover a new part of yourself. Tell your partner you are ready to grant one of their behavior-change requests, and do something today to show you mean it.*

I take time for twenty minutes of quiet contemplation today, considering the mystery of this paradox: "Meeting my partner's needs opens me to my own."

Why can't a woman be more like a man?

—GEORGE BERNARD SHAW

Isn't it ironic that men and women expect each other to live up to culturally determined gender role models and then criticize each other for fulfilling them? The sad truth is that gender differences—both inherent and cultivated—cause problems between partners. Men and women are raised in rival camps, steeped in narrowly defined roles and stereotypes, each assured of their superiority. Then they are released into the larger world to meet and mate. No wonder they end up making war, not love.

It is common for couples to have difficulty accepting differences in their partners without making value judgments about those differences. The assumption is that there is something *wrong* with the disparities, something that needs to be *changed* so our partners will be just like us.

But your partner's likes and dislikes, and their way of seeing and understanding life have their own integrity and legitimacy equal in value to your own. *Your partner is not you.* They see the world through different lenses. Your partner's way of being in and experiencing the world offers you an opportunity to expand yours. In the best of all possible worlds, a woman would be more like a man—and vice versa. Mutual understanding and respect open the door to that world.

᠅ *Have a couples dialogue with your partner about your different perspectives and reactions, your unique ways of doing things. Ask questions, see what you can learn about your partner's world. Emphasize validation in your conversation; make a special point of letting your partner know that you can see their experience is true for them, and that their point of view, while it may be different than yours, makes sense.*

Today as I take time to relax deeply, I admit that I don't have to learn a foreign language to communicate with my partner. I just have to listen. Underneath it all we speak the same language. I vow in prayer: "Today I will listen from my heart."

The miracle is this—the more we share, the more we have.

—LEONARD NIMOY

It sometimes seems that men and women have organized themselves into two armed camps. Wary and suspicious of each other, they keep to themselves, bonding in the ways peculiar to their sex, hoarding their secrets, and restricting memberships in their exclusive clubs. Women collect in their sewing circles or goddess-worship groups, privy to the arcana of menopause and cutwork embroidery. Men gather at the bar or the ball game, poring over batting statistics and leveraged buyouts. No one has all the information they need to see the big picture.

But you and your partner can be subversives in the war between the sexes. You can throw open the doors to the inner sanctum and give away the secrets. There is no better way to expand your own horizons than to enter your partner's world and investigate it fully. Think of yourself as exploring a foreign land in the company of an experienced guide, or taking a master class from an expert. The world is a complex and fabulous place—even in your own backyard, more is going on than you could ever discover on your own.

❧ *Have a couples dialogue about one specific thing the two of you have seen or done together recently—a movie, a party or event you both attended, the family room you're adding to the house. See if you can really tune in to your partner's experience and not only learn something about how your partner thinks but see how their view of the world complements and expands yours.*

Today, I enter a place of deep thanksgiving, accepting the gift of being who I am and the hope of getting to know more deeply who my partner is. I commit to enjoying the miracle of discovery.

What's so remarkable about love at first sight? It's
when people have been looking at each other for years
that it becomes remarkable.

— HELEN HAYES

Falling in love is easy, a piece of cake. We are carried along on
dreams, buoyed up by endorphins, sustained by the sheer mad thrill
of it all. But loving our partner in the midst of conflict, loving them
when we are threatened or disappointed, loving them when they're
not treating us as we would like, that's the challenge. It's the ability
to love and value our partner when they are of no value to us, just
because they exist and deserve love in their own right, that is the
true test of our character. Real love is the product of day-by-day,
year-after-year caring, talking, working out problems, extending
ourselves to grow and change, overcoming obstacles in our path.
That is remarkable.

❧ *Dialogue with your partner today about what you have been*
through in the time you've been together. Pick out the acts of love
and caring, the effort and attention that have made it remarkable.
Plan a small ritual or celebration to mark your accomplishment.

In sacred quiet today, with each breath I take, I see that our love is
more remarkable with each passing day, and give thanks for this
great blessing in my life.

People who fight with fire usually end up with ashes.

—ABIGAIL VAN BUREN

When we lash out at our partner in anger, when we are quick to criticize, we should not be surprised to find our relationship consumed in flames. Intimate relationships inevitably surface terrible hurts, and we fight for our survival by whatever means we know. But when we use the primitive weapons we learned in childhood, we usually end up with more pain than when we began.

Fighting fire with fire is actually a primitive technique of last resort, a weapon of war, not of peace and conciliation. When you fight fire with fire, the earth on both sides ends up scorched. The containment process can be used to do battle in a way that assures safety and victory for both parties. Dealing with all conflicts by using this anger management avoids the kind of spontaneous combustion that so quickly gets out of control. Years of accumulated anger are slowly dissipated. Our relationship becomes calmer and less volatile; our clearly expressed needs are clearly responded to.

❧ *Ask your partner for an appointment to do the containment process sometime today to express a frustration that you may have been handling inappropriately. Before you start, check the guidelines on Days 122–124.*

I am aware that sometimes I burst into flames of anger, scorching my partner with pain. Sitting quietly today, I access the courage to contain the flames of my rage, making sure that no matter how angry I feel, I keep my partner safe. I meditate on these words: "When my partner and I fight fair, we both win."

It is best to learn as we go, not as we have learned.

—ANONYMOUS

No matter how many books we've read or movies we've seen, no matter what we were told, we've learned most of what we know about intimate relationships from watching our parents. We had front-row seats to the show they put on, day after day. If we were lucky, they treated each other with respect and laughed together. They listened closely to what each other had to say, and they were able to resolve their arguments without resorting to yelling or tears. If, on the other hand, our parents treated each other disrespectfully and our home was filled with anger or fear, we absorbed a very different lesson. Whatever the circumstances, our relationships echo our past.

To some extent, we all learned unproductive, unloving relationship tactics that we brought to our adult partnerships: silence, threats, wheedling, complaining, nagging, crying, withholding, bargaining. One thing we may not have absorbed is that these tactics didn't work. They didn't create love or harmony in our home. Is there any reason to think they will work now, with our partner?

🐾 *Listen today for the echo of your parents' marriage. Select one behavior that you learned from your parents' marriage—angry silences, escaping from chores, indirect criticism. Ask your partner to do the same, and have a dialogue about how these habits have influenced your partnership, and how you can each learn a new Imago skill to change that behavior.*

As I retreat into my stillness today, I visualize myself as a sponge having soaked up tactics from my past that do not work in my partnership today. I take the sponge in my hands and squeeze it dry, and as it returns to its normal shape it draws in new consciousness.

A conscious relationship is not a sometime thing. The idea of forever may seem dull and prosaic, but the reality is that the achievement of real love requires regular, ongoing attention and maintenance. Our commitment must be indelible and steadfast, something our partner can rely upon.

When we have created a no-exit relationship, we are, surprisingly, liberated. We become truly free to explore who we are with our partner. The fear of abandonment or of being controlled dissipates, as does the energy that is spent when we are living with this vague and unspoken uncertainty. The result is not boredom or predictability but rather an atmosphere of spontaneity and fun that permeates our being together side by side, day by day, year after year.

How about a surprise for your partner today—perhaps a passion-filled love note taped to the bathroom mirror, a bottle of champagne (tied with a red satin bow) waiting when they come home from a hectic day at work, a hand-drawn coupon that can be exchanged for a romantic evening out . . .

During my time of prayer today, I hold an image of the sun rising and setting, rising and setting. When the sun sets each night, in its blaze of fiery color, I have no fear that it won't return the next morning at dawn. I bring this same constancy to my relationship, so my partner and I can count on each other as surely as we depend on the sunrise.

*Our aim is to recognize each other and for each one of
us to see and honor in the other what he is — the
counterpart and complement of the other.*

— HERMANN HESSE

One partner is superrational, the other wildly emotional; one is
sexually ravenous, the other near-virginal. It seems to make no
sense, and it is the source of much misery. But it is nature's way.
Though on the surface it appears to be a flawed construct, when you
look closer it becomes clear that this tension of opposites is an
elegant design for stimulating growth. As each other's complement
or counterpart, we possess the raw materials for collaborative healing. Better we should honor than rail against the contrasting qualities
in our partners that now provoke tension.

It's a simple truth: your partner is in your life for a reason—to
mirror your undeveloped side and to stimulate your spiritual growth
toward wholeness. The traits in your partner that are most opposite
of yours reflect that part of you that needs to evolve. The dynamics
of the Imago are such that each person's deepest need is always
matched with their partner's greatest weakness. And it is at this point
of greatest tension and resistance that the greatest growth becomes
possible. To become whole yourself you must stretch into that
atrophied part of you that your partner needs.

ᔕ *By now you are pretty familiar with your character defenses,
those parts of you that resist change. Exactly what is it that your
partner needs from you that is such a struggle for you to give? In
recognizing this point of tension, remind yourself again why the
two of you are a perfect match.*

**I take time today to dwell in a place of inner renewal. I draw from
the well of my soul to give me greater compassion and understanding
as I consider the purpose behind our differences. I focus on this
paradoxical truth: "My partner's needs are a blueprint for my own
growth."**

In love, you must give three times before you take once.

—BRAZILIAN PROVERB

Many of us are victims of arrested development. Insufficiently loved as children, inadequately taught how to love through the example of our parents and society, we didn't progress naturally from the infant stage of being loved to the adult stage of being the lover. We're stuck somewhere along that learning curve. Perhaps we got stuck at infancy, and all we know about love is that we're supposed to get it. If it's not there, we figure we'd better scream or sulk about it, or just forget it. Maybe our stopping place came at a point when we recognized that if we offered something in return for love—our charm, our cooperation, our services—we'd be successful. Few of us received enough love to feel that we had enough to give to others.

But it's never too late to learn this magical lesson. In a way it requires the suspension of disbelief, a setting aside of our ideas about give and take, profit and reward. In a conscious relationship we commit to loving our partner unconditionally, which means we commit to learning *how* to do so, for it isn't a part of our current repertoire. By rote at first, we show our affection to our partner, hold them in times of trouble, tell them they're wonderful, shower them with kindness—regardless of their behavior toward us. This seemingly mechanical, no-strings-attached care has a powerful impact both on our partner and on our own unconscious. It's like going back to school. As we practice love, we are imprinting in our unconscious— and in our partner's unconscious—the patterns that never got set down in childhood. We are literally cocreating the ability to love.

🍃 *Give your partner three caring behaviors today, without any thought of what you might get in return.*

Relaxing into my breathing, I see myself as a child in school listening to a wise person speak of love, and realize that I am finally learning truths about relationship that were not taught me in my youth. I see myself growing older and wiser, at last becoming an adult.

I like not only to be loved, but to be told I am loved.

—GEORGE ELIOT

Yes, love shows itself in deeds and gestures of affection and gifts. It is apparent in the time we spend with our partners, in the effort we make to bring in money, to take care of the kids, to handle our chores responsibly. But there's something about hearing those three little words, "I love you," that somehow connects with a different part of our brain or heart, that gives our love an added dimension or tangibility, and reaffirms that our partner unquestionably still cares.

We're not talking here about tossing off a *pro forma* "I love you" at the end of a phone conversation, the casual "Love ya," as we walk out the door, but rather a thoughtful, meaningful communication *in words* of your choice that express your love in a special moment.

In a conscious relationship, we don't assume that our partners know what we want: we tell them, clearly and directly. The same is true of declarations of love. "Well, of course my partner knows I love them," we say. Oh, really? Have you checked that out with your partner lately? Words of love are nourishment; like meals, they should be served up several times a day.

&. *Look deep into your partner's eyes today and say, "I love you"—simply and straight from the heart.*

I imagine my partner standing before me looking for something, and I intuitively know they want to hear my words of love. As I say "I love you," my partner's face breaks into a smile, their body relaxes, and a glow forms around them. I say these three words over and over: "I love you."

Well, here we have a typical Imago pair—the pursuer and the distancer. One approaches, and the other flees. One is always in need of reassurance ("You still love me, don't you?"); the other has a hard time giving it ("For crying out loud, you know how I feel about you"). They share the same issues from childhood, but their reactions are different.

All partners push against an invisible relationship boundary in an attempt to satisfy their dual needs for separateness and connection. Most of the time, each individual fixates on one of those needs: one person habitually advances in an attempt to satisfy their need for closeness and the other habitually retreats in an effort to remain separate. Some couples stay locked in this particular dance for the duration of their relationship. Others experience a startling reversal. When the partner who typically advances begins to retreat, the partner in retreat suddenly starts seeking the closeness they thought they had to run away from. It's as if the two partners are like a pair of magnets that must maintain a set distance between them. One or the other must always advance and retreat to keep a balance.

&ed Are you a pursuer or an distancer? See if you can make some change in your usual pattern today. If you're a pursuer retreat a little—stop asking for reassurances of love, don't nag at your partner to do things, go out to dinner and a movie by yourself, show some independence! If you're a distancer, reach out to your partner with words of love, plan something together, show some interest in being close. Notice that you can be closer together without either being smothering or running away.

In my quiet time, I look more directly at the push/pull that my partner and I struggle with around issues of closeness and distance. I recognize that many of these feelings are a part of our emotional history, and acknowledge this reality: "The space between us is an opportunity to create a loving dance."

We can only learn to love by loving.

— IRIS MURDOCH

Love has to be learned; it cannot be found in the natural repertoire of options we possess as creatures. But you can't learn it from books, not even this one. It requires on-the-job training and requires a lot of courage, because you have to transcend your instinctual impulses.

So what is this thing called love? First, it is an attitude that gives value to your partner independent of any value they have for you. Your partner does not exist for you, and their value is not based upon what they do or do not do. They were given existence by the universe, and their presence in your life is a gift, freely bestowed by their choice.

Second, it is a behavior that expresses that attitude in everything you do in your relationship, not just when they meet your needs. And it endures even when your partner is a source of frustration. It is usually born in the midst of conflict, not in the throes of passion.

Third, it is a commitment to the total welfare of your partner, including their emotional healing, psychological growth, and spiritual evolution, and this gift is bestowed without conditions. This means your partner is always safe in your presence, and their existence is at the center of your consciousness.

Fourth, what love is not: It is not feeling, thus it has to be distinguished from the emotions of romantic attachment. Real love is born after the death of romantic love. In a conscious relationship, feelings of appreciation and joy attend love, but they are not its substance.

❧ *Spend a few minutes today pondering your love for your partner.*

During my time of solitude today, I enter the safe place in mind, and when I am comfortable and serene, I bring my partner into the safe place with me. As I do, a golden ray of light shines down from above, filling me with light. As I relax more deeply, this ray emanates from me and shines on my partner, illuminating them with its warm golden glow until they are all that is in my consciousness. I become aware that this light is my love, coming from my deepest core, bathing my partner. Then I notice that the ray goes through my partner and shines back on me, then returns to my partner and then to me in a continuous circle of light until both of us are enveloped in a single glowing circle of light. I see my partner relaxing and I know they feel safe in my presence.

Love must be learned again and again; there is no end to it.

—KATHERINE ANN PORTER

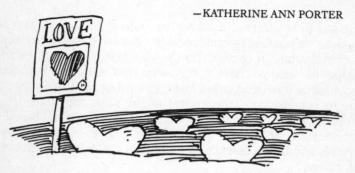

The old adage is that wishing won't make it so, but we humans are constructed in such a way that our new brain can (slowly) train our primitive old brain to change its habitual responses. When we actively practice visualizing something that we want, over time we actually create its coming to pass. In visualizing the loving energy between you and your partner every day, you open and strengthen new neural pathways. New connections are made, and the old pathways—along with the messages they carried—shrivel with disuse. The old messages—"My partner doesn't love me," "My partner will hurt me," "I won't ever be loved"—get drowned out by the new words and images.

❧ *Take a minute to repeat the visualization of love you learned yesterday. Write down what you saw, heard, and felt in the golden light of love with your partner. Repeat this same visualization daily, several times a day; in a few days you will have the procedure memorized so that you won't need to refer to the instructions. Over time your relationship will be transformed.*

Moving toward my source of strength within, I recognize the power of images to create new realities. I focus on this prayer: "Visualizing loving my partner creates love in our relationship."

When we describe what the other person is really like,
I suppose we often picture what we want. We look
through the prism of our need.

— ELLEN GOODMAN

All of us have had the experience of describing our beloved to friends and family in the most glowing terms, sure that we're articulating their reality. So why is it that our friends don't quite see the same thing we do? The reason is that what we are really describing is our need. We are in love with the idea that our partner will meet those needs. Of course they cannot—because they resemble in crucial ways the caretakers who were unable to love us in the first place, and because they don't have a clue to what we really need.

In a conscious relationship, partners recognize that the prism through which they view their partners reveals important information about the work they must do together. They understand that they need to receive love from exactly the kind of person their partner represents. Slowly but inexorably, reality love replaces the chimera of romance and then the anger of the power struggle, as our problematic partner becomes, through years of Imago practice, our fantasy partner.

🐚 *Make a list of three qualities you wish your partner had. Now match each quality with a need that you have. Pick one and ask your partner for a behavior-change request (Day 200) that addresses that need.*

In my twenty minutes of quiet contemplation today, I see that the qualities I want in my partner are attributes I need to develop in myself. Surrendering my criticism and complaints, I focus on this prayer: "I renew my commitment to do this holy work of becoming whole."

Sensual pleasures have the fleeting brilliance of a comet; a happy marriage has the tranquillity of a lovely sunset.

—ANN LANDERS

Marriage can feel so dull! No rockets going off, no pounding heart, no all-night sex marathons, no breathless anticipation. Ho-hum. We grow up in a culture where we're constantly exhorted to have excitement in our lives, a culture in which men and women are trained to judge themselves on their attractiveness and allure, to measure their relationships in terms of peak experiences. It's easy to lose sight of the slow-burning beauty of the sunset when we're always hearing praise of comets. Comets are rare, a flash in the pan. The sun sets every day, without fail, and its own display is often glorious.

🦢 *Make a list of five things your partner does today that make you feel cared about and loved. This evening, before you go to sleep, share them with your partner.*

Relaxed, with my eyes closed, I withdraw my energy from the manic pace and compulsions of the world and listen simply to the beating of my heart. I tune in to my breath and to the wondrous workings of my own human body—rhythms usually drowned out by my hectic life. I let my thoughts expand to my relationship: this too is a body in need of appreciation. Its pulsating breath and heartbeat offer tranquility and dependability in the midst of life's comets.

*Who knows but for a time you may have taken
yourself for somebody else? Stranger things have
happened.*

—HERMAN MELVILLE

"**I**m not the stingy one—you're the tightwad!" How can *you* accuse
me of being pigheaded?" Our partner is the perfect screen on which
to project the traits that are too incongruous with our self-image for
us to admit that we possess. It's convenient to see in our mates the
very qualities that we are blind to in ourselves. As long as we can
blame our partner for what's wrong, we don't have to confront our
own shortcomings, or do anything to change them.

When we deny unacceptable traits, we are taking ourselves for
somebody else—somebody who is whole. Only by accepting and
integrating our denied-self traits can we become the person we
thought we were. And only by loving in our partner what we cannot
admit to in ourselves can we do that.

🍳 *Jot down three qualities that irritate you most about your
partner—their habit of clamming up in an argument, their clumsiness, their awkwardness at parties. Can you see how any of
these traits might describe your own denied self?*

I acknowledge that self-love includes accepting all of myself. I consider this wisdom: "My partner mirrors my unwanted self and offers
the opportunity for true self-love."

So often we play hide-and-seek with our partner. One day we are close and loving; then something sets us off and we head for one of our exits—our office, an affair, a fantasy of leaving, a double hot-fudge sundae. In our hiding places we have the illusion of satisfying the desires our partner isn't fulfilling; but we're really just avoiding the pain of conflict.

Hide-and-seek is a children's game, and we are no longer children. Nothing is solved when we hide from our problems, or our partners. We need to come out of hiding and seek the satisfaction of our needs through resolving our conflicts with our partner.

❧ What are a few of the subtle, almost invisible exits you use to hide from your partner: taking forever to read the paper or shower or do the dishes, reading very long bedtime stories to the kids, acting tired or unapproachable, having too many friends or responsibilities? Resolve to close one of those exits today.

During my time of prayer, I become aware of the walls behind which I hide from my partner. As I breathe more deeply, the wall becomes transparent and I step forward with commitment to join my partner.

A caress is better than a career.

—ELISABETH MARBURY

The two-career couple, working twelve-hour days and networking on the weekends while their kids are raised by day care and baby-sitters, who have time only for a peck on the cheek and a schedule consultation when they come home, are becoming stock characters on the American scene. Many of us, regrettably, live out some version of this scenario. In placing so much emphasis on our jobs, having so much of our self-image bound up in our work, we often sabotage our relationships.

Expending such a high percentage of our energy in our work life is a misappropriation of our priorities. A growing body of research confirms that intimate relationships are essential to our physical health, emotional stability, overall sense of well-being, and spiritual growth. In a conscious relationship partners seek to allocate their resources in a way that is satisfying and productive for both partners. They seek to achieve a balance of time for work and play, time to be together and time alone. Sometimes it requires drastic change, a wrenching redirection of goals and plans: shorter hours, passing up promotions, living more frugally, working at home part-time. But they recognize that the intimacy and safety between them is a priceless asset. They care most about caress advancement.

&* *Examine your priorities. Have a dialogue with your partner about how you parcel out your time between work and relationship. Is career advancement causing your relationship to backslide? Make a list of what needs to happen to achieve the right balance between the two.*

In meditation today, I see a light shining on all the things around me I value, including my relationship with my partner. I make this commitment: "I will protect this treasure and keep a balance between work and love."

Most of us in committed, stable relationships settle for predictability, comfort, and companionship because we fear exploring the mysteries that we embody as man and woman, the exposure of our deepest selves.

—ROBIN NORWOOD

Predictability, comfort, and companionship in a relationship are not to be sneezed at, and many couples rightly consider themselves lucky to achieve these worthy goals. But in stopping at this point, they are settling for far less than commitment offers. Sometimes couples choose to maintain the status quo out of fear; they're content to have found peace and comfort, and they decide to quit while they're ahead. Other couples have no idea of the richness and closeness in store for them if they go the next step.

Couples in a conscious relationship commit themselves to full disclosure, to working through their fear and discomfort to explore the deeper mysteries of themselves and their partners. They do not underestimate the psychic strength necessary to make this formidable journey, but they know too that they are safe in exposing their deepest secrets; they understand that their partners welcome the restoration of their lost selves. They keep their eyes on the goal of this deep intimacy: real love.

&. *Take a bold plunge into the unknown today. Open up to your partner about something you've been afraid to disclose — your jealousy of their best friend, your secret desire to be famous, your preoccupation with a wild sexual fantasy. Invite your partner to share one such tidbit with you. In dialogue, welcome and validate each other's disclosure.*

In quiet today, I contemplate the idea that ignoring the potential for intimacy is a sacrilege. I hold this thought: "Intimate connection brings divinity into my relationship with my partner."

For some of us, the reflection in the fun-house mirror pretty much matches our self-image. Just as we deny the negative traits in ourselves that are too uncomfortable to own up to, we often disown positive traits that make us squirm. We do this because we were criticized or shamed for having them—our creativity was labeled "weird," our curiosity deemed "snoopy," our dreams "foolish." Implicitly trusting the opinions of others seemingly older and wiser than ourselves, we took on their judgments as own own, and buried our inner treasures and our potential.

Though friends or coworkers often mention our creativity or curiosity, it is too scary for us to see these traits in ourselves; it would be a slap in the face of our parents, and others who criticized us, to accept our disowned qualities. So we admire them from afar, worshipping what we cannot own up to in ourselves.

We are not whole without our missing traits, and our partner needs our curiosity, our creativity, our daring. With their encouragement and support, in contrast to our parents' response, we can reclaim them.

❧ On a sheet of paper, make a list of traits that you admire in movie stars, public figures, and friends. Then consider how these traits are true of you. Say each one of these traits out loud, preceded by "I am . . ." Share this list of traits with your partner.

I release myself from adoration and accept in myself the positive traits I assign to others. I embed this truth in my heart: "Adoration is a form of self-debasement."

*Above all that you guard, watch over your heart. For
out of it are the sources of life.*

— PROVERBS 4:23

You've spent almost a full year working through the Imago process
one day at a time. During this time you've acquired many new skills
that will help you acknowledge and respond to your partner's deepest
needs, and you've begun to enjoy your partner's reality.

In the process you are also learning to become an inner guardian
for your own heart. To protect its beauty and spiritual resiliency from
the dark emotions of blocked rage, despair, and bitterness that were
festering there a year ago, you have begun to give rational expression
to your frustrations and negative feelings. This reverses the deaden-
ing of the soul that comes from the harboring of ill will. Now the
divine essence, that vibrant aliveness at the core of your being has a
greater chance of being retained and expressed. On guard!

🙠 *Today I identify two ways I once habitually harbored ill will
toward my partner and evaluate how I have changed them. Have
I replaced them with two hitherto-unrecognized areas of appreciation? I make the conscious decision to focus on these and
mention them to my partner before going to bed. In doing this, I
nurture the glow of my heart.*

**In a time of stillness, I visualize my heart, threatened by the forces
of rage and bitterness that threaten to darken and destroy its inner
calm. I erect a watchgate flanked with soldiers to stand on guard,
allowing in only the emotions that edify my inner spirit. I focus on
this wisdom: "It is out of a protected heart that new life is born."**

The way to heaven is in your heart. Open and lift the wings of love!

—RUMI

In our society, what is outside is more highly valued than what is inside. Rationality, strategic thinking, driving ourselves to achieve our goals, are the hallmarks of our time. We frantically produce more and more, not so that we can relax but so that we can afford to consume more. If this is heaven on earth, we're in trouble.

We need time to go inside, to shore up and nurture our own interior, to acquaint ourselves with the inner heaven in our hearts, where we are connected to everything and to everyone. When we open and lift our wings, we know that love is the source of all.

❧ *Take some time today to just slow down. Breathe the air, smell the flowers, hear the birds sing, gaze at your partner, be fully aware of your surroundings. Just be.*

I shift my consciousness to my inner life, and for twenty minutes allow myself to experience the presence of everything, especially my partner, and open that part of myself that can generate healing love. I hold this thought: "The way to heaven is in my heart."

*The sunken moon returns, the broken branch
    grows back.
He who ponders this is not troubled in adversity.*

—BUDDHIST PROVERB

Shattered dreams, severed relationships, aborted plans: each of us has, at one time or another, come face to face with our failure and with our own inner darkness. At such bleak moments, we see hopelessness and despair stretching before us without end, with no sign of reprieve.

But unrelenting darkness is contrary to the laws of nature, which inexorably seeks repair. Even as the forest fire rages, the trees release their seeds so new growth can take root in the charred soil. Fresh blood and antibodies rush immediately to the site of a wound. In time, mighty oaks again shade the forest floor, and only the barest trace of a scar records our wound.

We are a part of nature; everything in us seeks self-repair. Every death—of a dream, a relationship, a plan gone haywire—can lead to rebirth. Our pain itself can kick in the emergency procedures that spur us to faster and deeper healing. Moving through the darkness brings us inexorably into the light—as the sunken moon unfailingly returns.

Contemplate for a few minutes the areas of darkness and disappointment in your relationship. Today's task is to look actively for the signs of new growth and repair that you may be blind to in your despair. Look for the smallest indicators—a hug from your partner before breakfast, the errand run without a reminder, the first buds of spring. Take care to note each sign of new life and healing in your relationship, and offer thanks to your partner today.

In quiet today, I face my inner darkness and give in to sadness, recognizing that only by acknowledging the pain of my unfulfilled expectations can I hope to begin the process of healing. I hold this thought: "Surrounded by tenderness and faith, my heart in time will self-repair."

Take your life into your own hands, and what
happens? A terrible thing: No one to blame.

                               —ERICA JONG

At this point, you have become aware of the major obstacle to intimacy in a committed relationship: assigning all the problems to your partner. Projection and blame are convenient, functional defenses that can absolve you of any responsibility for your troubles. But they also rob you of a special gift: your wholeness. The vast power of claiming your projections is that you become a more empowered person. Without parts of you projected onto your partner, there's more of you to integrate into your full personhood.

As you plan the direction your life will take in the future, design the journey thoughtfully. While you've made it past many treacherous switchbacks, through swamps of quicksand, and sidestepped a few avalanches this past year, know that peaks and valleys remain ahead, and how you handle blame will greatly influence the outcome. As you chart the course, keep the Imago process close at hand as your guidebook. And continue to protect the time each day for your own spiritual renewal. The two together will help ensure that you keep alive and vital a rich oasis of love in the vast landscape of your life.

◈ Think about the year ahead and make a conscious plan with your partner to continue work on your relationship. What options come to mind? Start this book again? Purchase a home video on relationships? Keep a journal? Time to take life into your own hands.

Moving to a place of stillness, I recognize that the lush, green oasis of love in the desert of my life is truly a sacred spot, providing the waters of restoration. I rest secure in this thought: "The power of love is my sure guide."

For a while, perhaps even for years, one partner may tolerate their mate's criticisms—the thinly veiled barbs, the troubled sighs, the litany of blame or discontent. It becomes such a habitual pattern— the constant complainer and the silent sufferer—that it seems part of the natural fabric of the relationship. But even the most tolerant or avoidant person has their limits. The most understanding, the most conflict-phobic person can explode unexpectedly, spewing out all that saved-up anger and unhappiness. Just because they don't show their feelings doesn't mean they don't have them, however masked or buried.

And then what? Where do they go from here? All couples need to find the balance between stuffing their feelings or making them felt gratuitously or indirectly—before the explosion comes. Remember, in a conscious relationship, all anger is expressed by appointment only, using guidelines that allow for direct but nonharmful communication.

🍃 *Have a container day (Day 271). Let the partner who usually avoids conflict be the sender. Tomorrow, switch roles.*

As I relax today, breathing deeply, I access the courage to hear directly my partner's anger, knowing that behind it is hurt. I honor their effort to get their needs met, and remember that anger is pain expressing itself.

Love at its highest point leads us to the brink of the great abyss, for it speaks to us directly of the infinite and of eternity. It is eminently religious.

—HENRI AMIEL

As you have worked your way through this book, with its many entries on the importance of love, you have gotten the idea, no doubt, that in the Imago process, love is serious business. This is consistent also with all great religious traditions, where it is the highest concept that can be imagined, often equated with the essence of the divine.

But what is love? How do you achieve it, and what happens when you do? Clearly there is an ancient consensus that love has something to do with how we should relate to others, and when it is achieved there is an outcome you can expect from the effort. In real love, others are to be seen as having a value independent of their usefulness to us. Giving to them is to be devoid of expectations of any response. Commitment to their total welfare, including their spiritual potential, is to be equated with commitment to one's own.

Clearly this is a high calling! And it may seem beyond our reach. But the way to achieve all this is simple though challenging—you simply have to love your partner the way they want to be loved, without conditions. The outcome that can be expected is paradoxical. Since your partner's needs will call upon you to develop your undeveloped self, you will become whole. In the process, the lover benefits from loving as much as the beloved benefits from being loved. Through reconnection to one's split-off parts, the lover becomes united simultaneously to the whole of the universe. That is love's highest point, the intersection with the infinite, and eminently religious experience.

❧ *Take some time today to look at the changes in your perspective that have been effected by stretching to love your partner as they have asked to be loved. Write down a few sentences. How do they compare to your views a year ago?*

In deep meditation today, I review where I was a year ago and where I am today. Though the journey has been hard and at times difficult, I can see that continuing on this path will further my spiritual evolution. I hold this thought as sacred: "Love restores my soul and connects me to the infinite."

Great souls have wills. Feeble ones have only wishes.
—CHINESE PROVERB

Do you ever find yourself envying actors who suddenly become big-name stars after one performance in a popular movie? The writer whose best-seller propels them to sudden fame? There is usually a more pedestrian story behind their apparent overnight success, that goes something like this: "I knew that I wanted to write by the time I was nine. Every day I'd write poems and short stories—pretty awful ones—but I kept at it. In high school I entered a bunch of essay contests, but I never won anything. During college I worked at the local paper at night for three dollars an hour. Finally I got a story published; they paid me sixty-five dollars. My first book sold fifteen hundred copies. . . ." You get the idea.

Success in our relationships is achieved the same way as success in any other area—through hard, persistent effort. A writer or actor—anyone with a long-term goal—learns his trade through education and experience, practicing his craft day after day, year after year. It is good to have a dream of love—or fame and fortune—because it tells us what we need to learn and do to achieve it, and it gives us a benchmark against which to measure our progress. But it is our will to keep on, to overcome obstacles, to maintain our faith and attention, that enables us to meet our goals. It is one thing to make a wish, quite another to find a way. Learning and practicing the Imago skills a little each day, no matter how busy or discouraged you might be, is one way of demonstrating the power of will.

🍋 *Identify one wish you have for your relationship—to spend more time together, to have more fun, to stop bickering about the evening chores, to talk more? Use your will to find a way to do something today to bring one of those wishes closer to reality.*

Today, I enter the place of my deepest spiritual strength and visualize myself empowered to succeed at my goals.

The heart never becomes wrinkled.

— MADAME DE SÉVIGNÉ

As time goes by, there is a natural diminishing—of our youth, our strength, our options. We can no longer do the things we used to do; we must put aside things that once we enjoyed, temper our dreams to match our capabilities and our resources. And yes, we get a bit wrinkled.

But the heart's capacity for love is one of the few things that increases with use and age. So stop hoarding your affections. Forget about conserving love—give it all away. Flood your partner with caring behaviors, and have fun doing it. This isn't for your partner, you see; they don't have to deserve it. This is a fitness plan for your own heart.

Treat your partner to a couple of minutes of positive flooding (Day 213) today. Circle around and around your partner, building excitement with every sentence. Have fun, and feel your heart overflow with love.

Today I contemplate my heart filled with love directed at my partner, and visualize this thought: "The more I love, the stronger and more beautiful is my heart."

There are more important tragedies than the tragedy of death. There are no more important victories than the victory of love.

—WILLIAM SLOANE COFFIN

At this point, you've put hours into learning the Imago process and honing new skills for your relationship. Your notebook is replete with lists of details that delineate your partner as a separate person. You've listed ways they love to have fun. And the things that most readily tick them off. You've spun all sorts of possible visions from your dream relationship; and you've faced the challenge of containing frustration and anger and being contained. You've put in so much effort learning to be intentional and grow more conscious.

You have demonstrated that human beings have the capacity to grow beyond their instinctual, self-protective natures, and develop the capacity to love. You have shown that the symbiotic tie can be broken, that profound empathy and genuine love for the other is possible, and you have begun to awaken to the broader world around you and grow to care for its existence. The incubation of this universal awareness in your relationship makes your marriage itself an incarnation of love; God made alive within our own being. This opens us to the transcendent, to the awareness of our interconnectedness and our interdependency with all of nature.

You deserve a gold medal, given your willingness to enter the marathon of conscious relating. And so today, victory is yours. Relish it.

❧ *Identify the item on your partner's behavior-change request list that was the most difficult for you to respond to. How do you feel about your response now? Is there more to do to complete the change your partner needs? Make an effort today to complete it.*

In serenity today, I contemplate my growth in my most difficult area. Although at times I confess that I feel I'm being pulled apart, I know the pain is opening the core of my being. I focus all my thoughts on this sober reality: "The struggle, the training, become the victory of love."

*In a sense we are alone, for our "inner freedom"
means that a love relation can no longer fetter us; the
other sex has lost its magic power over us, for we have
come to know its essential traits in the depths of our
own psyche. We shall not easily "fall in love," for we
can no longer lose ourselves in someone else, but we
shall be capable of a deeper love, a conscious devotion
to the other.*

—JOLANDE JACOBI

The message here is a profound one: *Love makes you whole.*

You came to your partner in need. You needed your partner to love
and care for you as your parents had not, to make up for what was
lacking in yourself, to make you feel safe and whole. When you found
out your partner had the same expectations of you, you were
frightened and angry. But through learning the skills of the Imago
process, in dialogue with your partner, in stretching into new behaviors, in finding daily time for yourself, you have been reclaiming your
true self bit by bit. Along the way, you have discovered that you don't
need your partner for the goods and services they provide; you are
not dependent on them for the male or female energy which you
lacked. Your partner has challenged you to find what you seek in
yourself, and you have indeed been finding what you need deep
within. You are no longer vulnerable to your needs or to the illusions
of romantic love. You have not, as you feared, lost yourself; rather,
you have found your partner, a separate and unique being whom you
can now love wholeheartedly. With each step, with each day, you are
falling out of need with your partner and into real love.

This way freedom lies.

೭ৼ *Ponder for a few minutes today the needs that you brought to
your relationship that are now fulfilled. Share this information
with your partner, and thank them for their love and healing, for
joining you on the journey to wholeness.*

**Sitting in stillness, I revel in my freedom from needs, in my fullness,
and take joy that my yearnings are at an end. I hold this thought:
"Love is the path to wholeness."**

*When the heart is flooded with love there is no room in
it for fear, for doubt, for hesitation. And it is this lack
of fear that makes for the dance.*

— ANNE MORROW LINDBERGH

Congratulations, you've just about made it through all 365 days!
You've been patient and diligent, so perhaps at this point you're
looking for signs that tell you you've achieved a conscious relationship,
or arrived at Real Love, or some other specific milestone on your
journey of partnership.

The measure of your progress won't hit you with lightning-bolt
clarity, but there are subtler signs that your work has manifested
itself in your relationship. Trust your intuition. You'll know you're on
the right track when you realize that safety is the bedrock of your
partnership, that you can live fearlessly with your partner and focus
your attention on loving rather than being loved. You'll know you're in
the dance of love when, giving to your partner, you forget to ask to
be given to in return.

🕭 *Snuggle with your partner before you fall asleep tonight. Share
with them the times in these past months when you've felt
completely safe. Praise your partner for understanding your
vulnerability and protecting you against the reopening of your
childhood wounds.*

**I visualize my partner and myself chained by fears that bind us
overwhelmingly to our needs. I see the love and safety we've cultivated
as the keys to unlock those chains. This ancient definition is mine
today: "Love asks nothing for itself."**

I learned this, at least, by my experiment: that as one advances confidently in the direction of his dreams, and endeavors to live the life which he has imagined, he will meet with a success unexpected in common hours . . . and he will live with the license of a higher order of things.

— HENRY DAVID THOREAU

You've been working with the Imago process on a daily basis for a year now. Though you're only a year older, the intensive work you've done has made you vastly wiser. You have recrystallized your dreams for your relationship and advanced in the direction of their fulfillment. You've taken the time to identify and express your feelings; you've learned to listen openly to your partner; you've taken steps to change behavior that is hurting you and your partnership. You've acquired a capacity for stretching that you didn't have a year ago. Your commitment, your sensitivity, and your connection to your inner spirit has deepened. While you may not yet have the perfect relationship—for our lives are always in process—think back to where you were a year ago. It is time to acknowledge how far you've come!

❧ *With your partner, review your relationship vision today. Note the ways in which you have already made your vision a reality. Make any new changes that reflect your present goals. Renew your commitment to this vision with a kiss, a glass of wine, a big hug.*

Taking time in this period of quiet, I visualize the relationship of my dreams. For a moment I live fully within it, and renew my resolve to bring my dream into reality. I enjoy this revelation: "If I can dream my life, I can live my dreams."

THE INSTITUTE FOR IMAGO
RELATIONSHIP THERAPY

The Institute for Imago Relationship Therapy was cofounded by Harville Hendrix and Helen Hunt in 1984. Its purpose is to help adults see and use their relationships to significant others, especially their intimate partners and children, as a resource for emotional healing, psychological growth and spiritual evolution. The Institute has certified over 1200 mental health professionals in Imago Relationship Therapy who offer therapy, workshops and professional training, worldwide.

For information on therapy, workshops, products and professional training, **please** contact the Institute by letter. The Institute for Imago Relationship Therapy, 335 North Knowles Avenue, Winter Park, Florida 32789, by phone: 1-800-729-1121 or 407-644-3537, by E-mail: IIRT@aol.com or Internet: www/imagotherapy.com.

Photograph by Jill Fineberg

HARVILLE HENDRIX, Ph.D., has spent more than thirty years as an educator and therapist, specializing in working with couples, teaching marital therapy to therapists, and conducting couples workshops across the country. Dr. Hendrix is the creator of Imago Relationship Therapy, which is known and practiced internationally, and the cofounder, with his wife Helen Hunt, and president of the Institute for Imago Relationship Therapy, based in Winter Park, Florida. He is the author of *Getting the Love You Want: A Guide for Couples*, and *Keeping the Love You Find: A Guide for Singles*, and has coauthored, with Hunt, *The Personal Companion: Meditations and Exercises for Keeping the Love You Find*, *The Couples Companion: Meditations and Exercises for Getting the Love You Want*, and *Giving the Love that Heals: A Guide for Parents*.

HELEN HUNT, M.A., M.L.A., has been involved as an activist in women's organizations such as The Ms. Foundation for Women, The Sister Fund, and The New York Women's Foundation. She is also involved with the interface between activism and spirituality, and offers seminars nationally on this subject. A contributor to the Imago process since its inception, she has been a cocreator of the concept both within couples therapy and how it applies to parenting. Helen and Harville have six children, and live in New Mexico.

THE COUPLES COMPANION
MEDITATIONS *and* EXERCISES *for*
Getting the Love You Want

In *Getting the Love You Want*, Harville Hendrix, Ph.D., helped thousands of couples nationwide achieve a new understanding of love relationships. Now, writing with his wife, Helen Hunt, he offers *THE COUPLES COMPANION*, a book of daily meditations that bring the positive power of *Getting the Love You Want* into your life every day, over the course of a year. Each of the three hundred and sixty-five entries will help you cultivate the conscious relationship you desire—and motivate the attitudinal changes that make a relationship last—as you:

- DISCOVER why you chose your mate
- RESOLVE the power struggle that is the barrier to greater intimacy
- LEARN to listen—*really* listen—to your partner
- RESTORE the wholeness of self through daily reflection
- INCREASE fun and laughter in your relationship
- ACHIEVE a common vision of your ideal relationship
- BEGIN the inner healing that leads to spiritual transformation— for both you and your partner
- BECOME "passionate friends" with your partner

Written with clarity and warmth, *THE COUPLES COMPANION* makes the work of a relationship a welcome part of your daily life, and transforms it into a joyous spiritual journey.

Praise for the celebrated bestseller *Getting the Love You Want*:
"I know of no better guide for couples who genuinely desire a maturing relationship."
—M. Scott Peck, author of *The Road Less Traveled*

VISIT US ON THE WORLD WIDE WEB
http://www.SimonSays.com

$14.00 U.S./$19.00 CAN.

14.00

0671868837

COUPLES COMPANION--MEDITATIO
HENDRIX, HARVILLE & HUNT, HE
RLA02 001213 B   QP   BRN 001
INGROO C8700U   001212

PRINTED IN U.S.A.